ERTOY

LANKY TINKER

BELLE TINKER

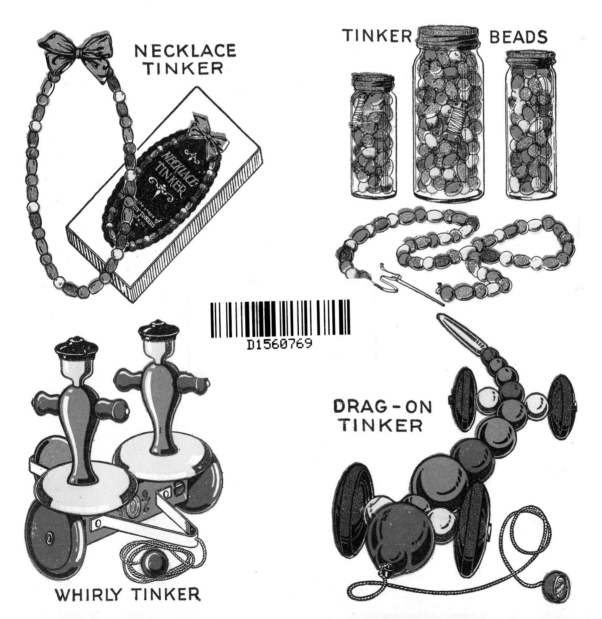

NECKLACE TINKER

TINKER BEADS

D1560769

DRAG-ON TINKER

WHIRLY TINKER

WITH THE "IN" SOUND INSIDE!

WHAM-O NEW
SHOOP SHOOP
HULA HOOP ®
WITH
U.S. PAT. No. 3079728
SOUND

INSIDE!

MAKES NEW Shoop Shoop
SOUND — AS IT GOES AROUND!

Shoop Shoop!

Shoop Shoop!

THE GREATEST TOY IN THE WORLD!

HULA-HOOP HOOP TOY

SPECIFICATIONS

STOCK No. 155
PACKED 3 DOZ TO
FLOOR DISPLAY
SIZE: 36⅞ x12x36⅞
WEIGHT: 31 LBS.

JIM HEIMANN · STEVEN HELLER

100 YEARS OF ALL-AMERICAN TOY ADS

100 JAHRE AMERIKANISCHE SPIELZEUGWERBUNG
100 ANS DE PUBS AMÉRICAINES

TASCHEN

TOY STORIES

AS AMERICANS MOVE FROM FARM TO CITY, WAGES INCREASE AND TOYS BECOME A BOOMING INDUSTRY. The familiar scene of awestruck children peering longingly into a toy store window filled with a cornucopia of commercial playthings, with each child aspiring to possess the doll, train, bicycle, or other piece of merchandise, is an iconic American image. For all kids (and some adults, too) toys trigger an irrepressible urge to have, hold, and thus consume. Not just simple diversions devised to bestow small pleasure, toys are motivators; toys are rewards; toys are big business, especially around Christmastime.

In the economically booming postwar 1950s there aired an afternoon TV game show where kid contestants were allotted five minutes to grab as many toys as their small arms could carry (whatever they could not hold was left behind). When the punishing sound of the buzzer signaled time had expired, the lucky prize-winners proudly displayed their booty for the audience to admire (and trigger their own desire to purchase them). Decades

later, Nickelodeon's *Super Toy Run* applied the same psychology to a more rapturous extreme with the chosen ones filling carts with the latest kid-*sumables*.

I was never lucky enough to be selected for the show—though not from lack of trying—but I experienced my own version. As compensation for enduring a torturous tonsil removal operation, I was allowed to select three toys from the legendary Rappaport's Toy Bazaar located for 90 years at Third Avenue near 79th Street in Manhattan—the same store that, until it closed in 1981, wrapped its wares in polka-dot paper (the inspiration for Stuart Davis's 1951 painting *Rapt at Rappaport's*). My mom and dad knew the co-owner, Harold Ostrover, who, in the spirit of the TV show, jokingly told me I had five minutes to decide what I wanted from the massive shelves filled with bounty. I made a mad dash, and as my heart pumped and adrenaline surged, I recalled the dozens of Saturday morning commercials and ads in *Life*, *Look*, and other magazines for the latest name-brand toys and tie-ins. My choices were based on what the top 10 toys were at the moment and the kind of status they would bring among my envious friends. Product status was derived from advertising campaigns—and such was the power of propaganda to direct behavior even when it came to toys.

Although toys fulfill many a child's usually harmless desires to play, make, and putter, there is nothing innocent about toy *advertisements*. They are gateways to a life of consumption—in this case, products designed to profit their maker even when camouflaged as educational. During those thrilling days of yesteryear, a rash of toys were promoted as positive developmental tools. Take the story in *Ladies' Home Journal* for July 1916 titled, "Teaching a Child Resourcefulness." "Every normal child is most happy when he is 'making' something or 'pretending' some situation even though there may be no visible result that harmonizes with the thought in the little mind," wrote Mildred Austin Shinn, adding that "little ones" derive more satisfaction from making playthings with materials found in the home.

Yet children also like getting playthings that are already designed, fully assembled, and branded. Many branded toys are advertised in aspirational ways and express life's privileges and benefits of wealth, race, or ethnicity. Competitive buying and owning is not just an adult syndrome—it starts with molding kids' behavior.

Toys may be objects of joy, yet children are not the paying customer. *Pic* magazine

1900

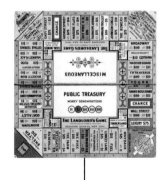

1904

1909

Joshua Lionel Cowen starts producing toy trains

Joshua Lionel Cowen startet die Produktion von Spielzeugeisenbahnen

Joshua Lionel Cowen commence à produire des trains miniatures

The first iteration of Monopoly appears as the Landlord's Game

Die erste Version von Monopoly heißt „Vermieterspiel"

Le Monopoly apparaît pour la première fois sous le nom de « Jeu du propriétaire »

Lionel promotes its toy trains as the "Standard of the World"

Lionel bewirbt seine Spielzeugeisenbahnen als „Standard of the World"

Lionel présente ses trains miniatures comme « la référence mondiale » in 1941 warned, "Although there have been great strides in the improvement of toys…the average parent still buys the toy that catches his own eye, and gives too little thought to the possible effect, good or bad, on the child for whom it is intended." The most important gift of a toy is to "teach your little one to get along with other children." In addition, toys should have an "actual everyday experience, or imitation of adults."

In the early age of mass national media, toy advertising was not as calculated as it became, in part because toys were *actually* more educational. Meccano's model building systems, created in 1898 by Englishman Frank Hornby, were among the most frequently advertised. One of the first major American toy advertisers was New York–based Erector Set (later bought by Meccano). Inducted into the National Toy Hall of Fame in 1998, the classic Erector Set, conceived by A. C. Gilbert, was made of metal girders and mechanical components held by little grub screws. "Businessmen and industrial psychologists hailed the toy that put play to work and encouraged children's 'constructive instincts,'" notes the National Museum of Play. The Erector Set premiered in 1913 through a campaign in the *Saturday Evening Post* and *Popular Mechanics*. These ads were aimed at children and their parents around the same time as Lincoln Logs and Tinker Toys. Erector Sets introduced boys (not girls) to engineering and structural principles of skyscrapers. Special kits with electric motors empowered users to

1912

A toy prize is included in every box of Cracker Jack

In jeder Packung Cracker Jack verbirgt sich ein kleines Spielzeug

Un jeu a été glissé dans chaque paquet de Cracker Jack

1915

Mass production of marbles made possible by invention of M. F. Christensen of Ohio

Eine Erfindung von M. F. Christensen aus Ohio ermöglicht die Massenproduktion von Murmeln

L'invention de M. F. Christensen, de l'Ohio, permet de produire des billes en série

1917

The Council of National Defense suggests eliminating Christmas during war

Der Council of National Defense schlägt vor, in Kriegszeiten auf Weihnachten zu verzichten

Le Conseil national de Défense propose d'annuler Noël tant que dure la guerre build trains, steam shovels, Ferris wheels, and zeppelins. Not pure play, these kits were aptitude tests for future careers.

There were dozens of ads for guns, both real and facsimile. The Winchester ("Oh, J-I-M-M-Y, come on over, we're goin' shootin'!") and Stevens rifles ("Hitting the Bullseye Since 1864") shot real bullets, while the King, Sterling, and Daisy rifles shot air and BBs. The ad for Daisy read: "Every healthy, natural, boyish boy wants and needs a gun," and in case BBs weren't enough armament, there was even a gun that came with a bayonet. Guns of all varieties were frequently sold. (Milton Bradley marketed a machine gun called Big Dick that fired wooden bullets for $3.)

There were safer play options, too. In magazines such as *Boys' Life*, Ives

Manufacturing Company and Lionel sold electric train sets. The Flexible Flyer sled, touted as fast and sturdy, was a fixture in almost every home. In addition, table tennis, fortune-telling games, and a genuine ($1.50) Native American Wigwam ("Just the thing for the Boys") were among the most popular products. Boys could also "Own a Speedy Car" to learn how to build and fly a three-foot model "Aero Car." There was no shortage of militaria, like the Fortress Sets made from Richter's Anchor Blocks.

During the Depression, catalogs were the Amazon of the day. Likewise, small-space ads in comic books and pulps sold mail-order toys like Zimmerman's Flying Machine, "A marvel of simplicity," a "scientifically" designed kite that "any boy or

1919	1920	1923
Louis and David Marx found Louis Marx and Company	Hornby toy trains are officially launched by Meccano	Madame Alexander, age 28, starts doll company in her kitchen
Louis und David Marx gründen die Louis Marx and Company	Hornby-Spielzeugeisenbahnen werden offiziell von Meccano eingeführt	Die 28-jährige Madame Alexander beginnt in ihrer Küche mit der Puppenherstellung
Louis et David Marx fondent Louis Marx and Company	Meccano lance officiellement les trains électriques Hornby	Madame Alexander démarre son atelier de fabrication de poupées à 28 ans, dans sa cuisine

girl could fly." Bicycles also came under the toy rubric. In 1919, Haverford Cycle Company sold its Black Beauty to boys only. With Skudder Car, "Every boy and girl in the block envies the youngster" who owns one. Girls were targeted with Dolly's Home. ("A Fairy-Tale Come True!") And speaking of girls, dolls were marketed as a best friend and confidant, like the famous Mary Jane. ("There's nothing you could give a little girl that she'd love so much as Mary Jane — nothing she'd hug so close to her heart.") Many toys for girls did indeed attempt to re-create the adult domestic experience. One kitchen miniature was touted as having "all the fun of a cabinet 'Just Like Mother's.'" Both boys and girls were targets for wagons — like the Sheboygan De-Lux Speedster — scooters, home playgrounds with swing sets, and Tinker Toys, which were artfully designed.

In the 1930s, toys were often premiums for buying other products, such as Wheaties, Ralston, and Quaker cereals. Frequently, comic strip characters lent their personas to toys — Dick Tracy sold aviation equipment — and with conflict looming in Europe, an increasing number of toys were warlike.

During World War II, however, most toy-making materials were limited because of government restrictions; throughout the war, neither toy manufacturing nor advertising was a high priority. While during the postwar boom, dolls, magic kits, and board games made a comeback.

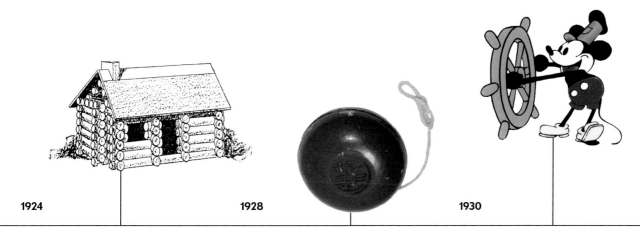

1924

1928

1930

Traditional values of the American frontier are used to sell Lincoln Logs

Lincoln Logs werden mit den traditionellen Werten der Pionierzeit beworben

Les valeurs traditionnelles de la conquête de l'Ouest font vendre les Lincoln Logs

Filipino immigrant Pedro Flores begins mass-producing the yo-yo in California

Der philippinische Einwanderer Pedro Flores beginnt in Kalifornien mit der Jo-Jo-Produktion

En Californie, l'immigré philippin Pedro Flores lance la production en série de yo-yo

Disney commissions a Mickey Mouse doll on the heels of Steamboat Willie

Nach Steamboat Willie gibt Disney eine Micky-Maus-Puppe in Auftrag

Disney commande une poupée Mickey dès la diffusion de Steamboat Willie

The late '40s and early '50s were times for money-saving fun in specially made banks, building structures with Playskool blocks, taking photographs with Roy Rogers's "pow'ful" box camera, or looking through neighbors' windows with his branded binoculars. New materials developed during the war were coming into the world with iconic brands in tow. Hasbro's Mr. and Mrs. Potato Head planted their roots in 1954 as one of the company's top 10 toys. By 1957, Slinky, invented in 1943, was doing its fair share of advertising. And by 1958 Silly Putty ads were helping to push the success of the popular solid-liquid toy. The technology was possible for an electric doll that could walk (and soon talk), like Effanbee's Norma. By 1955, Mickey Mouse ears came

into the cultural landscape, along with dozens of other branded clothing/costumes, like Davy Crockett frontier kidswear and Roy Rogers one- and two-gun holster ensembles.

In the 1960s — coinciding with advertising's Creative Revolution — toy ads became more sophisticated in design and content. A 1962 ad for Mattel showed children of color with dolls of the same skin tone. The Cheerful Tearful doll campaign was another Mattel advancement, as sophisticated as any adult ad. A 1967 ad for Lego with the headline, "Lego, the toy they won't be tired of by Dec 26th" not only looked adult but was as smart as any "Big Idea," too. (The tagline lived up to the promise "Lego…the thoughtful toy.") As the years rolled on, advertisements for

1931

Wood-jointed Betty Boop doll debuts; fans go dizzy with excitement

Betty-Boop-Puppen mit Holzgelenken werden produziert – sehr zur Freude der Fans

La poupée Betty Boop aux articulations en bois sort enfin! Les fans se pâment

1933

Initially called Lexiko, Scrabble is created by an out-of-work architect

Scrabble, ursprünglich Lexiko genannt, wird von einem arbeitslosen Architekten erfunden

Un architecte au chômage crée le Lexiko, qui deviendra le Scrabble

1934

Straight out of a comic book, the Buck Rogers toy ray gun hits shelves

Die Strahlenpistole von Buck Rogers schafft es vom Comicbuch in die Regale der Spielzeugläden

Tout droit sorti des comics, le pistolet à rayon laser de Buck Rogers arrive en boutique life-lesson products like Barbie, Midget Mustang, Julia (based on a TV show of the same name with an African American star), and the Signature Junior electric portable sewing machine, among others, were popular because they mimicked the adult world. Fisher-Price *Sesame Street* products and others were aimed at adults who were familiar with the advertising industry's creative visual language.

This new sophistication was not exclusively targeted at children. Parents were the quartermasters in charge of toy allotment, and they were easily convinced by advertisements that echoed their own consumption habits. During the late 1970s and well into the '90s, computer games were, however, advertised for both — especially around Christmastime.

Children may continue to tear advertisements out of magazines and newspapers and strategically place them around the house to signal their preferences before birthdays and holidays, but digital-age toy propaganda is more likely to come via email based on data collected from algorithms that can predict personal wants. Toy store windows are not the same as once upon a time, and kids today are more likely to surf the windows on their computer screens than stand spellbound before those vintage places of retail wonder and delight.

1934

An import from England, the board game Sorry! is introduced by Parker Brothers

Das Brettspiel Sorry!, ein Import aus Großbritannien, wird von Parker Brothers herausgebracht

Parker Brothers lance le jeu de plateau Sorry! importé d'Angleterre

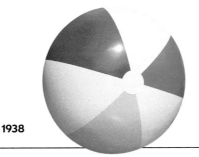

1938

Simple yet versatile, the inflatable beach ball is invented by Jonathon DeLonge

Einfach, aber vielseitig: Jonathon DeLonge erfindet den aufblasbaren Wasserball

Simple mais polyvalent, le ballon de plage gonflable est inventé par Jonathon DeLonge

1940

The Red Ryder BB gun makes its debut; young boys rejoice

Das Luftgewehr Red Ryder BB kommt auf den Markt; die Jungen sind begeistert

Le fusil à plombs Red Ryder BB arrive sur le marché, à la grande joie des garçons

Because girls would love
a friend to dance with,
Mattel makes SWINGY.™

She swings! She swings her arms...
she swings her feet with the "Swingy Step."
She tosses her shining hair from side to side,
and dances like no other doll in the world.
Swingy comes with her very own pop record,
with music and lyrics to match her mood. And
when *Swingy* finishes dancing, she'll walk, too.

TOY STORIES

Die Amerikaner ziehen vom Land in die Stadt, die Löhne steigen, und die Spielwarenindustrie boomt.

Kinder, die sich vor dem Schaufenster eines Spielwarenladens die Nase platt drücken und sich nichts sehnlicher wünschen, als die darin ausgestellte Puppe, die Spielzeugeisenbahn oder das Fahrrad ihr eigen zu nennen – eine typisch amerikanische Szene und ein symbolhaftes Bild, das jeder versteht. Bei allen Kindern (und auch so manchem Erwachsenen) erzeugen Spielsachen den unwiderstehlichen Wunsch, sie zu besitzen, zu halten, zu konsumieren. Spielzeuge sind nicht einfach nur kleine Ablenkungen und Vergnügungen, sondern sie sind Motivatoren, Belohnungen, und sie sind – vor allem vor Weihnachten – ein lukratives Geschäft.

In den 1950ern, den boomenden Nachkriegsjahren, flimmerte eine Spielshow über US-amerikanische Fernsehbildschirme, in der die teilnehmenden Kinder fünf Minuten Zeit hatten, um so viele Spielsachen zusammenzuraffen, wie ihre kleinen Ärmchen halten konnten (nur die durften sie dann behalten). Nachdem ein Klingelton signalisiert hatte, dass die Zeit um war, präsentierten die glücklichen Gewinner ihre Beute stolz dem Publikum, wodurch dessen Kauflust geweckt werden sollte. Jahrzehnte später wandte Nickelodeon in *Super Toy Run* dieselbe Psychologie an, nur durften die Kandidaten diesmal mithilfe von Einkaufswagen noch mehr neuartiges Spielzeug an sich reißen.

Ich hatte nie das Glück, für diese Show ausgewählt zu werden – obwohl ich mich redlich bemühte –, erlebte aber meine eigene Version davon. Als Belohnung dafür, dass ich eine qualvolle Mandeloperation über mich hatte ergehen lassen, durfte ich mir drei Spielsachen bei Rappaport's Toy Bazaar aussuchen – dem legendären Laden, der bis zu seiner Schließung 1981 90 Jahre lang auf Manhattans Third Avenue, Ecke 79th Street residierte und seine Waren in gepunktetes Papier einpackte (das Stuart Davis 1951 zu seinem Gemälde *Rapt At Rappaport's* inspirierte). Meine Eltern kannten einen der Besitzer, Harold Ostrover, der in Anspielung auf die TV-Sendung scherzhaft zu mir sagte, ich hätte fünf Minuten Zeit, mir aus dem Sortiment in den endlos langen und bis zum Bersten gefüllten Regalreihen etwas auszusuchen. Folglich spurtete ich los und rief mir, während mein Herz wie verrückt schlug und Adrenalin meinen Körper durchflutete, unzählige Werbespots, die samstagmorgens im Kinderprogramm ausgestrahlt wurden, und Anzeigen in *Life*, *Look* und anderen Zeitschriften in Erinnerung, die die neuesten Markenspielsachen und Merchandising-Produkte bewarben. Meine Wahl richtete sich ganz nach den Top Ten der damals angesagtesten Spielzeuge und dem entsprechenden Status, den mir diese bei meinen neidischen Freunden bescheren würden. Und was angesagt war, bestimmten Werbekampagnen – ein schönes Beispiel für den unmittelbaren Einfluss von Propaganda auf das menschliche Verhalten, sogar wenn es um Spielsachen ging.

Spielwaren erfüllen das in der Regel harmlose Bedürfnis von Kindern zu spielen, zu basteln und herumzuwerkeln, aber die *Werbung* für Spielzeug ist alles andere als unschuldig. Sie ist das Tor zu einem lebenslangen Konsumverhalten – in diesem Fall von Produkten, die ihren Herstellern auch unter dem Deckmantel des pädagogisch Wertvollen satte Profite einbringen. In der guten alten Zeit der Spielzeugwerbung, einer Zeit, in der pädagogische Theorien Anklang fanden, wurden zahlreiche Spielwaren als Instrumente der kindlichen Entwicklung angepriesen. Im Juli 1916 erschien zum Beispiel in der Zeitschrift *Ladies' Home Journal* ein Artikel namens „Den Einfallsreichtum der Kinder fördern": „Jedes normale Kind ist dann am glücklichsten, wenn es etwas ‚macht' oder eine Situation ‚spielt', auch wenn es vielleicht kein sichtbares Resultat gibt, das mit dem Gedanken in seinem kleinen Köpfchen harmoniert", schrieb Mildred Austin Shinn und fügte hinzu, dass die Kleinen am liebsten mit ganz normalen Haushaltsgegenständen spielen. Kinder mögen aber auch perfekt entworfene und bereits fertig zusammengesetzte Spielsachen bestimmter Marken. Die Werbung vieler Markenprodukte versprechen Privilegien, die mit Wohlstand und einer bestimmten ethnischen Herkunft einhergehen. Beim Kaufen und Besitzen von Statussymbolen zu konkurrieren, ist kein reines Erwachsenenphänomen. Die Grundlagen dafür werden bereits im Kindesalter geschaffen.

Spielzeuge sollen Spaß machen, doch Kinder sind nicht die zahlenden Kunden. So warnte die Zeitschrift *Pic* 1941: „Obwohl bei der Verbesserung von Spielzeug große Fortschritte gemacht wurden … kaufen Eltern im Durchschnitt immer noch Spielsachen, die ihnen selber gefallen, und machen sich zu wenige Gedanken über die möglichen Auswirkungen, gut oder schlecht, auf die Kinder, für die die Sachen eigentlich bestimmt sind." Die wichtigste Eigenschaft eines Spielzeugs sei es, „ihren Kleinen beizubringen, mit anderen Kindern auszukommen". Darüber hinaus sollten Spielsachen „eine echte Alltagserfahrung oder eine Nachahmung von Erwachsenen" ermöglichen.

In der Anfangszeit der flächendeckenden Massenmedien war die Spielzeugwerbung noch nicht so berechnend wie später, was zum Teil daran lag, dass sie *tatsächlich* pädagogisch sinnvoller war. Die Bausätze von Meccano, 1898 vom Briten Frank Hornby erfunden, gehörten zu den am meisten beworbenen Spielwaren. Eine der ersten großen amerikanischen Werbekampagnen wurde für die in New York produzierten Bausätze von Erector (die Meccano später aufkaufte) aufgefahren. Das klassische, von A. C. Gilbert erfundene und 1998 in die National Toy Hall of Fame aufgenommene Erector Set bestand aus Metallbalken und mechanischen Komponenten, die von kleinen Gewindestiften zusammengehalten wurden. „Geschäftsleute und Arbeitspsychologen lobten das Spielzeug, das Spiel und Arbeit verband und die ‚Bauinstinkte' der Kinder weckte", kommentiert das National Museum of Play. Das Erector Set wurde 1913 lanciert, begleitet von Werbekampagnen in der *Saturday Evening Post* und *Popular Mechanics*, die auf Eltern *und* Kinder abzielten. Ungefähr zur selben Zeit kamen auch Lincoln Logs und Tinker-Toys auf den Markt. Erector Sets brachten Jungs (nicht Mädchen) das Ingenieurwesen und die Konstruktionsgrundlagen von Wolkenkratzern nahe, Spezialbausätze mit Elektromotoren erlaubte den Bau von Zügen, Dampfbaggern, Riesenrädern und Zeppelinen. Diese

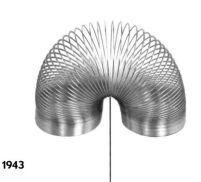

1943

1948

1949

The Slinky is invented after springs for a ship fall off a shelf

Der Slinky wird erfunden, nachdem Schiffsfedern aus einem Regal fallen

Un ingénieur naval invente le Slinky après avoir vu tomber un ressort d'une étagère

Nosco produces bargain toys, duping kids to buy "100 Toy Soldiers for $1"

Nosco produziert Billigspielzeug, darunter „100 Spielzeugsoldaten für $1"

Nosco produit des jouets à bas prix et les enfants se ruent sur ses « 100 petits soldats à 1 dollar »

A new tabletop game has millions of Americans shouting, "I got Cooties"

Ein neues Brettspiel lässt Millionen von Amerikanern schreien: „Ich habe Läuse"

À cause du nouveau jeu Cootie, des millions d'Américains crient « J'ai des poux ! »

Bausätze waren nicht als reines Spielvergnügen, sondern als Eignungstests für zukünftige Berufe gedacht.

Es gab Dutzende von Anzeigen für Gewehre, sowohl für echte als auch in Spielzeugausführung. Die Winchester- („Oh, J-I-M-M-Y, come on over, we're goin' shootin'!") und Stevens-Gewehre („Hitting the Bullseye Since 1864") schossen scharf, während King, Sterling und Daisy Luftgewehre waren, die Diabolos oder Rundkugeln verschossen. In der Werbung für Daisy hieß es: „Jeder gesunde, normale, echte Junge will und braucht ein Gewehr", und für Käufer, denen Luftgewehre nicht martialisch genug waren, gab es sogar ein Gewehr mit Bajonett. Waffen aller Art verkauften sich bestens. (Milton Bradley vermarktete ein Maschinengewehr namens Big Dick, das mit Holzkugeln schoss und nur drei Dollar kostete.) Auch andere Militaria wie zum Beispiel die Forts, die mit Richters Ankersteinen errichtet wurden, waren beliebt.

Aber natürlich gab es auch weniger kriegerische Spieloptionen. In Zeitschriften wie *Boys' Life* bewarben die Ives Manufacturing Company und Lionel ihre elektrischen Eisenbahnen. Der Schlitten Flexible Flyer, als schnell und stabil angepriesen, gehörte fast zur Standardausrüstung in amerikanischen Haushalten. Zu den populärsten Produkten zählten außerdem Tischtennissets, Wahrsagespiele und ein echter Indianer-

Wigwam für nur 1,50 Dollar („Genau das Richtige für Jungs"). Jungen konnten auch stolze Besitzer eines Speedy Car werden oder das 1 Meter lange Aero Car bauen und fliegen.

Kataloge waren das Amazon der Wirtschaftskrisenära. Kleine Anzeigen in Comic- und Groschenheftchen bewarben Versandhandelsprodukte wie Zimmerman's Flying Machine: „Ein Wunder an Einfachheit", ein „wissenschaftlich" entworfener Drachen, den „jeder Junge und jedes Mädchen steigen lassen" konnte. Auch Fahrräder fielen in die Kategorie Spielwaren. 1919 verkaufte die Haverford Cycle Company ihr Model Black Beauty nur an Jungs. „Jeder Junge und jedes Mädchen im Wohnblock beneidet den Youngster", der damals stolzer Besitzer eines Skudder Car war. Nur für Mädchen bestimmt war hingegen Dolly's Home („Ein wahr gewordenes Märchen!"), und Puppen wie die berühmte Mary Jane wurden als Busenfreundinnen vermarktet („Nichts, was Sie einem kleinen Mädchen schenken könnten, würde sie je so liebhaben wie Mary Jane – nichts würde sie so sehr herzen und an sich drücken.") Viele Spielsachen für Mädchen versuchten, die häusliche Erwachsenenwelt nachzuahmen. Eine Miniküche versprach „genauso viel Spaß wie Mutters Küchenschrank". Sowohl Mädchen als auch Jungen waren die Zielgruppe für Bollerwagen

1950

1953

1954

Bagel-maker Dan Thompson invents folding pingpong table on wheels

Bagel-Bäcker Dan Thompson erfindet einen zusammenklappbaren Pingpongtisch auf Rädern

Le fabricant de bagels Dan Thompson invente la table de ping-pong pliante sur roues

Wiffle Ball created for postwar American suburbs; translation: fewer broken windows

Wiffle Ball ist die Baseballvariante für die Vororte der Nachkriegszeit: weniger zerborstene Scheiben

La Wiffle Ball est destinée aux banlieues résidentielles : moins de carreaux cassés

Davy Crockett TV show sets off coonskin hat craze

Die TV-Serie *Davy Crockett* macht Mützen aus Waschbärfell zum Trend

Le feuilleton télévisé *Davy Crockett* lance la mode de la toque de trappeur (zum Beispiel der Sheboygan De-Lux Speedster), Roller, Schaukeln für zu Hause und die ansprechend designten Tinker-Toy-Bausätze.

In den 1930ern gab es Spielsachen oft als Beigabe zu anderen Produkten wie den Frühstücksflocken von Wheaties, Ralston und Quaker. Häufig wurden Spielwaren mit Comicfiguren beworben – Dick Tracy verkaufte Flugausrüstungen – und vor dem Hintergrund des drohenden Kriegs in Europa war eine zunehmende Anzahl von Spielsachen militärisch ausgerichtet. Während des Zweiten Weltkriegs waren die meisten Materialien der Rüstungsindustrie vorbehalten, die in dieser Zeit vor der Spielzeugproduktion Priorität hatte. Die Spielzeugherstellung und -werbung verloren an Bedeutung. Im Nachkriegswirtschaftsboom erlebten Puppen, Zauberkästen und Brettspiele jedoch ein Comeback.

In den späten 1940er- und frühen 1950er-Jahren war es angesagt, in kindgerechten Sparschweinen Geldmünzen zu sammeln, mit Bauklötzen von Playskool Türme zu errichten, mit Roy Rogers' „pow'ful" Kastenkamera Fotos zu schießen oder mit den Ferngläsern derselben Marke die Nachbarn auszuspähen. Neue, im Krieg erfundene Werkstoffe und neue Marken tauchten auf. Hasbros Mr. und Mrs. Potato Head etablierten sich ab 1954 als einer der Top-Ten-Bestseller des Unternehmens. 1957 nahm das 1943 erfun-

dene Slinky ordentlich Werbefläche in Anspruch, und 1958 halfen Anzeigen dem die Konsistenz verändernden Silly Putty (Hüpfkitt) zum Erfolg. Von technischem Fortschritt zeugten elektrische Puppen wie Effanbees Norma, die laufen (und bald auch schon sprechen) konnten. 1955 erschienen Micky-Maus-Ohren auf der Bildfläche, zusammen mit Dutzenden anderen Accessoires und Kostümen von beliebten Figuren, darunter Trapperkleidung im Stil von Davy Crockett und Roy-Rogers-Pistolengürtel.

Im Zuge der Creative Revolution in der Werbebranche wurde in den 1960er-Jahren auch die Spielzeugwerbung in Design und Inhalt kreativer und intelligenter. Eine Mattel-Anzeige von 1962 zeigte dunkelhäutige Kinder mit Puppen derselben Hautfarbe, und die Werbekampagne für die Puppe Cheerful Tearful, ebenfalls aus dem Hause Mattel, war genauso clever wie jede Werbung für Erwachsene aus der Zeit. Eine Lego-Anzeige von 1967 mit der Headline „Lego, das Spielzeug, von dem Kinder am 26. Dezember noch nicht genug haben werden" sah nicht nur erwachsen aus, sondern war auch genauso smart wie eine große Idee (und passte zum Slogan „Lego … das gut durchdachte Spielzeug"). In den folgenden Jahren waren unter anderem die Werbungen für Barbie, Midget Mustang, Julia zur gleichnamigen TV-Serie mit afroame-

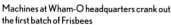

1957

1959

1960

Machines at Wham-O headquarters crank out the first batch of Frisbees

Aus der Wham-O-Zentrale kommt die erste Ladung Frisbees auf den Markt

Les machines de l'usine Wham-O crachent la première série de frisbees

Fisher-Price introduces Little People to help children think big

Fisher-Price präsentiert Little People, um Kindern die größeren Dimensionen zu zeigen

Fisher-Price lance les Little People, pour que les enfants voient les choses en grand

Rock-a-Stack teaches children about colors while developing motor skills

Rock-a-Stack bringt Kindern die Farben bei und trainiert gleichzeitig ihre motorischen Fähigkeiten

Avec la Pyramide Arc-en-Ciel les enfants apprennent les couleurs et développent leur motricité rikanischen Stars und die tragbare elektrische Näh-maschine der Marke Signature Junior beliebt, weil sie die Welt der Erwachsenen imitierten. Die *Sesamstraße*-Produkte von Fisher-Price und andere richteten sich an Erwachsene, denen die kreative visuelle Sprache der Werbeindustrie vertraut war.

Diese neue Werbekultur zielte nicht ausschließ-lich auf Kinder, denn die Eltern waren schließlich die Verwalter des Spielzeugbudgets und ließen sich als solche vor allem von einer Werbung überzeugen, die ihr eigenes Konsumverhalten spiegelte. Von den spä-ten 1970er- bis in die 1990er-Jahre hinein wurden Computerspiele sowohl für Kinder als auch für ihre

Eltern beworben – vor allem zur Weihnachtszeit. Auch heute noch reißen Kinder vielleicht Anzeigen aus Zeit-schriften oder Katalogseiten aus und verteilen sie vor Weihnachten und Geburtstagen strategisch im Haus, doch die Spielzeugpropaganda des digitalen Zeitalters kommt eher per E-Mail, basierend auf Algorithmen, die individuelle Wünsche ermitteln können. Die Schau-fenster von Spielwarenläden strahlen nicht mehr die-selbe Faszination aus wie einst, und die Kids von heute starren eher gebannt auf ihren Computerbildschirm, als sich sehnsüchtig vor den Auslagen altmodischer Spielzeug-Paradiese die Nasen platt zu drücken.

1961

America jumps onto the Slip 'N Slide

Ganz Amerika reitet auf der Slip 'N Slide-Wasserrutsch-Welle

Toute l'Amérique saute sur le Slip 'N Slide

1962

The Chatter Telephone becomes the first phone for many baby boomers

Das Chatter Telephone ist für viele Babyboomer das erste Telefon

Le Chatter de Fisher-Price sera le premier téléphone de bien des baby-boomers

1965

Riding a wave of audio-toy popularity, Mattel releases the educational See 'n Say

Mattel nutzt den Audiospielzeugtrend und bringt das pädagogisch wertvolle See 'n Say heraus

Surfant sur la popularité des jouets audio, Mattel sort le jeu éducatif L'Horloge parlante

Teddy
Walking Sailor

**No. 102 Teddy Walking
Sailor**

A jolly tar, just in from a long
cruise and with the sea roll
still in his legs. His funny
action is a delight to grown-
ups as well as to the children.

9½ inches high

The Ted Toy-lers INC.
NEW BEDFORD, MASS., U.S.A.

TOY STORIES

Les Américains quittent la campagne pour la ville, le pouvoir d'achat augmente et l'industrie du jouet explose.

L'image des enfants collés à la vitrine d'un marchand de jouets, dévorant des yeux le grand déballage d'objets ludiques de tous acabits, chaque gamin désirant plus que tout la poupée, le train ou le vélo à pédales, a valeur d'icône aux États-Unis. Les jouets déclenchent chez tous les enfants (et certains adultes) une irrépressible envie de toucher, d'avoir et donc, de consommer. Loin de n'être que des diversions destinées à procurer un petit plaisir, les jouets sont des modèles, des récompenses et représentent un marché énorme, tout particulièrement à la période de Noël.

Dans l'économie florissante des mythiques Fifties, la télévision diffusait une émission où les jeunes participants avaient cinq minutes pour attraper autant de jouets que leurs petits bras pouvaient en porter. Quand le terrible buzzer final retentissait, les gosses présentaient fièrement leur butin au public (provoquant sa soif d'achat). Plusieurs dizaines d'années plus tard, le *Super Toy Run* de la chaîne Nickelodeon appliquera la même approche pour un concept plus jubilatoire encore, où ce seront des caddies que les petits élus rempliront jusqu'à ras bord.

Je n'ai pas eu la chance d'être sélectionné pour l'émission – ce n'est pas faute d'avoir essayé – mais j'ai eu droit à une expérience similaire. Pour me réconforter après une douloureuse ablation des amygdales, j'ai pu choisir trois jouets au Rappaport's Toy Bazaar. Pendant 90 ans, jusqu'à sa fermeture en 1981, cet illustre magasin de jouets de la Troisième Avenue, à Manhattan, a enveloppé sa façade de papier cadeau à pois (ce qui inspira sa toile *Rapt At Rappaport's* à Stuart Davis en 1951). Mes parents connaissaient un des propriétaires, Harold Ostrover, qui, en clin d'œil au jeu télévisé, m'a annoncé que j'avais cinq minutes

pour choisir ce qui me ferait plaisir dans cette caverne d'Ali Baba. Je suis parti en trombe, mon cœur battait à tout rompre, l'adrénaline me tambourinait aux tempes et j'ai repensé à toutes ces pubs du samedi matin à la télé, dans *Life*, *Look* ou d'autres magazines, pour les derniers jouets à la mode des marques les plus prisées. J'ai fait mon choix en fonction des dix jouets les plus recherchés du moment et du statut qu'ils me conféreraient auprès de mes copains envieux. Le lien entre produit et statut social est une création de la publicité – et c'est ainsi que la propagande parvient à dicter des comportements, même lorsqu'il s'agit de jouer.

Si les jouets comblent le désir inoffensif qu'un enfant a de manipuler, fabriquer ou bricoler, les publicités pour les jouets n'ont rien d'innocent. Entre les mains des publicitaires, ils deviennent des passerelles vers une vie de consumérisme – des produits destinés à enrichir leur fabricant et non l'esprit des bambins, quoi qu'ils en disent. Au cours de ces glorieuses années passées, toute une gamme de jouets a été vendue comme stimulant le développement cognitif ou intellectuel. Prenez cet article paru en juillet 1916 dans le *Ladies' Home Journal*, intitulé «Apprendre la débrouillardise à un enfant»: «Tout enfant normalement constitué est heureux quand il "fait" quelque chose ou qu'il "imite" des gestes, même si la pensée du petit être ne se traduit par aucun résultat tangible», écrit Mildred Austin Shinn, ajoutant même que les «petits» tirent davantage de satisfaction à fabriquer leurs jouets avec ce qu'ils trouvent à la maison.

Ne nous leurrons cependant pas, les enfants aiment aussi recevoir des jouets finis, neufs, populaires. Bien des marques vendent leurs produits comme des signes extérieurs d'ambition, reproduisant les privilèges liés à la richesse, à l'origine ethnique ou au genre. L'achat compétitif n'est pas l'apanage des adultes, il s'installe dès que les marques modèlent les désirs des enfants. Les jouets ont beau être faits pour eux, ce ne sont pas les enfants qui consomment. Le magazine *Pic* le soulignait en 1941 : « Malgré les importantes améliorations apportées au jouet, (…) le parent moyen achète encore l'objet qui l'attire, lui, sans penser à l'effet, bon ou mauvais, qu'il aura sur l'enfant auquel il est destiné. » Le jouet n'est un vrai cadeau que s'il « apprend à votre petit à socialiser avec les autres enfants », poursuit l'auteur, et qu'il intègre « une part d'expérience quotidienne réelle ou d'imitation des adultes ».

Aux premières heures des mass media nationaux, la pub pour les jouets n'est pas aussi calculée qu'elle le deviendra, notamment parce que les jouets d'alors sont *vraiment* plus éducatifs. Les jeux de construction Meccano créés en 1898 par l'Anglais Frank Hornby font alors partie des produits les plus visibles. La marque new-yorkaise Erector (plus tard rachetée par Meccano) est un des premiers gros annonceurs américains du secteur. Intronisé au National Toy Hall of Fame en 1998, le kit Erector original, conçu par A. C. Gilbert, était composé de poutrelles métalliques et d'éléments mécaniques qu'on assemblait avec de petites vis sans tête. « Les

milieux d'affaires et les psychologues de l'industrie ont vanté les mérites de ce jouet qui valorise l'effort et encourage les "instincts bâtisseurs des enfants" », note le Musée national du jeu. Le kit Erector est sorti en 1913, accompagné par une campagne dans le *Saturday Evening Post* et *Popular Mechanics*. Ces publicités sont destinées autant aux parents qu'à leurs enfants, tout comme celles pour les deux autres succès de l'époque, Lincoln Logs et Tinker Toys. Les kits Erector familiarisent les garçons (pas les filles) avec l'ingénierie et la structure des gratte-ciel. Des kits spéciaux comprenant des moteurs électriques permettent de construire des trains, des excavateurs, des grandes roues et des zeppelins. Tout cela ressemble davantage à un test d'aptitude professionnelle qu'à du jeu.

On trouve aussi foison de pubs pour des armes, vraies ou factices. Les carabines Winchester (« *Oh, J-I-M-M-Y, come on over, we're goin' shootin'!* ») et Stevens (« En plein dans le mille depuis 1864 ») tirent des balles réelles, tandis que les fusils King, Sterling et Daisy sont à air comprimé ou à plomb. La pub pour Daisy affirme que « tout vrai garçon sain de corps et d'esprit a envie et besoin d'une arme » et si les plombs ne suffisent pas, il y a le fusil équipé d'une

1968

Mattel muscles its way into the boys' market with Hot Wheels

Mattel erobert mit Hot Wheels den Spielzeugmarkt für Jungen

Mattel tente de s'imposer aussi auprès des garçons avec Hot Wheels

1970

The Nerf ball is released; indoor sports thrive

Der Nerf-Ball erobert den Markt; der Indoorsport boomt

La balle Nerf sort en boutiques ; le sport en salle prospère

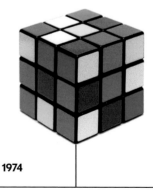

1974

Hungarian professor Ernõ Rubik invents Rubik's Cube for students

Der ungarische Professor Ernõ Rubik erfindet für Studenten den Zauberwürfel

Le professeur hongrois Ernõ Rubik invente son célèbre cube pour ses étudiants baïonnette. Les armes en tous genres se vendent très bien – Milton Bradley commercialise même pour 3 dollars une mitraillette baptisée Big Dick qui tire des balles en bois.

Il existe toutefois des options de jeu moins risquées, comme les trains électriques de Ives Manufacturing Company et Lionel promus dans des revues comme *Boys' Life*. Presque toutes les familles possèdent leur luge Flexible Flyer, rapide et robuste. Les tables de ping-pong, les jeux divinatoires et l'authentique (1,50 dollar) Wigwam amérindien («Parfait pour les garçons!») font aussi partie des classiques de l'époque. Les garçons peuvent «posséder leur propre bolide» après avoir construit et appris à piloter l'Aero Car, modèle réduit d'un mètre de long. L'armée n'est pas en reste, avec les kits Fortress des Anchor Blocks créés par Richter.

Pendant la Dépression, on se rue sur les catalogues comme sur Amazon aujourd'hui. Des petits espaces publicitaires sont aussi ménagés dans les *comics* et les *pulps*, qui proposent de commander des jouets par correspondance, comme la Machine Volante de Zimmerman, «un miracle de simplicité» conçu «scientifiquement» (un cerf-volant) que «tous les garçons et les filles sauront faire voler».

Les vélos entrent aussi dans la catégorie ludique. En 1919, la Haverford Cycle Company ne vend sa bicyclette Black Beauty qu'aux garçons, mais «tous les garçons et les filles du quartier envieront» celui ou celle qui a la Skudder Car. Pour les filles, il y a Dolly's Home («Un conte de fées devenu réalité!»); les poupées sont vendues comme une meilleure amie, une confidente, à l'image de la célèbre Mary Jane («Rien de ce que vous pourrez offrir à une petite fille ne la ravira autant que Mary Jane – rien qu'elle puisse serrer aussi fort contre son cœur.»). La plupart des jouets pour filles tentent d'imiter la vie domestique des femmes adultes, comme cette cuisinette équipée de «placards super amusants, comme celle de maman». Les chariots de diverses formes – comme le Sheboygan De-Lux Speedster – les trottinettes, les portiques de jeux et les astucieux Tinker Toys sont eux destinés aux garçons comme aux filles.

Dans les années 1930, les marques, notamment de céréales comme Wheaties, Ralston ou Quaker, proposent des jouets en bonus. Souvent, des personnages de comics prêtent leur image aux annonceurs – Dick Tracy fait, par exemple, la promotion de pièces d'avion. Avec le conflit qui couve en Europe, les jouets sont de plus en plus belliqueux, mais pendant

1976

1978

1981

Art student Xavier Roberts makes prototype for Cabbage Patch Kids

Kunststudent Xavier Roberts erstellt den Prototyp für die Cabbage Patch Kids

L'étudiant en arts Xavier Roberts réalise le prototype pour les Patoufs (d'abord appelés Copinous)

Whoever eats the most marbles wins in Hungry Hungry Hippos

Wer in Hungry Hungry Hippos die meisten Murmeln frisst, gewinnt

Avec les Hippos Gloutons, celui qui mange le plus de billes a gagné

Care Bears originate as greeting card art, two years before plush toy debut

Zwei Jahre vor ihrem Debüt als Plüschtiere gibt es die Glücksbärchis als Postkartenmotive

Les Bisounours figurent sur des cartes de vœux et deviennent des peluches deux ans plus tard la Seconde Guerre mondiale la plupart des matériaux servant à la fabrication des jouets sont rationnés par le gouvernement; le jeu et la pub ne sont plus une priorité. Une fois la paix signée, en revanche, l'économie repart en flèche et les poupées, boîtes de magie et jeux de société font leur retour.

À la fin des années 1940 et au début des années 1950, on s'amuse à mettre de l'argent de côté dans des minibanques spéciales, à construire tours et châteaux avec les briques Playskool, à prendre des photos avec le « suue-per » appareil de poche Roy Rogers ou à espionner par la fenêtre des voisins avec ses jumelles brevetées. De nouveaux matériaux ont été développés pendant la guerre, donnant naissance à des géants du secteur: les monsieur et madame Patate de Hasbro se sont imposés en 1954 comme un des dix jouets les mieux vendus de la marque. En 1957, Slinky, inventé en 1943, fait l'objet d'une publicité soutenue et, en 1958, c'est aussi une campagne rondement menée qui pousse le versatile Silly Putty (le Mastic idiot) sur le devant de la scène. L'industrie dispose de la technologie nécessaire pour proposer une poupée électrique qui marche (et ne tardera pas à parler), comme la Norma d'Effanbee. En 1955, les oreilles de

Mickey entrent dans le paysage culturel, ainsi que des dizaines d'autres costumes et accessoires inspirés de mascottes et d'icônes comme Davy Crockett ou Roy Rogers.

Dans les années 1960, alors que la pub fait sa révolution créative, la promotion des jouets devient plus travaillée sur le fond et la forme. Une pub de 1962 pour Mattel montre ainsi des enfants de diverses couleurs de peau tenant des poupées de la même carnation. La campagne sophistiquée pour la poupée Cheerful Tearful, digne d'une grande, témoigne aussi des progrès de Mattel. Le slogan choisi par Lego en 1967, « Lego, le jouet qui ne les aura pas lassés le 26 décembre » est un message adulte, malin comme une « grande idée » (d'autant que la promesse d'une « créativité sans limites » était tenue). Les années passent et les pubs pour des produits supposés enseigner la vie comme Barbie, Midget Mustang, Julia (d'après l'héroïne afro-américaine de la sitcom éponyme), ou la machine à coudre électrique portable Signature Junior, sont populaires parce qu'ils imitent le monde adulte. Les produits dérivés *Sesame Street* de Fisher-Price, entre autres, s'adressent à des adultes réceptifs au langage visuel employé par l'industrie publicitaire.

1983

1984

1985

Slap bracelets are invented by Stuart Anders, a high school shop teacher in Wisconsin

Die Klackarmbänder werden von Stuart Anders, einem Highschool-Lehrer aus Wisconsin, erfunden

Les bracelets Slap sont inventés par Stuart Anders, professeur de lycée dans le Wisconsin

Pound Puppies are created by Mike Bowling, a Ford car assembler

Mike Bowling, Automonteur bei Ford, kreiert die Pound Puppies

Les Pitous sont créés par Mike Bowling, ancien assembleur chez Ford

Garbage Pail Kids trading cards make big bucks on bad taste

Die Sammelkarten der Garbage Pail Kids machen viel Geld mit schlechtem Geschmack

Les cartes à échanger des Patoufs, où comment faire fortune avec du mauvais goût

Cette nouvelle sophistication n'est donc pas destinée exclusivement aux enfants. Ce sont les parents qui tiennent les cordons de la bourse et ils se laissent aisément convaincre par des campagnes qui font écho à leurs propres habitudes de consommation. De la fin des années 1970 à la moitié des années 1990, les jeux vidéo sont promus pour plaire aux grandes personnes comme aux petites, surtout en fin d'année. Les enfants déchirent peut-être toujours les pages des

catalogues et des magazines pour ensuite les laisser négligemment traîner aux endroits stratégiques de la maison à l'approche de leur anniversaire ou de Noël, mais à l'ère numérique la propagande arrive souvent dans un e-mail, acheminée par des algorithmes nourris aux données personnelles. Les devantures des magasins de jouets ne sont plus comme autrefois et les enfants d'aujourd'hui lèchent plus souvent leur écran d'ordinateur que les vitrines de ces lieux magiques.

1989

1991

1993

Nintendo releases Game Boy for gamers on the go

Nintendo bringt für Gamer unterwegs den Game Boy heraus

Nintendo édite la Game Boy, pour les joueurs qui ont la bougeotte

Super Soakers drench the media with an aggressive advertising campaign

Eine aggressive Kampagne wirbt in den Medien für Super-Soakers-Wasserpistolen

Les fusils à eau Super Soaker inondent la presse d'une publicité agressive

Beanie Babies have soft opening at various toy shows

Beanie Babies werden auf diversen Spielwaren-messen präsentiert

Les peluches Beanie Babies sont accueillies avec douceur dans divers salons du jouet

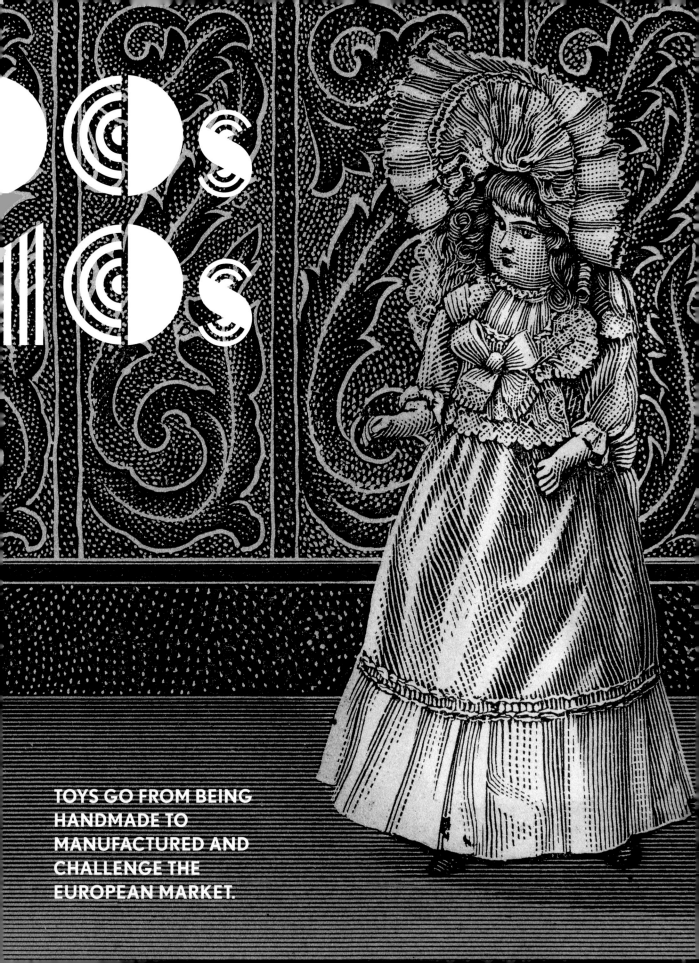

TOYS GO FROM BEING
HANDMADE TO
MANUFACTURED AND
CHALLENGE THE
EUROPEAN MARKET.

A MERRY CHRISTMAS FOR THE CHILDREN

Lettie Lane's Most Beautiful Doll
In Her Party Clothes

Designs by
The Fashion Editors

Drawings by
Sheila Young

Here is a Coat Long Enough to Cover Daisy's Party Dresses Completely. There are Also a Twisted Ribbon Hair Band and a Bonnet to Fit Her Head

A Dainty Dolly Varden Dress for Daisy, With a Pink Vanity Bag and Such a Lovely Hat

For a New Year's Party Make Daisy an Indian Dress Out of Brown Cambric Like This

In This Way She Can Impersonate Red Riding Hood on Her Way to Grandmother's

Making Daisy's New-Year Frolic Clothes

LIKE all little-girl dolls Daisy is in a great flutter of excitement over her first party, wondering what it will be like and whether she will enjoy herself or not. There will be lots and lots of cakes and candies, a tall Christmas tree lighted with candles, and, best of all, no one is expected to wear her regular party dress trimmed with lace and fussy bows—which makes one's mother say, "Now please don't tear or soil your dress, Daisy darling"—but to wear a real play dress, such as is worn by the little girl in the story book, in which one can jump and run. As Daisy loves little Red Riding Hood one dress is to be made like the dress Red Riding Hood wore on the day she visited her grandmother and met the wolf. This dress is to be of green cambric, with a pinafore of printed calico and a red satine cape and cap, and Daisy will have a tiny basket in which to put the dainties for Grandmother.

For another day there is the Indian girl's dress made of brown cambric and trimmed with bias strips of plaid. A white muslin belt, decorated with patches of embroidery, and a band for the hair with two funny little feathers on the side make this a very joyful dress. For trimming, the cambric is slashed to look like fringe. As only a tiny bit of flowered lawn is needed Daisy could also have a "Dolly Varden" dress trimmed with pretty white ruffles, and she would look "just too sweet" with a little hat, like the one above the bag, tied around with a wide ribbon band and bow. She will need a dinner dress of pale green challis with lace collar and cuffs. Last of all is the coat of plaid woolen goods, with red collar and cuffs trimmed with black braid.

Would You Like Daisy for Christmas?

YOU can have a golden-haired Daisy, with eyes that open to look at you and close when you lay her down, if you will read carefully and follow these directions: SEND US THREE YEARLY SUBSCRIPTIONS FOR THE LADIES' HOME JOURNAL, ACCOMPANIED BY A REMITTANCE OF FOUR DOLLARS AND FIFTY CENTS ($4.50), and the doll and patterns for all the clothes which are illustrated on this page will be sent to you, with all the shipping expenses prepaid. Of these three subscriptions AT LEAST TWO MUST BE FOR PERSONS WHOSE NAMES ARE NOT ALREADY ON OUR SUBSCRIPTION LIST. The third subscription may also be a new subscription, or it may be a renewal of a subscription which is already on the list. This renewal may be an extension of a subscription which has not yet expired, in which case be sure to call our attention to this fact, that duplicate copies may not be sent.

Remember the Points

There must be three yearly subscriptions; $4.50 must accompany the order; at least two of the subscriptions must be for persons not on our subscription list; the doll must be requested in your letter.

The doll, eighteen inches tall—more than twice as large as she is above—and dressed as shown on the left (in a white muslin slip, with white lace stockings and white slippers), with patterns for all the clothes illustrated on this page, will be sent with the charges prepaid.

Address all communications in regard to this doll to "Lettie Lane," in care of The Ladies' Home Journal, Philadelphia, Pennsylvania.

NEW CENTURY, OLD TOYS

DOLLS ARE THE MOST ANCIENT PLAYTHINGS EVER DEVISED.
Yet these miniature replicas of humans and animals dating back millennia were not originally made for children. At first, they embodied spiritualism, superstition, and ritual. Comfort and joy came later. At the turn of the century, advertisements triggered psychological urges in innocent tykes to bond with their make-believe friends and imaginary siblings. Made from wood, porcelain, and soft, huggable fabrics, dolls were imbued with female characteristics. In the early 1900s, it was no surprise that dolls were the bedrock of a nascent toy industry. During this same period, French bisque dolls with swivel heads and movable arms, legs, and eyes (that would open and close depending on whether they were standing or reclining) were all the rage for little girls. *The Ladies'*

1900

1901

1901

Plasticine, a British modeling clay for children, is first produced commercially

Plasticine, eine britische Knetmasse für Kinder, kommt auf den Markt

La plasticine, une pâte à modeler britannique pour enfants, est lancée sur le marché

Walt Disney is born in Chicago

Walt Disney erblickt in Chicago das Licht der Welt

Walt Disney naît à Chicago

Englishman Frank Hornby patents Mechanics Made Easy, soon to be Meccano

Der Engländer Frank Hornby lässt Mechanics Made Easy, das spätere Meccano, patentieren

L'Anglais Frank Hornby fait breveter Mechanics Made Easy, qui deviendra Meccano

World magazine offered such dolls for free to anyone who recruited nine yearly subscribers. Free rag dolls were also advertised as incentives for the purchase of various products, including Cook's Flaked Rice.

Animal dolls were popular, too. A hot advertised item, the Teddy Bear, was the most beloved soft toy. The bear, a gender-neutral kid's staple, originated from a story that President Theodore "Teddy" Roosevelt, while on one of his frequent hunting trips, refused to shoot a bear that had already been captured, tied up, and knocked unconscious. Roosevelt believed that shooting the captured animal was unsportsmanlike. When the incident became public, it was lampooned by Clifford Berryman in a cartoon in *The Washington Post.* This influenced husband and wife stuffed-animal makers Morris and Rose Michtom to create what they called "Teddy's Bear," which eventually became a toy sensation. Roosevelt spared his bear, but guns for boys were among the biggest-selling toys of the era. ("A gun that a fellow can be proud of…" read a *Boys' Life* ad for the .22 caliber Remington rifle.)

1902

1902

1903

Iron windup toys are popular at the turn of the century

Aufziehbares Blechspielzeug ist um die Jahrhundertwende beliebt

Les jouets mécaniques en fer blanc sont populaires au début du siècle

President Roosevelt's hunting trip spawns new toy: the teddy bear

Präsident Roosevelts Jagdausflug führt zu einem neuen Spielzeug: dem Teddybären

D'une partie de chasse du président Roosevelt naît l'indétrônable nounours, le Teddy Bear

Crayola introduces its box of color crayons

Crayola bringt seine Schachtel mit acht bunten Wachsmalstiften heraus

Crayola sort sa boîte de huit crayons de couleur

On a less violent track, boys were also encouraged through advertisements to engage in mind-bending engineering, invention, and construction as an introduction to future careers. Structo Boys' Engineering Outfits enabled "real boys" to learn the physics of manufacturing. Electric train sets also flooded the market. In 1917, as America went off to the Great War, *The American Boy* magazine announced that there would be "No toys from Europe this year," but "No one in America need go without playthings." For pennies, the M. W. Dunton Company sent drawings and directions for making submarines, monoplanes, and other wonders. The Robbins Manufacturing Company offered "Your Own Private Line To Your Pal's House" with its $1.50 electric telephone (picturing a boy and girl in conversation on the box). And for those lads and lassies that had musical prowess, the Southern California Music Company offered a complete "Rolando" Ukulele-Banjo Outfit for just $10.

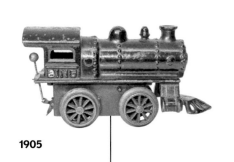

1905

1908

1908

German company Bing is the world's largest toy manufacturer

Die deutsche Firma Bing ist der weltweit größte Spielzeughersteller

L'Allemand Bing est le plus gros fabricant de jouets du monde

American Flyer enters the toy-train marketplace with a more affordable product

American Flyer mischt den Eisenbahnmarkt mit einem erschwinglicheren Produkt auf

American Flyer arrive sur le marché du train électrique avec un produit moins cher

British construction-toy company Meccano appears

Meccano, ein britischer Hersteller von Konstruktionsspielzeug, erscheint auf der Bildfläche

La compagnie de jeux de construction britannique Meccano est créée

NEUES JAHRHUNDERT, ALTES SPIELZEUG

US-Spielwaren werden nicht mehr in Handarbeit, sondern maschinell hergestellt und fordern die europäische Konkurrenz heraus.

Puppen gehören zu den ältesten Spielsachen überhaupt. Doch ursprünglich waren Miniaturversionen von Menschen und Tieren nicht für Kinder gedacht, sondern dienten als kultische oder rituelle Objekte, die Spiritualität und Aberglauben entsprangen. Zu Freuden- und Trostspendern wurden sie erst später. Um die Jahrhundertwende erweckten Werbeanzeigen in unschuldigen Rotznasen das Bedürfnis, Puppen zu ihren imaginären Freunden und Geschwistern zu machen. Die aus Holz, Porzellan und weichem Knuddelstoff gemachten Puppen bekamen weibliche Züge und bildeten Anfang des 20. Jahrhunderts das Fundament der aufkeimenden Spielzeugindustrie. Französische Bisque-Puppen mit drehbaren Köpfen und beweglichen Armen, Beinen und Augen (die sich öffneten, wenn die Puppe aufgerichtet wurde, und sich schlossen, wenn sie lag) waren bei kleinen Mädchen der Renner. Wer für die Zeitschrift *The Ladies' World* neun neue Abonnenten pro Jahr an Land zog, bekam eine solche Puppe als Prämie. Auch Stoffpuppen (traditionell aus Stoffresten gemachte *rag dolls*) wurden als Werbegeschenke eingesetzt und fungierten als Kaufanreiz für diverse Produkte wie zum Beispiel Cooks Reisflocken.

Stofftiere waren ebenfalls beliebt, vor allem der heiß beworbene Teddybär. Dessen beispielloser Aufstieg zu einem für Mädchen und Jungen gleichermaßen ansprechenden Kultspielzeug geht auf eine Geschichte zurück, die über Präsident Theodore „Teddy" Roosevelt überliefert ist. Er soll sich auf einem seiner häufigen Jagdausflüge geweigert haben, einen Bären zu erschießen, der bereits gefangen, gefesselt und bewusstlos war. Roosevelt fand, dass es unsportlich sei, das wehrlose Tier zu erschießen. Der Vorfall wurde publik und von Clifford Berryman in einer Karikatur in der *Washington Post* dargestellt. Dies inspirierte die Stofftiermacher Morris und Rose Michtom, „Teddy's Bear" zu kreieren, der sich zur Spielzeugsensation entwickelte. Trotz Roosevelts Weigerung, den Bären zu erlegen, gehörten aber auch Spielzeuggewehre für Jungs zu den Verkaufsschlagern der Ära. („Ein Gewehr, auf das man stolz sein kann …", hieß es in einer Werbung für ein Kaliber-.22-Gewehr der Marke Remington in der Zeitschrift *Boys' Life*.)

Auf einer weniger martialischen Schiene wurden Jungs in Werbeanzeigen auch dazu animiert, sich – als Grundlage für zukünftige Berufe – mit Technik, Erfindungen und Baukonstruktionen zu beschäftigen. Die Elektrobausätze von Structo sollten „richtigen Jungs" die Mechanismen der Industrieproduktion nahebringen. Elektrische Eisenbahnen überfluteten den Markt ebenfalls. 1917 traten die USA in den Ersten Weltkrieg ein, und die Zeitschrift *The American Boy* verkündete patriotisch, dass es „dieses Jahr kein Spielzeug aus Europa" geben würde, aber trotzdem „niemand in Amerika ohne Spielsachen auskommen" müsse. Die M. W. Dunton Company verschickte für Pfennige Baupläne für Modelle von U-Booten, Eindeckern und anderen Wundern der Technik. Die Robbins Manufacturing Company hatte für 1,50 Dollar ein elektrisches Telefon im Angebot und warb mit dem Slogan „Dein direkter Draht zum Haus deines Freundes" (auf der Verpackung waren ein Junge *und* ein Mädchen beim Telefonieren abgebildet). Und für den musikalischen Nachwuchs bot die Southern California Music Company das komplette Ukulele-Banjo-Set Rolando für nur 10 Dollar an. Wer konnte da schon widerstehen?

▶ Ives Manufacturing Company, 1914

Build a Model of a real Racing Automobile

A REGULAR speed-demon that will fly across the floor, or around in a circle like the big ones on the track or speedway. Build a late model, "classy" roadster-type car; or a big, powerful motor truck that dumps the load; or a dandy farm tractor that will haul heavy loads. Structo Auto Builder Outfits make it easy for you to build any of these wonderful toy models.

Building a Structo Automobile, Truck or Tractor is the next best thing to building a real one. They have parts like real cars. You assemble the parts and learn the principles of automobile construction. Some have sliding-gear transmission and differential just like a real car; others have direct shaft drive with die-cast gears on the rear axle. All have strong, powerful motors, regular steering knuckles, artillery type wheels and other features of regular machines. They run fine, too; up-grade or on the level. You crank the motor, shift the gears, "throw her in high," and off she goes! Run them indoors or outside.

Build a Structo Model Automobile, Truck or Tractor and you'll find out lots of things about real cars, have fine fun while you are building, and lively sport after you get it built.

Made Like A Real Automobile

Here's the rear end of Model No. 12. See the sliding gear transmission and the "big car" differential gears. They're just like the gears on a big car. Throw in the gear; two speeds forward and reverse. All controlled by one gear-shift lever.

STRUCTO TOYS

MAKE MEN OF BOYS

AMERICAN TOYS

Structo Auto Builder Outfits are the kind of toys every boy's dad likes to see him have because they teach useful knowledge and keep a fellow interested for a long time. And you can take them apart and put them away if you want to. Each Outfit is complete with everything you need to build one Model, even a screw driver and wrench. You assemble the parts the way a real mechanic does and then have a Model machine that looks, runs and *is* just like a real car.

Just look at these fine Models. Read the specifications for each one. Make your selection now. Write Structo on your Christmas list. Tell everyone *that's* what *you* want. Ask for Structo Auto Builder Outfits in the Toy Department, the Hardware Store, or in any store that sells worthwhile toys. Get Structo for Christmas and you'll have heaps of real fun.

West of Denver, Colo., and in Canada, prices are a little higher.

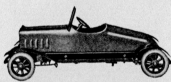

Structo Bear Cat Auto, Model No. 10

A sturdy, powerful, roadster-type car, finished in red enamel with black trimmings. Single-unit motor; direct shaft drive with die-cast gears on rear axle. Stop and start lever. 16 inches long. 12¼-inch wheelbase. **Price $6.50**

Structo DeLuxe Auto, Model No. 12

Just like a real car; underslung body, slanting windshield, folded top, extra wheel and other features. 16 inches long. 12¼-inch wheelbase. Triple-unit motor; "big car" transmission and differential; two forward speeds and reverse; gear-shift control lever. Orange, with black trimming. **Price $10.00**

Structo Farm Tractor, Model No. 11

The most powerful tractor of its size. Pulls three loaded trailers up-grade or on the level. Runs 18 minutes on one winding. Big, triple-unit motor, directly connected to drive wheels by low speed gears. Stop and start lever. Steered by steering wheel or long lines attached to steering bar. Green finish. **Price $7.50**

Trailers for Structo Tractor, Model No. 15

The Structo Tractor will pull wagons, toy cannon, engines and other similar toys; or you can build a separate Trailer and haul heavy loads like a real tractor. Trailers sold separately. **Price $1.00 Each**

Structo Dump Truck, Model No. 14

Just like a real truck! Runs smoothly and steadily. Carries heavy loads up-grade or on the level. Triple-unit motor; sliding gear transmission with forward and reverse speeds. Special load dumping attachment. 16 inches long. 12¼-inch wheelbase. Finished in red. **Price $12.00**

MADE BY STRUCTO MANUFACTURING COMPANY, FREEPORT, ILL.

NOUVEAU SIÈCLE, ANCIENS JOUETS

Les jouets ne sont plus façonnés à la main mais fabriqués en usine et s'attaquent au marché européen.

La poupée est le jouet le plus ancien jamais conçu. Pourtant ces petites répliques d'humains et d'animaux façonnées il y a plusieurs millénaires n'étaient pas destinées aux enfants. Elles étaient investies de spiritualité, de superstition et de ritualité. Le réconfort et la joie sont venus plus tard. Au tournant du siècle, la publicité déclenche dans l'esprit des petits innocents le besoin irrépressible de nouer des liens avec ces amis et frères et sœurs imaginaires. Confectionnées en bois, en porcelaine, en tissus doux et moelleux, les poupées sont dotées de caractéristiques féminines. Au début des années 1900, tout naturellement, elles sont le socle d'une industrie du jouet encore balbutiante. À l'époque les petites filles ne jurent que par les poupées françaises en biscuit dont on peut bouger la tête, les bras et les jambes et dont les paupières se ferment quand on les couche. Le magazine *The Ladies' World* en donne une à quiconque recrute neuf abonnées pour un an. Les poupées de chiffon sont souvent offertes pour l'achat de divers produits de consommation courante, comme les flocons de riz Cook's.

Les poupées animalières sont populaires aussi. La peluche qui réjouit les publicitaires comme les bambins, c'est le Teddy Bear, le fameux nounours asexué créé après que le président Theodore « Teddy » Roosevelt, féru de chasse, a refusé de tirer sur un ours qui avait déjà été capturé, attaché et assommé, jugeant que tuer un animal inconscient contrevenait aux lois du sport. L'incident devient public, Clifford Berryman en fait une caricature dans le *Washington Post*, et les fabricants de peluches Morris et Rose Michtom créent « l'ours de Teddy », qui devient la star du secteur. Roosevelt a épargné son ours, mais les armes font partie des jouets favoris des petits garçons. (*Boys' Life*

publie, par exemple, un encart pour la carabine Remington calibre 22, « une arme dont un petit gars peut être fier ».)

Dans un registre plus pacifique, la pub encourage les garçons à se montrer inventif et à relever des défis d'ingénierie ou de construction pour se faire une idée de leur future carrière. La boîte de jeu Boys' Engineering Outfits de Structo permet aux « vrais garçons » d'apprendre les lois physiques de la construction. Les trains électriques en kit envahissent aussi le marché. En 1917, alors que les États-Unis s'engagent dans la Grande Guerre, le magazine *The American Boy* annonce qu'il n'y aura « aucun jouet venu d'Europe cette année », mais que « personne en Amérique ne sera privé de joujoux ». Pour quelques pennies, la société M. W. Dunton envoie schémas et instructions pour fabriquer des sous-marins, des monoplans et d'autres merveilles. La Robbins Manufacturing Company, elle, offre « ta propre ligne privée pour appeler ton copain » avec son téléphone électrique à 1,50 dollar (dont la boîte montre un garçon et une fille en conversation). Pour les musiciens et musiciennes en herbe, la Southern California Music Company propose son ensemble ukulélé-banjo « Rolando » pour 10 dollars. Le tout *Made in America*.

◀ Structo Manufacturing Company, 1919

Great Bic

ycle Offer

STEVENS

◄◄ Arrow Cycle Company, 1916

◄ J. Stevens Arms and Tool Company, 1902

"With our arms you need fear no accidents," boasts the J. Stevens Arms and Tool Company. Providing further evidence of the rifles' safety, in the ad the parents are nowhere to be found while the kids are left to play with their new "toys," which, Stevens says, are "necessary articles for their enjoyment."

„Bei unseren Waffen brauchen Sie keine Angst vor Unfällen zu haben", brüstete sich die J. Stevens Arms und Tool Company. Wie um dies zu beweisen, sind in der Anzeige keine Eltern in Sicht, während die Kinder mit ihren neuen „Spielsachen" hantieren, die laut Stevens „unverzichtbare" Artikel der Kinderbespaßung sind.

« Avec nos armes, aucun risque d'accident », se vante la J. Stevens Arms et Tool Company. Pour illustrer le slogan publicitaire les parents sont hors champ tandis que les enfants s'amusent avec leurs nouveaux « jouets », des « articles nécessaires à leur plaisir », clame Stevens.

Harrington and Richardson Arms Company, 1905

RUBBER BROWNIES

These Amusing Little Fellows Created in Fine Red Rubber.

An Entertaining Toy. A Novel and Attractive Book-case or Mantel Ornament.

L I F E L I K E

D U R A B L E

Height of Figures, 6 inches.
10 in a Set, $5.00, or Sold Singly at 50c each.
Send for Our Catalog of Fine Rubber Toys.

THE B. F. GOODRICH CO.
AKRON, OHIO.

The B. F. Goodrich Company, 1901

▶ Schoenhut, 1907

By 1907, German immigrant Albert Schoenhut, a third-generation wood-carver who moved to Philadelphia in 1866 to fix toy pianos, had established one of the largest toy companies in the U.S. His specialty was meticulously constructed circus-themed wood dolls called the Humpty Dumpty Circus, which were sold individually or in sets.

1907 besaß der deutsche Einwanderer Albert Schoenhut, ein Holzschnitzer in dritter Generation, der 1866 nach Philadelphia gekommen war, um Spielzeugklaviere zu reparieren, eine der größten Spielzeugfirmen der USA. Seine Spezialität waren liebe-voll ausgearbeitete Holzfiguren mit Zirkus-Thematik, die unter dem Label „Humpty Dumpty Circus" einzeln oder als Sets verkauft wurden.

En 1907, l'immigré allemand Albert Schoenhut, troisième génération de menuisiers arrivé à Philadelphie en 1866 pour réparer des pianos jouets, a créé une des plus grosses entreprises de jouets des États-Unis. Son produit phare est une collection de poupées en bois sur le thème du cirque, le Humpty Dumpty Circus, vendues à l'unité ou par lots.

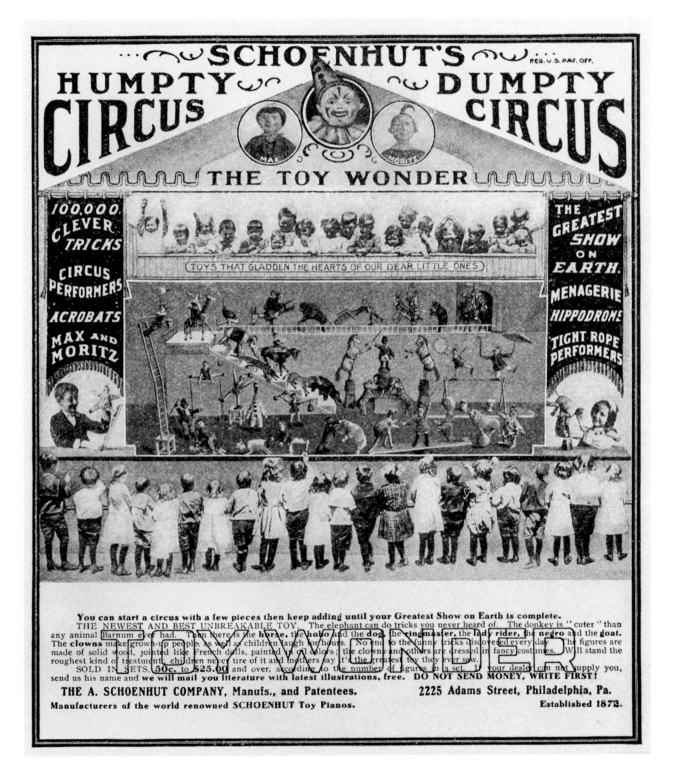

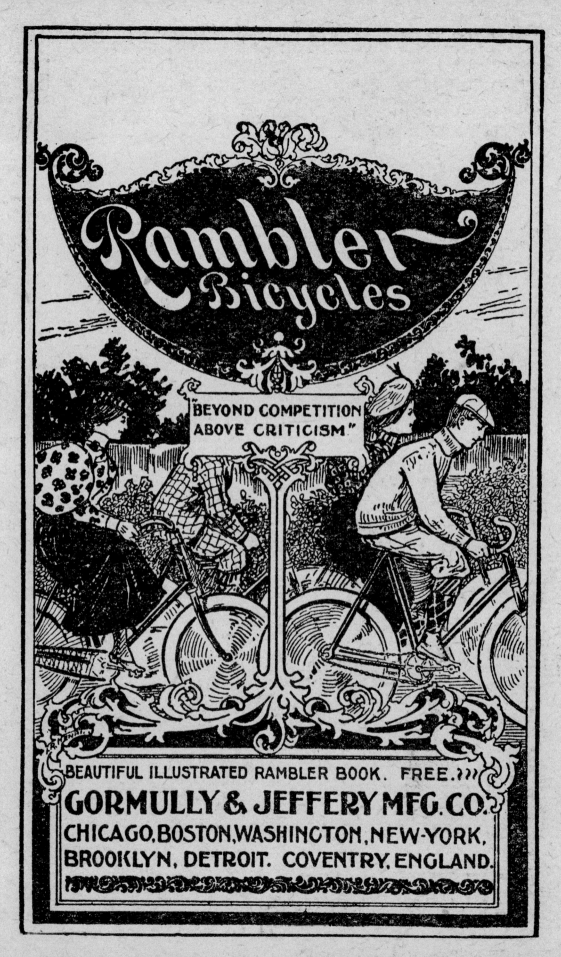

◄ Gormully and Jeffery, 1900

F. R. Bird, 1907

President "Teddy" Roosevelt's hunting trip in 1902 spawned one of the most iconic toys of all time after he refused to shoot a bear that had been tied to a tree. A cultural touchstone, he would later use the teddy bear as a calling card for the 1904 election.

US-Präsident "Teddy" Roosevelts Jagdausflug von 1902, bei dem er sich weigerte, einen angebundenen Bären zu erschießen, führte zur Erfindung eines der beliebtesten Spielzeuge aller Zeiten. Roosevelt benutzte den Teddbären im Wahlkampf 1904 sogar als sein Markenzeichen.

En 1902, une partie de chasse du président « Teddy » Roosevelt déclenche la naissance d'un des jouets les plus universels, clin d'œil à l'ours attaché à un arbre que le président refusa de tuer. Celui-ci n'hésitera pas à utiliser l'iconique nounours comme mascotte lors de la campagne pour sa réélection, en 1904.

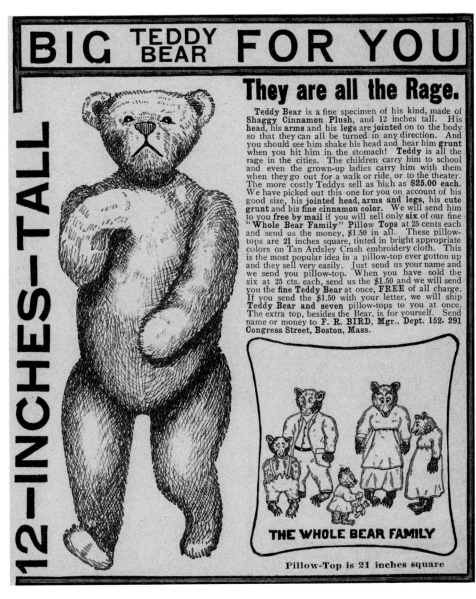

MYSTO MAGIC

The Best Tricks of Famous Magicians

Here's a Gilbert Toy that makes a big hit with boys who like to give shows and do real magic tricks just as they are done on the stage. Gilbert Mysto Magic Sets contain scores of the famous tricks of the greatest magicians. They mystify people—seem marvelous to them—and make them say about you, "Isn't it wonderful how he does that!"

Have Fun—Give Shows—Earn Money

You can give a complete evening's entertainment with these sets and earn money in your home, or at parties, socials, churches and theatres.

Gilbert Mysto Magic Set No. 2004 is one of the best sets of all. The great Magic Manual given with this set tells you how to perform all of the fine tricks described herewith; it also includes instructions for many other wonderful tricks which you can do without special apparatus—such as the Multiplying Dollar Bill, Disappearing Tumblers, Invisible Flight and the world-famous Excelsior Rope-Tying Trick. It also contains a humorous monologue for the magician's use.

This set sells for $5. (In Canada $7.50). Other Magic Sets $1, $2, $3, $10. (Canada $1.50, $3.00, $4.50, $15.00.)

Here are some of the contents of Magic Set No. 4:
Indian Beads, Okeito Coin Box, Chinese Ring on String, Multiplying Billiard Ball, Vanishing Coin from Glass, Phantom Cards, Mysto Jacks, Pass-Pass Coins, Vanishing Handkerchief, Mysto Vanishing Coin, Wonder Change, Princess Card Trick, Phantom Ring, Startling Card Trick, Knockout Card Trick, Pick-it-Out, Papel Blanco, Odin's Discs, Invisible Hen, Diminishing Billiard, Sphinx Card Trick, Marble Vase, Chinese Linking Rings, Cassette, Drum Head Tube, Magician's Wand.

A Wonderful Book The Big Manual of Magic Knowledge that comes with all Gilbert Magic Sets is the greatest book on Magic ever printed. Ask your folks to give you one of these sets for Christmas —or save your money and buy one yourself. Sold by Toy and Department Stores everywhere.

Magic and Trick Catalog—FREE
Write for it today. It tells about all the different Gilbert Magic Sets. Give name of your regular toy dealer when you write.

The A. C. Gilbert Co., 300 Blatchley Ave., New Haven, Conn.
Canadian Representatives: Menzies & Co., Limited, Toronto, Ontario

Remove the Back Stop and Ten Pins and you can then play all the CARROM GAMES on

Archarena Star COMBINATION BOARD with

NEW GAMES Including New TOP GAMES on all Boards.

Making an added value for the purchaser of from $1.25 to $2.00 on each Board, and yet the same price as last year.

Never has so much been combined on one Board, for the money.

See Santa Claus List on Other Page.

NEW STYLES, 1900, ELEGANT MAHOGANY FINISH.

No. 1, 24-in. Board, - - - - -	22 Games,	$2.50
No. 2, 28-in. Board, with Flag Travelette,	28 Games,	3.50
No. 4, 28-in. Board, with Flag Travelette,	32 Games,	4.75

Reverse the Board and you play CROKINOLE

and other games, using our Carrom Rings.

Carrom Rebound Beats Them All.

The *No. 4* is finished in elegant *Marquetry*, imitation of inlaid wood, for the Checker Board and Flag Game. The handsomest Board ever offered to the Public.

We manufacture also separate, the magnificent Folding Card Board New Game of "Flag Travelette."

Patents applied for in U. S., Canada England, Germany and France.

FLAG TRAVELETTE is gotten up in TWO EDITIONS, a Folding Board 18 inches square.

No. 1—IMITATION CLOTH BOUND EDITION (Express paid East of Omaha) - $1.00
No. 2—CLOTH BOUND, Gold Embossed, " " " " " - 1.50

with ALL THE IMPLEMENTS for the 27 DIFFERENT GAMES,

including Ten Pin Set, Carrom Rings, Arrow Indicator, Spinning Tops, and Book of Rules.

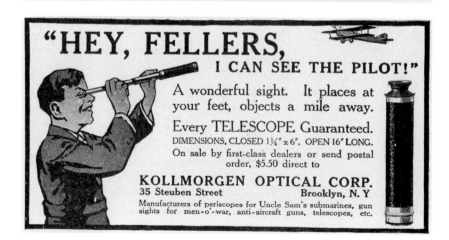
The Pittsburgh Lamp, Brass, and Glass Company, 1919

Kollmorgen Optical, 1919

▶ *Ladies' Home Journal*, 1911

A Christmas Tree for the Dolls

By Eleanor Colby

HERE is a Christmas tree all ready to be hung with toys, and here are the toys all ready to be hung on the tree—and that is a pretty good combination.

First cut out the tree and paste it very neatly to a piece of paper nearly as large as this page. Then lay the sheet you have pasted under some heavy books while you cut out the toys and the decorations. Take plenty of time to do this and use sharp scissors.

When you have everything very neatly cut you may arrange the presents on the tree in just the way you like best, placing the large things, such as the hobby horse and the sled, under the tree.

If you wish to make your tree particularly grand you may cut tiny little bits of tinfoil, tinsel or gilt paper and paste them on.

The grown-ups will wish they were children when they see what fun you are having.

BOYS! BUILD REAL FORTS

If ever a boy wanted to have loads of fun—here's his chance. Any boy can build modern forts like this with Richter's Anchor Blocks—the new Fortress Sets. Put some lead soldiers in the forts,—use a bean shooter for a cannon, and you can have as exciting war games as you wish.

These blocks are entirely different from ordinary blocks. They are made of real stone and they last forever. You can build bomb proof forts, armored turrets, anti-aircraft stations, fortified bridgeheads, citadels, trench works and coast defenses. You can have hours of pleasure and study the war game from a practical standpoint with them.

RICHTER'S ANCHOR BLOCKS

For building castles and towers, bridges, viaducts and all sorts of modern buildings, other sets of Anchor Blocks—of red, buff and blue, reproduce in miniature any structure built of stone or brick. They are easy to put up and easier to take down,—no pegs or screws or nuts or bolts. With one set of Anchor Blocks you can build an almost endless number of models. Book of designs furnished with every set.

A Dandy Christmas Gift Ask your folks for a set of Anchor Blocks for Christmas. Prices 50c to $5.00. Fine Fortress Sets $1.50, $3., $6., $12. Fill in and mail the coupon below for illustrated catalog or send money order if you wish to order now.

F. AD. RICHTER & COMPANY,
Dept. 116, 74 Washington St., New York

F. AD. RICHTER & CO.,
Dept. 116, 74 Washington St., New York

Send me your free booklet giving full particulars about Anchor Blocks.

Name..

Address ....

City.............................State ....

F. AD. Richter and Company, 1917   ▶ Robert H. Ingersoll and Brother, 1917

"He's got an Ingersoll Radiolite"

There's joy in that boy's heart—for every boy loves his Ingersoll Radiolite Watch! And the other boys envy him —as they would you.

You—and every other boy—need an Ingersoll Radiolite. It gets you to school on time and it brings you home on time. You never miss that first tense minute of a ball game. You catch trains and boats. Oh! it's *real* to have one of these men's watches.

And Ingersoll Radiolites tell time in the dark. No matter how black the night or the room, they always show the time clearly. Look at the day-and-night photograph of the Ingersoll Waterbury Radiolite Model. Real *radium* in the *Radiolite* hands and figures makes them glow as long as you have the watch.

It's just this *radium* that makes them photograph in the dark. Take your Radiolite into a pitch black room and lay a photographic plate over it for 20 minutes. When it's developed you'll have the same picture you see here.

Ask Dad to get you one of these wonder watches. Cut out the *24-hour-trial* coupon and take it to your dealer. He'll return Dad's money if you don't agree that this is the greatest watch you ever saw. Take the coupon to your dealer now.

IN THE LIGHT   IN THE DARK

To Parents! Give your boy one of these *man*-watches. They're not boys' watches— but the best watches for boys. Why wait till the chap is 21? Let him have the joys and benefits of his own watch now. He needs one as badly as you do. And it'll make him into a *punctual*, better boy.

Cut out this coupon—Hand it to your dealer

ROBT. H. INGERSOLL & BRO.

New York   Boston   Chicago   San Francisco   Montreal

Not a Boy's Watch~but the best Watch for Boys~and Girls, too.

Show your Radiolite to the other boys in a pitch dark room. They will envy you.

Show your Ingersoll Radiolite to your teacher. Tell her how you can be right on the dot— just like a railroad train—both day and night.

You boys who are camera experts—take your Radiolite into a pitch dark room. Lay a piece of black paper and a photographic plate over it. Leave it for an hour. Then develop. The result proves there's real radium in Radiolite.

Girls love Radiolite Watches, too. Every girl should have a small, stylish, accurate Radiolite in her purse and on her dresser. She'll always know the time accurately, both day and night.

"Boys—Buy only American-Made Toys"

YOU'D give a lot to wear gold chevrons, wouldn't you? But you were under age—you helped over here. Are you going to quit helping now? The way you can help best is by buying American things. *That* way your money buys shells for the army of American business—your father's business too, that maintains America as the first nation in the world.

For example, take toys. The American toy industry is a growing important one. But it can't grow without you—your help means victory or defeat for America. American toys are the very best made — the sturdiest — they are accurate in design — carefully finished and painted. They give you the greatest fun. Whenever you want a toy—whenever sister wants a toy—do one thing first. Go to the store that sells only American-made Toys. You're proud you're a real American. Make your toys real Americans, too.

Buy American-Made Toys

◀ Toy Manufacturers of U.S.A., 1919

In the early 20th century, American toy companies competed not just with each other, but with European manufacturers — especially Germans, who produced the bulk of the world's toys. In the aftermath of World War I, consumers were urged to "Buy American" — not just for economic reasons, but because "they give you the greatest fun."

Zu Anfang des 20. Jahrhunderts konkurrierten amerikanische Spielzeugunternehmen nicht nur gegeneinander, sondern auch mit europäischen Herstellern – vor allem mit deutschen, die in dieser Branche weltweit führend waren. Nach dem Ersten Weltkrieg wurden die Konsumenten aufgefordert: „Buy American" – und zwar nicht nur aus ökonomischen Gründen, sondern auch, weil man mit Spielzeug made in USA angeblich „den meisten Spaß" hat.

Au tout début du XXe siècle, les fabricants de jouets américains sont en concurrence entre eux, mais aussi avec les Européens – en particulier les Allemands, plus gros producteurs de jouets au monde. Au lendemain de la Première Guerre mondiale, il faut « acheter américain », pour des raisons économiques, mais aussi parce que c'est avec les jouets américains qu'on « s'amuse le mieux ».

The Toy Tinkers, 1919

MECCANO

Toy Engineering For Boys

BOYS! You can build this great Eiffel Tower with Meccano, and all the other models on this page. They are perfect models of the real thing, and they *work*. The electric elevator in the Tower runs right up to the top with its load and then down again. The Automobile Chassis has Differential, Worm Steering Gear, etc., and shows just how Dad's car works. The Steam Shovel raises, lowers and swings the dirt as it digs. And the Tractor is a sturdy little power plant that will pull your toys like a switch engine.

YOU Can Build This Eiffel Tower

Each Meccano Outfit Is Complete

No Study Necessary

You don't have to study or know a thing about Engineering to build Engineering models with Meccano. You get a big, illustrated Manual of Instructions which makes it all clear and easy; your fun begins the moment you open your Meccano outfit.

425 DANDY MODELS

These are only four of the fascinating models you can build with Meccano. Along with all Meccano Outfits from No. 1 upwards, you get illustrated instructions for building 325 models; then comes Book No. 2 with 100 Prize Models, and more are steadily being added to the system. Always something new!

The story of Meccano has been told by the inventor himself in a fascinating, illustrated book, which we will mail you without charge on receipt of your name and address. It is called "The Meccano Wonder Book," and contains hours of interesting reading. Write for one today, so you can go over it with Dad early. Also ask for rules of Meccano competitions and cash prizes given for most original models.

Get This Superb BOOK FREE!

Steam Shovel That DIGS

Electric Tractor

Prices of Meccano Outfits

No.		Price
00,		$ 1.00
0,		1.50
1,		3.00
1X,		4.50
2,		6.00
2X,		7.50
3,		9.00
3X,		12.00
And up to		40.00

Sent prepaid on receipt of price, if not at your dealer's.

The Meccano Motors give you still more fun. They are the most powerful toy motors made. Build right into your models and make them run like real machinery.

MOTORS

Electric, Reversing,	$4.00
Electric, Non-Reversing,	2.00
Clockwork Motor,	3.00
Transformer,	2.00

MECCANO COMPANY, Inc.
Division A
71 West 23rd Street
New York, N.Y.

Automobile Chassis
—a perfect model of the real thing

Meccano, 1919

▶ The Mysto Manufacturing Company, 1915

In 1913, the year Erector launched, construction was completed on the tallest skyscraper in the world at the time: the Woolworth Building in New York City. Separating its product from other construction toys, Mysto Manufacturing Company prided itself on the likeness of its models to "actual skyscrapers."

1913 wurde der Bau des damals höchsten Wolkenkratzers der Welt, des Woolworth-Gebäudes in New York, abgeschlossen und im selben Jahr brachte die Mysto Manufacturing Company ihre Produktlinie Erector auf den Markt. Die Firma war besonders stolz darauf, dass ihre Modelle an real existierende Wolkenkratzer angelehnt waren.

En 1913, l'année où l'Erector sort, s'achève la construction du plus haut gratte-ciel de l'époque, le Woolworth Building de New York. Soucieux de se démarquer des autres jeux de construction, la Mysto Manufacturing Company se vante que le sien ressemble aux « vrais gratte-ciel ».

American Biscuit Company, 1915

▶ Kiddie-Kar, 1919

H. C. White Company originally specialized in stereoscopes, but when Clarence White invented the Kiddie-Kar in 1915, it was such a smashing success that the business shifted toward production of this toy. It was marketed toward girls and boys — a rarity in a sea of gender-specific playthings.

Die H. C. White Company war ursprünglich auf Stereoskope spezialisiert, doch das 1915 von Clarence White erfundene Kiddie-Kar war ein solcher Erfolg, dass die Firma sich auf die Produktion dieses Spielzeugs verlagerte. Die Werbung für das Dreirad richtete sich an Jungen und Mädchen – in der damaligen Zeit des genderspezifischen Spielzeugs eine Seltenheit.

La spécialité originelle de la compagnie H. C. White est le stéréoscope, mais quand Clarence White invente le Kiddie-Kar en 1915 le succès est tel que l'entreprise lui consacre une part de plus en plus importante de sa production. Rareté pour l'époque, le tricycle est vendu pour les garçons et les filles.

MY father has a motor-car
 And mother too can steer it.
My sister owns a bicycle
 But I may not go near it.

Upon a red velocipede
 My brother rides about
And even baby has a cart
 When nursie takes her out.

I am too big for go-carts, and
 My mother says, too small
To have a tricycle like Nan's
 Because I'd maybe fall.

So when I used to want to travel
 Up or down the street
I almost always had to go
 Just only on my feet.

But now I've something of my own
 That takes me near or far,
I don't suppose you'd guess, but it's
 A reg'lar Kiddie-Kar!

I had a fight with Bobby Lee
 He'd always want to ride it
And took it almost every day
 Until I had to hide it.

And then one time I just went up
 And asked his daddy whether
He couldn't have one too, and now
 We Kiddie-Kar together!

Be sure this mark
is on the seat.

KIDDIE KAR, first built by a father for
 his own child, is not a grown-up's idea
of what a child ought to like, but a simple
conveyance which satisfies a natural instinct
of the child. It fills a period not taken care
of by any other vehicle.

It is perfectly safe, even for a baby one
year old. It is close to the ground and
almost impossible to tip over. There is
nothing to pinch fingers or tear clothes.
No sharp corners, no splinters—every surface is sand-papered. No adjustments to
get out of order. No paint to come off.

It is the only practical indoor vehicle.
It gives the child healthful exercise outdoors. It is used the whole year round.

Don't wait till Christmas. Get one for
your child to ride these brisk October days.

You will find Kiddie-Kar wherever juvenile vehicles are sold.

REAL KIDDIE-KARS ARE MADE ONLY BY WHITE

Made in five sizes
No. 1—for 1-2 years, $1.25
No. 2—for 2-3 years, 2.00
No. 3—for 3-4 years, 2.50
No. 4—for 4-5 years, 3.00
No. 5—for over 5 years, 3.50
Higher west of the Mississippi

The only genuine KIDDIE-
KAR is made by the H. C.
White Company of North
Bennington, Vt. The name
KIDDIE-KAR is a registered
trade mark; it is always on
the seat. The KIDDIE-KAR
is protected by four patents.

MADE IN AMERICA FOR AMERICAN GIRLS AND BOYS

The American Mechanical Toy
Company, c. 1918

▶ Dennison Manufacturing Company,
1919

The American Woman, 1913

Dolly's Home was a premium meant to induce readers of *The American Woman* magazine to sign up for more subscriptions. The ad speaks directly to children, which was a clever marketing technique knowing full well the effects a little begging and pleading would have on its consumer base.

Dolly's Home bekamen Leserinnen von *The American Woman*, die neue Abonnenten anwarben, als Prämie. Die Anzeige richtete sich direkt an die Kinder – eine clevere Marketingstrategie, die mit der Wirksamkeit von kindlichem Quengeln spekulierte.

Dolly's Home est au départ un bonus destiné à encourager les lecteurs du magazine *The American Woman* à en convaincre d'autres de s'abonner. La publicité s'adresse aux enfants, une technique marketing avisée sachant l'impact que peut avoir une petite moue suppliante sur sa cible.

▶ Ives Manufacturing Company, 1918

▶▶ Lionel, 1928

Ives Toys
MAKE HAPPY BOYS

TRAINS AND ACCESSORIES

THE train illustrated below consists of a Locomotive, Buffet Car, Parlor Car, and Observation Car and 8 pieces of curved and 4 pieces of straight track (2 gauge, 2¼″ from center to center), one terminal section, control switch and connecting wire.

Go to your dealer today and ask to see IVES TRAIN No. 701. If he can't supply you, send us $25 00 and we will ship direct to you.

"Side-track that freight!
Here comes the express!"

1920s

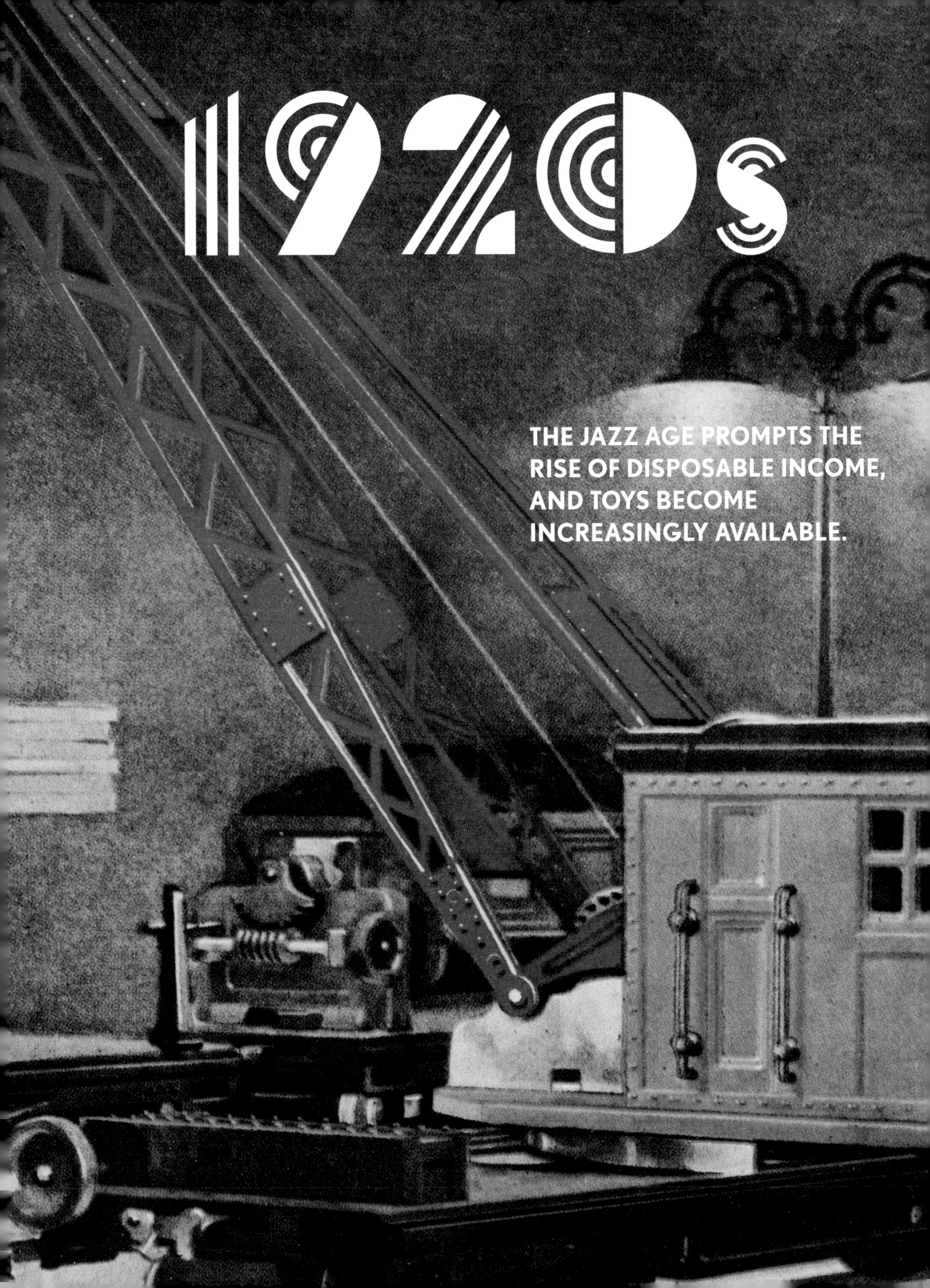

THE JAZZ AGE PROMPTS THE
RISE OF DISPOSABLE INCOME,
AND TOYS BECOME
INCREASINGLY AVAILABLE.

Tinker Toys ∾ 1928

SIREN

BELLE

JUMP ROPE

BABY DOLL

TOM

AUTO RACER Nº 3

LITTLE ARTIST TINKER
TWELVE SILHOUETTES TO COLOR
SERIES ONE
GIRLS AND BOYS

LITTLE ARTIST

PUPPY

LIFE GUARD

TINKERTOY THE WONDER BUILDER
THE TOY TINKERS
EVANSTON ILL U.S.A.

DOUBLE TINKERTOY THE TEN THOUSAND WONDER BUILDER
TOY TINKERS INC
EVANSTON ILL U.S.A.

BUNNY

MULE

TINKERTOY

DOUBLE TINKERTOY

BILLY GOAT

PONY

WHIRLY

DOGS

WONDER TOY

ADVERTISEMENTS CREATED DURING THE PREVIOUS TWO DECADES WERE THE BABY STEPS OF A GROWING TOY INDUSTRY, REPRESENTING A PERIOD WHEN THE WANTS OF CHILDREN WERE BALANCED WITH THE MEANS OF BUSINESS. It was a time when the requisite imports from Europe, particularly Germany, were stopped because of the Great War, necessitating the rise in "American made" products and a new nationalism. With victory came the spoils; the 1920s witnessed a phenomenal increase in American industry and a rise in population. The United States emerged from the Great War with its resources intact and the economy growing.

Advertising was the bulwark of American commercial power, and though not as many dollars were spent on toys as other consumables, toy manufacturing and sales were substantially on

1920

1920

1922

Parker Brothers hold ping-pong tournaments where contestants must use their equipment

Parker Brothers veranstalten Pingpongturniere, deren Teilnehmer nur Equipment von Parker benutzen dürfen

Parker Brothers organise des tournois de ping-pong où les participants doivent utiliser ses produits

Hornby toy trains are officially launched by Meccano

Hornby-Spielzeugeisenbahnen werden offiziell von Meccano eingeführt

Meccano lance officiellement les trains électriques Hornby

First realistic infant doll is created by Grace Storey Putnam, called Bye-Lo Baby

Die erste lebensechte Babypuppe, Bye-Lo Baby, wird von Grace Storey Putnam kreiert

Le premier poupon réaliste, le bébé Bye-Lo, est créé par Grace Storey Putnam the rise. Certain playthings were promoted more than others, of course. Among them, the red Radio Flyer wagon, invented by Antonio Pasin, was mass-produced out of stamped metal for less than $3 — a bargain. Competing wagon companies were also advertised during the '20s, along with bicycles, tricycles, velocipedes, junior cycles, and the old favorite, roller skates, like the KoKoMo Chieftain brand. ("Off Like a Shot" with "Redskins.") The same year as Radio Flyer, A. C. Gilbert Company, producer of the prodigiously advertised Erector kit, introduced its first "educational" chemistry set full of laboratory material, including explosives, which was a staple Christmas or birthday present for boys and some girls. Not as educational, yet no less enjoyably addictive, the yo-yo garnered major success as much through advertising as word of mouth in 1928. Filipino American Pedro Flores, founder of the Yo-Yo Manufacturing Company, referred to his product as the "Wonder Toy," with continued sales to this day.

On a slightly more serious note, toy companies advertised their wares as sources for "Happiness and Health." Merremaker, for example, marketed the Complete Home Play-ground,

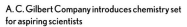

1923

A. C. Gilbert Company introduces chemistry set for aspiring scientists

Die A. C. Gilbert Company stellt für angehende Chemiker einen Experimentierkasten vor

La société A. C. Gilbert lance la boîte pour petits apprentis chimistes

1925

Paper dolls reach the height of their popularity throughout the 1920s

Anziehpuppen aus Papier sind in den 1920ern enorm beliebt

Les poupées de papier sont au sommet de leur popularité dans les années 1920

1926

All Metal Products Company: "Every Boy Wants a Pop Gun"

Slogan der All Metal Products Company: „Jeder Junge möchte eine Spielzeugpistole haben"

All Metal Products Company : « Tous les garçons veulent un pistolet à bouchon »

Row-cycle, and 6-Play Gym, obviously anticipating the war against obesity to come, while Mitchell sounded the bell for "Healthy Fun for Children." Heroics were a point of sales, too. "I am keeping up with Lindy," — referring to Charles Lindbergh's historic solo flight across the Atlantic Ocean — was the slogan for Metalcraft Corporation's Airplane Construction Sets. Despite some of the foreigners who invented them, the toys of the age were "American made," a kind of propaganda for the American Century. In the 1920s, toys often had a higher purpose, and the children who played with the guns and planes during the post–World War I era became the generation that would fight World War II. Through toys, they were indoctrinated to embrace nationalism and loyalty to the United States, even when hit hard by the Great Depression.

1927

1928

1929

Toy airplanes are a hot item after Charles Lindbergh's flight across the Atlantic

Nach Charles Lindberghs Atlantikflug sind Spielzeugflugzeuge heiß begehrt

Charles Lindbergh franchit l'Atlantique et les ventes d'avions miniatures s'envolent

The Joy buzzer zaps its first hapless victim

Der Joy Buzzer erschreckt sein erstes nichts ahnendes Opfer

Au rayon farces et attrapes, la poignée de main électrique fait sa première victime

The first modern pop up children's book featuring illustrations is published

Das erste moderne Pop-up-Kinderbuch erscheint

Le premier livre illustré et animé pour enfants est publié

WONDER TOY

Dank höherer Einkommen können sich amerikanische Haushalte im Jazz-Age mehr Spielwaren leisten.

Die Werbung der beiden vorhergehenden Jahrzehnte waren die ersten Schritte einer wachsenden Spielwarenindustrie. Damals hielten sich die Wünsche der Kinder und die Möglichkeiten der Industrie die Balance. Im Ersten Weltkrieg wurden Importe aus Europa und vor allem aus Deutschland gestoppt, was sowohl den amerikanischen Nationalismus als auch die heimische Produktion ankurbelte. Mit dem Sieg kam auch der wirtschaftliche Aufstieg: Die 1920er-Jahre sahen eine phänomenale Expansion der US-amerikanischen Industrie und einen Bevölkerungsanstieg. Die USA hatten den Ersten Weltkrieg mit intakten Ressourcen und einer wachsenden Ökonomie überstanden.

Werbung war das Bollwerk der amerikanischen Wirtschaftskraft und obwohl für Spielzeug nicht so viele Dollar wie für andere Konsumgüter ausgegeben wurden, stiegen die Absatzzahlen in der Spielwarenbranche deutlich. Manche Spielsachen wurden natürlich mehr beworben als andere, zum Beispiel die hübschen roten Handwagen von Radio Flyer, erfunden von Antonio Pasin, die in Massenproduktion aus Metallplatten ausgestanzt und für unter 3 Dollar verkauft wurden – ein echtes Schnäppchen! Konkurrierende Handwagen wurden in den 1920ern ebenfalls beworben, zusammen mit Fahrrädern, Dreirädern, Laufrädern und einem alten Favoriten, den Rollschuhen, zum Beispiel der Marke KoKoMo Chieftain (Pfeilschnell mit „Redskins"). Im selben Jahr wie Radio Flyer brachte die A. C. Gilbert Company (Hersteller der intensiv beworbenen Erector-Bausätze) ihren ersten „pädagogischen" Chemiekasten auf den Markt, der jede Menge Labormaterial inklusive explosiver Komponenten enthielt und sich zum Standardweihnachts- oder -geburtstagsgeschenk für Jungen (und auch einige Mädchen) mauserte.

Pädagogisch nicht ganz so wertvoll, dafür aber sehr unterhaltsam war das Jo-Jo, das 1928 sowohl durch Werbung als auch durch Mundpropaganda zum Erfolgsschlager wurde. Der von den Philippinen stammende Amerikaner Pedro Flores, Begründer der Yo-Yo Manufacturing Company, bezeichnete sein Produkt als „Wonder Toy", das bis heute verkauft wird.

Ernstere Töne anschlagend, bewarben andere Spielzeugfirmen ihre Waren als die Quelle für „Glück und Gesundheit". So bot zum Beispiel Merremaker einen vollständigen Spielplatz für zu Hause, ein Ruderfahrrad und ein sechsteiliges Kletter- und Spielgerüst an und antizipierte damit den kommenden Kampf gegen Übergewicht, während Mitchell „gesunden Spaß für Kinder" propagierte. Auch Heldentaten wurden vor den Werbekarren gespannt. Der Slogan „I am keeping up with Lindy" („Ich halte mit Lindy mit") bezog sich auf Charles Lindberghs historischen Flug über den Atlantik und bewarb die Flugzeugbaukästen der Firma Metalcraft Corporation. Obwohl einige von Ausländern erfunden wurden, waren die Spielwaren der 1920er-Jahre „American made" (in den USA hergestellt) – eine Propaganda für das amerikanische Jahrhundert. Sie dienten zudem oft einem höheren Zweck: Die Kinder, die nach dem Ersten Weltkrieg mit Waffen und Flugzeugen spielten, waren die Generation, die im Zweiten Weltkrieg kämpfte. Durch Spielzeug hatte man sie trotz der Wirtschaftskrise auf stolzen Patriotismus getrimmt.

▶ Schoenhut, 1928

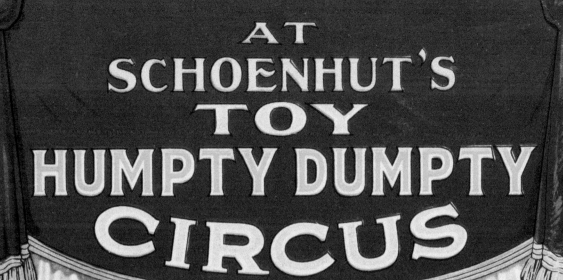

AT SCHOENHUT'S TOY HUMPTY DUMPTY CIRCUS

10,001 ASTONISHING TRICKS
UNBREAKABLE JOINTED FIGURES

LE JOUET MIRACLE

L'ère du jazz invente le revenu disponible et le jouet se démocratise.

Au cours des vingt années précédentes, l'industrie du jouet, en pleine croissance, a fait ses premiers pas timides dans la publicité, une période où les désirs des enfants s'équilibraient avec les ressources du commerce. À cause du gel des importations de produits européens, allemands en particulier, provoqué par la Grande Guerre, il a fallu combler ce manque avec des produits de fabrication américaine, portés par un nationalisme nouveau. La victoire s'accompagne d'un beau butin : les années 1920 connaissent une expansion phénoménale de l'industrie et une forte poussée démographique. Les États-Unis sortent du premier conflit mondial avec des ressources intactes et une économie florissante.

La publicité est le bastion de la puissance commerciale américaine et si le marché du jouet pèse moins lourd que d'autres secteurs, il enregistre une croissance substantielle de sa production et de ses ventes. Certains jouets sont promus avec davantage d'insistance que d'autres. C'est notamment le cas du chariot rouge Radio Flyer conçu par Antonio Pasin, produit en série à partir de tôle emboutie pour moins de 3 dollars – une affaire. Ses concurrents sur le segment « chariot » paient aussi pour gagner en visibilité pendant les années 1920, tout comme les fabricants de bicyclettes, tricycles et autres vélocipèdes, avec une mention spéciale pour les patins à roulettes, comme ceux de la marque KoKoMo Chieftain. (« Off Like a Shot » – comme une flèche – avec les « Redskin ».) L'année où sort le Radio Flyer, la compagnie A. C. Gilbert, qui produit le très populaire kit Erector, présente sa première boîte de chimie « éducative » remplie de matériel de laboratoire et de produits chimiques, notamment explosifs, qui devient aussitôt un classique des Noëls et anniversaires, surtout pour les garçons. Pas aussi éducatif mais tout aussi addictif, le yoyo accède à la gloire grâce à la pub et au bouche à oreille en 1928. L'Américain d'origine philippine Pedro Flores, le fondateur de la Yo-Yo Manufacturing Company, qualifiait son produit de « jouet miracle ». Il se vend toujours aujourd'hui.

Un peu plus sérieusement, les fabricants de jouets présentent leurs produits comme des sources de « bonheur » et de « santé ». Ainsi Merremaker, anticipant à l'évidence la guerre prochaine contre l'obésité, propose un « terrain de jeux complet à domicile », un rameur-cycle et le portique 6-Play Gym, tandis que Mitchell promet « des loisirs sains pour les enfants ». Les héros aussi font vendre : le slogan de Metalcraft pour ses maquettes d'avions, « Je marche dans les pas de Lindy », fait référence au survol historique de l'Atlantique par Charles Lindbergh. S'ils ont parfois été inventés par des étrangers, les jouets de l'époque sont *Made in America* et participent à la propagande autour du « siècle américain ». Dans les années 1920, le jouet sert souvent un objectif plus vaste et les enfants qui ont joué avec les armes et les avions de la Première Guerre mondiale seront les adultes qui les prendront et les piloteront pendant la Seconde. Les jouets les ont endoctrinés pour qu'ils embrassent la cause nationaliste et sacrifient loyalement leur destin à celui des États-Unis, même aux pires heures de la Dépression.

◄ The Toy Tinkers, 1925

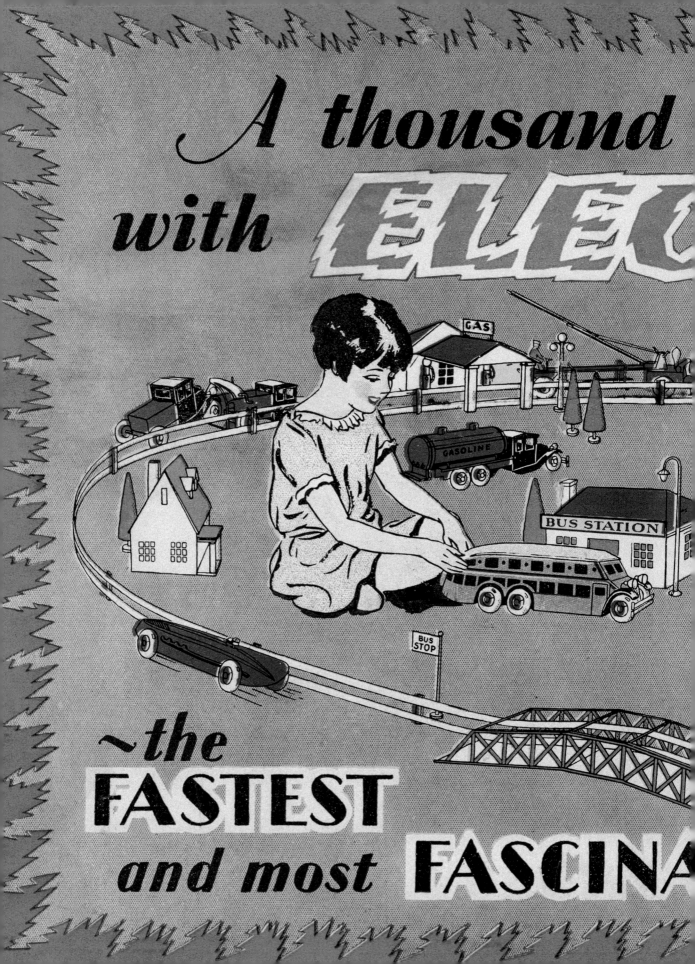

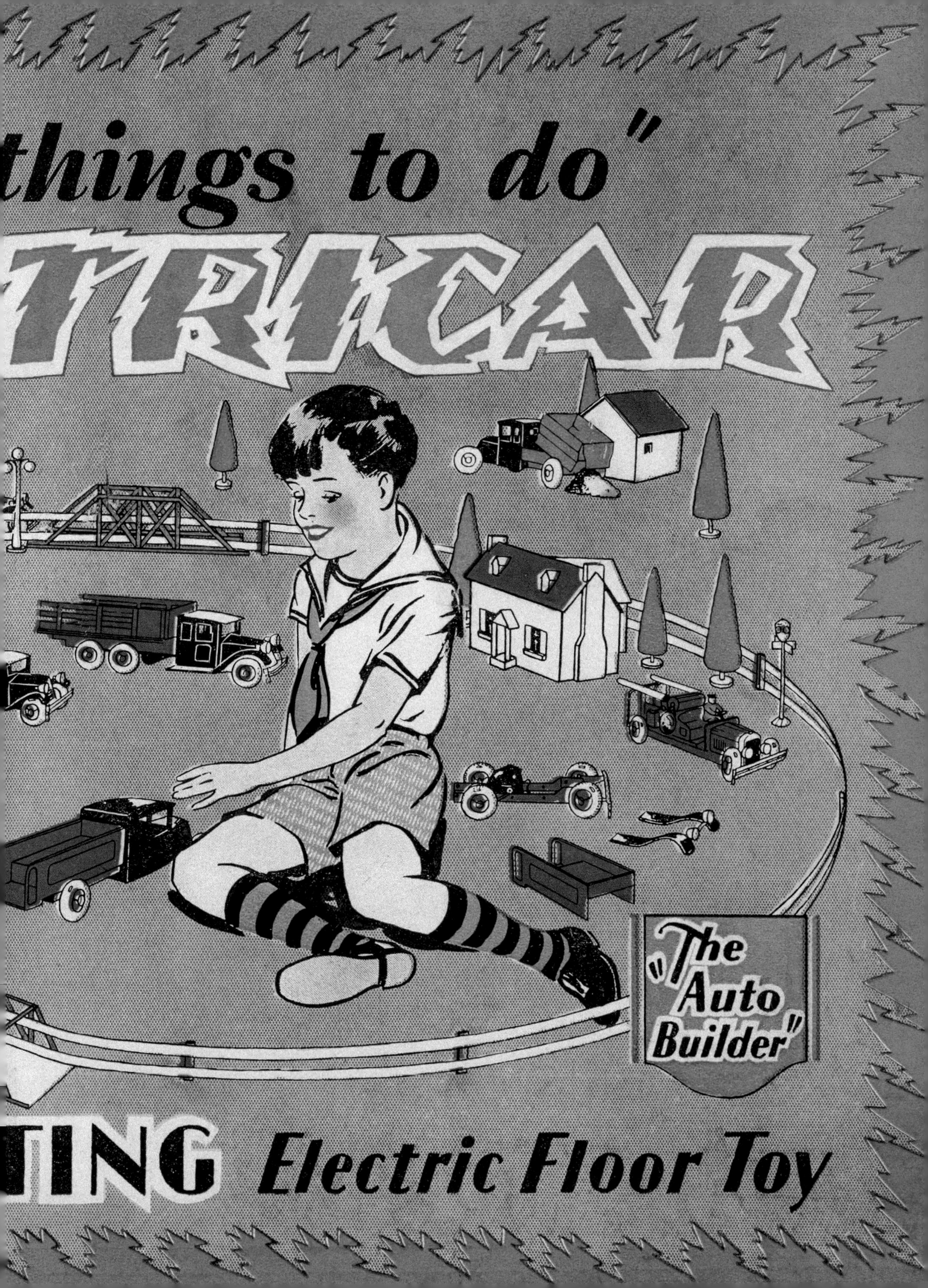
things to do"
TRICAR
"The Auto Builder"
TING Electric Floor Toy

KoKoMo Stamped Metal Company, c. 1927

Tootsietoy, c. 1928

King Paper Specialties Company, 1929

Courtesy of W. & J. Sloane Linoleum.

Tom Thumb has two new Surprises

A Real Playhouse

big enough for You

for

$4.50

and

A New Doll House

just like it

for

$1.25

Tom Thumb Playhouse for You

Photograph in actual colors shown above

It is large enough for you and your playmates to use for your very own Playhouse. It has a real door that opens. Windows without glass for light and air. Made of tough corrugated fibre board of the same strength as used in large shipping cases.

The house is collapsible and is easily put away when not in use. It fits in its own flat container so that it can be put away under the bed or in a closet. It is light and easily set up. The four walls come as one piece and the roof fits on top. Set up, it is 41" high, 36" wide and 29" deep. Can be used indoors, on the porch or outdoors.

The price is the nice part. Only $4.50 delivered to you postpaid. Use the order coupon below.

KING PAPER SPECIALTIES COMPANY
Room 700, Gunther Building, 11th and Wabash   **CHICAGO, ILLINOIS**

King Paper Specialties Company, Room 700, Gunther Building, 11th and Wabash, Chicago, Ill.

Gentlemen:—

Please find enclosed check or money order for $............for which please send me the items checked below.
( ) Tom Thumb Play House $4.50. ( ) Tom Thumb Doll House $1.25
( ) Special combination of both $5.00

Name ....

Street ....

City .... State ....

Tom Thumb Doll House

This big Doll House looks almost exactly like the Playhouse. Beautiful colors, strong, durable fibre board. You open the front door just as in a regular house and see five rooms, one large two story living room, and four small rooms, two on each floor. The side windows have cellophane.

It is 18¼" high, 17" wide and 14" deep. This large, beautiful, true-to-life Doll House, costs only $1.25 postpaid. Use the order coupon.

Only $1.25 postpaid

Milton Bradley, c. 1923

▶ Bradleys, 1928

BRADLEYS
"You Can't Find Better Games"

Babe Ruth's Own Baseball Game

Here is the newest thing in games, boys! A baseball game played with cards and little disc players, just as interesting and exciting as if you were out on the diamond pitching against the "King of Swat" himself. How the fellows will love to come in and play this game with you!

No. C4225 Price... $1.50

Spoof

This is a card game which is entirely different from anything you've ever played, and it's lots of fun. Any number of boys and girls can play it, and it is just about the fastest game you have ever played. The cards pass from player to player, and whoever is quickest has the best chance to win.

No. C4240 Price........ $1.00

Wooden Blocks for Little Folks

Sixteen blocks with rounded corners and edges, for spelling, for making numbers and building things. Each block 1¾ inches square.

No. C316 Price............ 50c

This set contains 30 rainbow blocks. Has more pictures than Set C316, and makes more words or numbers.

No. C330 Price......... $1.00

C316

Just think of it! There are 50 blocks in this set. All nicely rounded, with a scroll design instead of the rainbow pattern. Size of each block 1¾ inches.

No. C3150 Price....... $1.50

C3150

HORSESHOE
A facinating Star Line Game

C375

Indoor Horseshoes

With this fine game you can play horseshoes all the year round, indoors as well as outdoors. There are four fine shoes and two pegs to ring them with. Entertaining when you just practice, and real fun when your friends or folks play with you.

No. C375 Price...................... 50c

ARCADE CAST IRON TOYS

Mack Chemical Truck
No. 245

A brother to the toy Mack Fire Apparatus Truck. The two make a fine combination. Gong rings when truck is set in motion, emergency ladders are removable and the hose reel unwinds.

Finish: Bright red and gold. Specifications:—Length 13¼″, height 4¼″.

Austin Autocrat Road Roller
No. 291

The very latest in toy road rollers, tractor type. A true simulation of the Austin Autocrat Road Roller. The boys will have no end of fun in rolling out new streets in the sand pile.

Finish: Body grey, wheels green. Specifications:—Length 8″, height 3¼″.

Mack Stake Body Truck
No. 246

Here comes another Mack. They're always popular. The stake body is removable and the box ample in size to carry small freight. Finished in green, trimmed with gold. Furnished with rubber tires at small additional cost. Specifications:—Length 11½″, height, 4½″.

Fordson Tractors in 3 sizes
15, 25, & 50¢ Retailers

The toy Fordson miniatures reproduced from the original popular Arcade Toy Fordson, just like the real Fordsons—gray body with red wheels. Specifications:—15c size #273 4″x2½″ high; 25c size #274 4¾″x3¼″ high; 50c size #275 6″x3½″ high.

HOTEL BRESLIN - ROOM 718

◄ Arcade Cast Iron Toys, 1928

Metalcraft, 1929

Two years after Charles Lindbergh's mon-
umental flight across the Atlantic Ocean,
the Metalcraft Corporation of St. Louis
catered to kids who were captivated by
the unprecedented feat. They are
implored to learn mechanics, "the secret
of Lindy's success," with their very own
airplane model kits.

Zwei Jahre nach Charles Lindberghs le-
gendärem Flug über den Atlantik machte
die Metalcraft Corporation in St. Louis
als Zielgruppe Kinder aus, die von dieser
sensationellen Leistung begeistert waren.
Mit Bausätzen für Flugzeugmodelle sollten die Kids Mechanik lernen und „das
Geheimnis von Lindys Erfolg" lüften.

Deux ans après l'historique traversée de
l'Atlantique par Charles Lindbergh, la
Metalcraft Corporation de St. Louis ravit
les gosses fascinés par cet exploit sans
précédent. Elle les enjoint à apprendre
la mécanique, « le secret du succès de
Lindy » avec ses maquettes d'avions.

► Wolverine, 1927

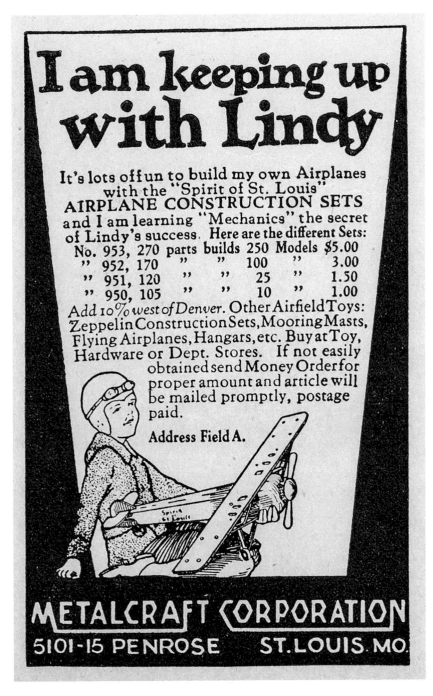

"Sandy Andy" Toys and Games

TRADE MARK   REG. U.S. PAT. OFF.

Toy Laundry Sets

4-PIECE SET
Contains metal wash tub 3⅜ x7¼ in.; blue enamel outside, white inside; clothes reel; metal surface wash board 4⅛ x8 in., and bundle of six clothes pins. Complete set packed in carton.

N74544—Doz.—$8.50

LARGER 4-PIECE SET
Contains metal wash tub 4¾ x 10 in., blue enamel outside, white inside; clothes reel; glass surface wash board 5⅛ x11 in., and bundle of six clothes pins. Complete set packed in carton.

N74545—Doz.—$16.00

6-PIECE SET
Contains metal wash tub 4¾ x10 in., blue enamel outside, white inside; clothes reel; glass surface wash board 5⅛ x11 in.; 12 clothes pins in bag; galvanized wringer with rubber rollers; and clothes basket. Complete in carton.

N74546—Per dozen—$38.50

8-PIECE SET
Contains metal wash tub 4¾ x 10 in., blue enamel outside, white inside; clothes reel; glass surface wash board 5⅛ x11 in.; 12 clothes pins in bag; galvanized wringer with real rubber rollers; clothes basket 11½ x7½ x4½ in.; ironing board with metal stand, and improved type sad iron. Complete set packed in carton.

N74547—Per dozen—$52.00

"Sandy Andy" Trick Animals
Mechanical-Motion Pull Toy
10 in. long, 3 in. wide, 7¼ in. high.

Made entirely of metal, beautifully lithographed. Formed figures without sharp edges. Rubber tire wheels. Action combines sound and movement. Polar Bear rings the bell by hitting it with hammer while colored ball bounces up and down on nose of Seal. Rapid continuous action and sound. Packed one in colored display carton.

N74550—Per dozen—$16.00

"Sandy Andy" Vacuum Cleaner
TRADE MARK   REG. U.S. PAT. OFF

28½ in. high. The first practical Toy Vacuum Cleaner. Light enough for any child, yet strong and well made. Operates by friction and suction; sounds like a real one and actually picks up dust, ashes and papers from rugs and carpets. Beautifully enameled in deep, rich, solid colors. Aluminum finished base. Enameled wood handle. Bag detachable.

N74548
Per dozen
$38.50

Just Like a Real One!

"Sandy Andy" Merry-Go-Round
Mechanical-Motion Pull Toy
10 in. long, 3 in. wide, 7 in. high.

Made entirely of metal, beautifully lithographed. Formed figures without sharp edges. Rubber tire wheels. Action combines sound and movement. Merry-Go-Round turns rapidly while clown rings the bell by hitting it with the hammer. Rapid, continuous action and sound. Packed one in colored display carton.

N74549—Per dozen—$16.00

Beautifully Lithographed, All-Metal Games

"The Motor Race"
Automobile Race Game Complete with Checkerboard and Checkers.

Four automobiles race around the speedway, spinning dials indicating moves. A fast-action lively game for little folks. Four automobiles included. Board 16½ in. square. Packed in display box.

G-5768—Per dozen—$16.00

The Junior Motor Race
Same as above, smaller size. Board 11 in. square. Four automobiles included; checkerboard on reverse side. Packed in display box.

G-5661—Per dozen—$8.00

"Speed Boat Race"
Motor Boat Race Game Complete with Checkerboard and Checkers.

Four speed boats race over a regular course encountering the hazards of a real race. An exciting game for all children. Four boats included. Board is 16½ in. square. Packed in display box.

G-5854—Per dozen—$16.00

Colored Checker Board Lithographed on Reverse Side of All Games

"Across the Channel"
Swimming Race Game Complete with Checkerboard and Checkers.

Interesting, instructive game based on celebrated Across Channel swimming races. Very realistic and exciting. Four swimmers included. Board is 16½ in. square. Packed in display box.

G-5853—Per dozen—$16.00

Box of 24 Embossed Checkers included with the four large games.

"Round-the-World Fliers"
Aeroplane Race Game Complete with Checkerboard and Checkers.

Four Aeroplanes race around the world following course of the U. S. Army Flyers. Very exciting and educational game. Four aeroplanes included. Board is 16½ in. square. Packed in display box.

G-5769—Per dozen—$16.00

Jr. "R'n'd-the-World Fliers"
Same as above, smaller size. Board 11 in. square. Four aeroplanes included; checkerboard on reverse side. Packed in display box.

G-5662—Per dozen—$8.00

"Sandy Andy"

TRADE MARK   REG. U.S.PAT. OFF.

Toys and Games

Automatic Action —they work by gravity!

These are the Original and Famous Sandy Andy Automatic Sand and Marble Toys

9 in. high

11 in. high

14¾ inches high

Sandy Andy "See Saw"
The newest sand toy. Dumps sand from hopper to can with fast, "see saw" action. White sand and a sand scoop included. Packed in display box which opens flat to form tray. Colors: pink, blue, orange.

N74532—Per dozen—$8.00

Sandy Andy Incline
The original of all automatic sand toys. Car runs up and down dumping sand as long as hopper is supplied. Can of white sand included. Packed in display box which opens flat to form tray.

N74533—Per dozen—$11.30

Sandy Andy Incline with Engineer
A larger model of this toy. Faster, more fascinating action. Can of white sand included. Packed in display box which opens flat to form tray.

N74534—Per dozen—$16.00

N74535—As above 17¾ in. high Per dozen—$20.00

12¼ in. high

Dumping Sandy
Dumps sand with a snappy, up and down action. Can of white sand and a sand scoop included. Packed in display box which opens flat to form tray.

N74536—Per dozen—$12.00

"OVER AND UNDER"
Wonderful mechanical toy; perfect working motor. Car runs down upper incline, drops to lower track and continues to end; then reverses to opposite end, where motor raises car for another trip. Action repeats many times with one winding. 25 inches long.

N74542—Per dozen—$16.00

"Over and Under Lift" 30½ inches long

The "jack-knife" bridge raises car, then closes together forming straight track down which the car travels, dropping to long track below. Car continues to end and returns, while bridge opens as pictured above, ready for next trip. Operated by strong spring motor and gear wheels.

N74543—Per dozen—$30.60

13⅜ in. high

Sandy Andy Sand Crane
Most interesting of all sand toys. Sand runs into shovel; shovel arm swings in semi-circle and engineer dumps the sand. Can of white sand and a sand scoop included. Packed in display box which opens flat to form tray.

N74537—Per dozen—$20.00

Bowler Andy Mill 21 inches high
Automatic Marble Toy. Car travels up and down and windmill turns continually. Eight steel marbles included.

N74539 Per dozen $23.40

BIZZY ANDY TRIP HAMMER
10½ in. high
Automatic marble toy. Hammer transfers 6 clay marbles from chute to base with fast, snappy action; marbles included.

N74540 Per dozen $8.00

BIZZY ANDY JUNIOR 7 in. high
Automatic marble toy and game. Swinging arm carries marble to base. 8 clay marbles included.

N74541 Per dozen $3.80

"PANAMA" PILE DRIVER
Panama Pile Driver 16¾ in. high
Automatic Marble Toy. Hammer and "engineer" both move up and down rapidly. Realistic pile driver action; 8 steel marbles included.

N74538 Per dozen $19.50

MAKE THIS A
BOOK
CHRISTMAS

Printed in U.S.A.

National Association of Book
Publishers, 1927

▶ The Toy-Kraft Company, 1926

A main selling point for the Toy Kraft
Garden Set was its hand-painted finish,
referred to as its "artistic richness of
color." Indeed, the vibrant pink and
blue veneer created a sense of fun and
excitement for the little ones who
played with the wheelbarrow alongside
their parents in the garden.

Ein Hauptverkaufsargument für das
Gartenset von Toy Kraft war die Hand-
bemalung, die als „künstlerische Farb-
kraft" beworben wurde. Und in der Tat:
Der leuchtende Anstrich in Pink und
Blau begeisterte so manchen Knirps,
der mit seiner Schubkarre neben den
Eltern im Garten spielten.

Les décors peints à la main du Toy Kraft
Garden Set et la « richesse artistique de
leurs couleurs » sont un atout commercial majeur. Le rose et le bleu pétants de
la petite brouette sont une source
supplémentaire d'exaltation pour les
petits qui jardinent avec leurs parents.

Garden Time

Glorious sunshine—smiling skies—caressing breezes—happy summer days for tiny tots with the Toy Kraft Garden Set!

Mothers will find this unusual wheel-barrow with its attendant tools an ideal summer plaything for small children. It will provide healthy amusement and an incentive which will keep little minds constructively and safely occupied for hours at a time.

Its uniqueness of design and artistic richness of color will also be a constant source of pleasure to them.

Sturdily built to stand hard knocks and, like every "Toy Kraft" toy, *hand painted* with highest grade enamels and lacquers that are unaffected by repeated washings.

Size of wheel-barrow;—Length 21 inches. Width 7 inches. Height 10 inches.

"Toy-Kraft" Toys are sold by leading toy and department stores, but if you are unable to obtain them locally, write us direct and we will see that you are supplied.

THE TOY-KRAFT COMPANY

Factory and Studio
WOOSTER, OHIO

Mary, Mary, so contrary,
How does your garden
grow? With Silver Bells
and Cockle Shells —
And Marigolds all in a
Row!

The Brand New
SUCK·A·THUMB
BABY
with rubber arms
that feel
so real!

SUCKS·THUMB

CLASPS·HANDS

ENJOYS·PACIFIER

SHE·SLEEPS

You will lose your heart to this
brand new baby doll

Needlecraft Magazine, c. 1920

▶ Lionel, 1921

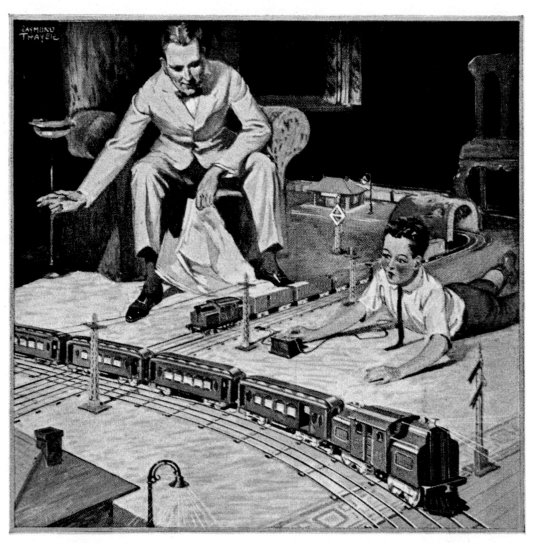

CHRISTMAS MORNING you and your son will be running his new Lionel Electric Railroad together. You'll get as much fun out of it as he does, for Lionel Railroads are the most wonderful sport in the world for youngsters.

Moreover, Lionel Trains combine the greatest enjoyment the boy can have with instruction that he will value all his life.

For twenty-two years Lionel has been "Standard of the World"—the unquestioned leader in electrical and mechanical perfection. Lionel outfits run from any electric light socket with Lionel "Multivolt" Transformer — or from dry or storage batteries.

Ask to see the "Twin-Motor" locomotive that pulls 20 cars, fast or slow, backward or forward, at a touch of the controller. You will be surprised to find that a complete Lionel outfit with this wonderful locomotive costs no more than outfits of like size with single motor locomotives of other makes.

Lionel complete outfits, despite their supreme high quality, are very low-priced. You may start as modestly as you wish and add to your boy's outfit each birthday and Christmas. Demand Lionel at your dealers. Give the boy a wonderful Christmas.

Be sure to send post card for the handsome
Lionel 40-page catalog printed in four colors.

THE LIONEL CORPORATION :: 48-G, E. 21st STREET
NEW YORK CITY

LIONEL ELECTRIC TOY TRAINS
& Multivolt Transformers

TOY SETS IN GIFT BOXES

No. N93999 $8.00 per dozen sets
Sets Comprise—6 Animals, 6 Floating Toys, 4 Boats,
5 Novelty Food Platters
Each Set in a Gift Box
6 Sets (Four Kinds Assorted) in a Carton

RATTLE

AND

TOY

ASSORTMENTS

IN ATTRACTIVE

DISPLAY

CABINETS

No. N93995
$4.00 per Cabinet of one doz.
The Newest
Novelty Rattles
in a Grand Stand Effect Display Cabinet
Average Length of Rattles 7 inches

No. N93996
$4.00 per Cabinet of one dozen
The Sanitary Rattle Assortment
Beautifully Decorated and Novelty Rattles
Each in a Cellophane Envelope
Average Length of Rattles, 7 inches

No. N93997
$7.00 per Cabinet of three doz.
Comprising—2 Doz. Floating Toys
to Retail at 10c Each
1 Doz. Floating Toys
to Retail at 25c Each
TOTAL—3 Dozen Assorted Toys
Attractively Colored.
Average Length of 10c Size—4 inches.
Average Length of 25c Size—7½ inches.
A Colorful Water-proof Dish is Set in a Conspic-
uous Place in Cabinet into which Water can be Poured,
making an Attractive Display of Toys Floating About

No. N93998
$8.00 per Cabinet of two dozen
(2 dozen at $4.00 per dozen)
A Varied Assortment of Large Size Attractively Colored Toys and Playthings in a
Cabinet. Average Length 5½ inches

◄ Dupont Viscoloid Company, 1929

Samuel Gabriel Sons and Company, 1922

Rolling Animal"

"Roly Poly Bear"

"Roly Poly Rabbit"

"Roly Poly Dog"

Write for Catalogue "Rocking Animal"

COASTERS

SPEED!

Fine roller bearings give these Coasters and Scooters a wonderful speed. Boy, what fun it is to get them going and then sail down the walk! And talk about strength. They are husky all the way through, built of fine materials, and machined to work easily and smoothly.

M1931

C111

The Jack Rabbit

There is no finer coaster, boys. This Jack Rabbit gets its name from its speed. Steel all the way through. Steel double-disc wheels and big rubber tires. Roller bearings, good springs, and strong, tubular steel handle. Quiet and easy rolling. Body measures 33½x14½ inches.
No. M1931 Price...... **$8.75**

Balloon Tire Scooter

Balloon tires, just like on the best automobiles. This scooter is a real speed bus. Well built and strong, it rolls along easily on roller bearings and does not mind bumps. See the parking stand?
No. C111
Price.................................**$2.00**

Badger Scooter

Here is the Scooter de luxe. A big fellow over 40 inches long. It is built unusually strong, of heavy steel. The 10-inch wheels, with their rubber tires, have large roller bearings which give it exceptional speed. Steers easily. Has parking stand, brake and rubber foot mat. This is the scooter you really should have. See if Mother and Dad can't arrange it with Santa.
No. C4100
Price.....................**$3.75**

M810

The Ace

This dandy speedster is 14 inches wide and 34 inches long. It is built entirely of steel, has fine roller bearings, 10-inch wheels, and ¾-inch rubber tires. Here is healthful, joyous fun for you!
No. M810 Price................**$5.25**

C4100

Fox, 1928

▶ The Dayton Toy and Specialty Company, 1928

New  Line

"SON-NY" AND "DATON" LINES WILL BE NATIONALLY ADVERTISED TO CONSUMER IN THE LEADING JUVENILE MAGAZINES

INCREASE YOUR 1928 SALES WITH OUR NEW "SON-NY" LINE TRUCKS AND WAGONS

EACH ITEM IMPROVED IN CONSTRUCTION AND FINISHED IN BRILLIANT COMBINATIONS OF ATTRACTIVE COLORS.

NEW AND FINEST LINE DRAWN BED WAGONS

OUR LINE IS LARGER AND BETTER THAN EVER BEFORE AND OUR NATIONAL ADVERTISING CAMPAIGN WILL HELP YOU SELL BOTH THE "SON-NY" AND "DATON" LINES.

"SON-NY" SAND DUMP WAGON WILL MAKE AN EXCELLENT SPRING AND SUMMER SELLER, WHICH WILL ASSURE LARGE VOLUME AND REAL PROFITS.

THE DAYTON TOY AND SPECIALTY COMPANY
1114-1120 BOLANDER AVENUE
DAYTON, OHIO, U. S. A.

Knapp, 1925

▶ Faultless Rubber Company, 1920

No. 647 Peerless
No. 647GD—Equipped with Gear Drive
(See Page 3)

Specifications

Length Overall—56 inches.

Finish—Brewster green, trimmed in apple green, red and gray.

Wheels—12¾ inch roller bearing, disc. 1¼ inch balloon tires. Finish green to match body.

Packing—One in crate, K. D. Weight per crate, 125 lbs.

Equipment

No Dead Center gear with adjustable rubber pedals. Cantilever springs, front and rear. Nickel-plated radiator with screen mesh front. Nickel-plated two piece adjustable windshield with side wings. Die formed crown fenders and running boards. Composition tilting steering wheel with gas and spark control. Nickel-plated three bar bumper. Gear shift and emergency brake levers. Adjustable rear view mirror. Windshield wiper. Adjustable spot light. Nickel-plated step and scuff plates. Head lamps. Cowl lamps. Instrument board. License tag. Full upholstered leather seat. Nickeled guard rail in rear. Spare wheel with tire and cover. Combination tail light and stop and slow signal. Special horn. Oil can with bracket. Eagle radiator cap. Blue Streak motor hummer. Fender mirror.

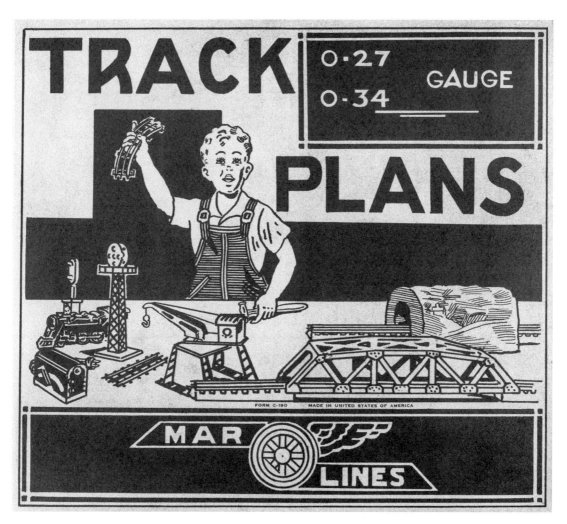

◄ Toledo Metal Wheel Company, 1926

Louis Marx and Company, 1929

BUILD a model village, boys
substantial, handsomely fin
nated houses. Steel constru
out. Roofs are removable, so that
may be easily reached. Lionel Bu
Villas will greatly enhance the a
your Model Railroa

**No. 186 Illuminated Bungalow
Set**—Comprises 5 No. 184 bungalows,
beautifully finished in assorted colors. Complete
with interior lights and connecting wires. Attractively packed.
Price
$7.50
Code Word "HAMLET"

No. 184
high, 4¾ in
Complete with
necting wires.

No. 191 Illuminated Villa—Beautifully designed. 7⅛
inches long, 5⅛ inches wide and 5¼ inches high. Roof is removable. Complete with interior lighting fixture, lamp
and connecting wires. Price $3.35
Code Word "SOLID"

**No. 89
Flag-Staff and Flag**—
For use with Lionel model
villages or to place in
front of a Lionel Station.
Flag-staff is 14 inches
high. Silk flag may be
lowered by cord attached,
which can be fastened to
hook near the
base. Price
$.75
Code Word "ARTHUR"

No. 189 Illum
—A model that
perfect. 5½ in
high. Complete v
necting wires.
Price . . . .
Code W

37

these
Illumi-
rough-
light
s and
ce of

No. 192 Illuminated Villa Set—A handsome assortment of model houses. Comprises
1 No. 191 villa, 1 No. 189 villa, and 2 No. 184 bungalows. All complete with interior lights and connecting wires. Very attractively packed.
    Price **$8.75**
       Code Word "VILLAGE"

d Bungalow—4 inches
. Beautifully decorated,
light and con- **$1.50**

"HOME"

No. 90

**Flag - Staff and
Flag** — The flag-
staff (14 inches
high) is remov-
able, and fits into
an ornamental base
mounted on a
miniature grass
plot with flower
border. **$1.25**
Price .
    Code Word
       "PLOT"

la
cturally
47⁄8 inches
or light and con-

$2.95

SE"

New ALL METAL DOLL BED ROOM SUITES

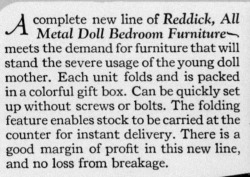

A complete new line of *Reddick, All Metal Doll Bedroom Furniture* meets the demand for furniture that will stand the severe usage of the young doll mother. Each unit folds and is packed in a colorful gift box. Can be quickly set up without screws or bolts. The folding feature enables stock to be carried at the counter for instant delivery. There is a good margin of profit in this new line, and no loss from breakage.

Furnished in Assorted Colors—Chinese Red and Nile Green

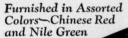

On Display During
New York Toy Fair
Breslin Hotel, Room 709
During Chicago Toy Fair at the
Palmer House

MICHIGAN WIRE GOODS CO.
Associated with THE WASHBURN COMPANY

NILES - - - MICHIGAN

Little Miss Ann-Drock
KITCHEN TOY SETS

New

Sets finished in the popular bright colors — Apple Green and Mandarin Red. Each carton contains one-half of each.

ANDROCK Kitchen Toy Sets

A complete new line of Kitchen Tool Toy Sets, finished in bright colors and attractively merchandised. These sets are made up of useful and practical miniatures of the familiar Androck Kitchen Tools for grownups. The bright colors in which these tools are finished and the colorful gift boxes in which each set is packed form an irresistible appeal to gift seekers. Always *popular* and *profitable*, this new line will make even greater sales records for our customers this year.

On Display During New York Toy Fair Breslin Hotel Room 709

During Chicago Toy Fair at the Palmer House

Set No. 10
Duck Cookie Cutter
Man Cookie Cutter
Kitchen Spoon
Wood Masher
Soup Strainer
Pastry Board
Mixing Bowl
Cake Turner
Rolling Pin
Egg Beater
Cake Pan
Spatula
Pie Tin
Muffin Pan
Flour Sifter
Cookie Sheet

One-half dozen Sets in a carton.
Weight, 25 lbs.

THE WASHBURN COMPANY - CHICAGO, ILLINOIS

◄ Michigan Wire Goods, 1928

The Washburn Company, 1928

ARKITOY
PLAY LUMBER

The Amazing New Wood Construction Toy

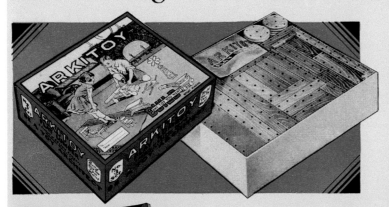

Boys and girls, here is something entirely different. Arkitoy play lumber comes in various sizes, designed around a new construction principle. Each piece is accurately drilled, nicely finished, and you join them with rustproof bolts and nuts. There is no limit to the many, lifelike models you can build, models which actually work, from folding furniture to a whole railroad. Just think of a model or toy, and go ahead and build it. Build a new one and get a diploma as Junior Toy Architect. And maybe you'll win one of the big cash prizes for the best new models submitted.

Arkitoy Set No. C97-(2) is the most popular size. There are 122 pieces of lumber, a combination hex wrench and screw driver and 7 dozen bolts. And there is no end to the number of different models you can build with this beautiful set. The plan book shows a great many of them. If you like to build, be sure to ask Santa for a set of Arkitoy.

No. C97-(2) Price................................**$2.00**

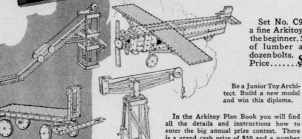

Set No. C95-(1) is a fine Arkitoy Set for the beginner. 50 pieces of lumber and 3½ dozen bolts. Price......**$1.00**

Set No. C98-(3) contains 235 pieces and 12 dozen bolts. This big set builds almost anything. Price......**$3.50**

No. C99-(4) is the Set De Luxe. 398 pieces and 15 dozen bolts. Santa Claus has nothing finer. Price..**$5.00**

Be a Junior Toy Architect. Build a new model and win this diploma.

In the Arkitoy Plan Book you will find all the details and instructions how to enter the big annual prize contest. There is a grand cash prize of $50 and a number of smaller ones. Ask Santa for a set of Arkitoy and compete for these prizes.

Show these models to Dad and see what he thinks of this wonderful construction set with which you invent your own models.

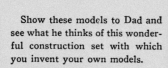

Invent and Build your Own Toys with ARKITOY

G. B. Lewis Company, 1928

▶ Liberty Playthings, 1929

New Device

Gives Liberty Boats Year Round Use and Sale

The new Liberty detachable undercarriage and wheels slip easily onto the keel of the boat, changing it into a pull toy for use in the home and on the sidewalk. Furnished free with all boats except No. 1 and No. 22.

These Features Make *Liberty* THE PROFITABLE LINE

BRILLIANT, flashing colors. . .Unsinkable All-Wood Hulls. . .Real Play Features offering a wide variety of indoor and outdoor play uses . . .Power supplied by finely-built, long distance motors. . .Complete price range—from $1.50 to $10.00.

Retails at $7.50

No. 7 Liberty Fire Boat

A durable pumping mechanism, concealed in the hull and operated by the center plunger, draws in water through suction line in bottom and throws a stream 25 feet through the revolving nozzle mounted on front deck. Length 22 inches.

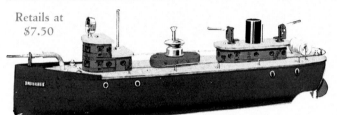

The Toy Line with Real Play Features

Retails at $3.50

No. 2

Liberty Tug and Scow

Carries a real load anywhere. Small enough to be navigated in the bath tub and sturdy enough for any outdoor sea. The powerful motor drives the Tug swiftly through the water, either alone or with the Scow in tow. Tug is 12 inches long. Scow is 12 inches long.

No. 22 Liberty Seaplane

This different water toy has two wooden air propellers, powered by substantial steel and brass motors, which drive it swiftly through the water. Its sturdy hull, 20 inches long, tapers down to a big rudder which gracefully guides the ship. Wing spread 22 inches.

No. 5 Liberty Freighter

The several hatches with sliding covers permit the carrying of mixed cargo. The twin propellers powered by two substantial steel and brass motors easily drive the Freighter through the water. All wood, non-crushable, unsinkable hull with 3-ply, non-warping veneer deck. Length 27 inches.

Retails at $5.00

Retails at $10.00

LIBERTY PLAYTHINGS, INC., NIAGARA FALLS, N. Y.

P.L.4

The Ideal Xmas Gift

AND ONLY

$7.50

FIVE OTHER SIZES

Brunswick Junior Playmate Tables
Solve Your Problem

GIVE your children the greatest present of all this Christmas— a Brunswick Junior Playmate Billiard Table—a magnet with the power to center and hold their interest in the home—the power to keep them under your guiding influence during their formative years.

Play with them, too. Billiards is a family game—a healthful game—a mental stimulant—an eye sharpener —and an eye opener to parents who have forgotten that playing together is the best way of sticking together.

Brunswick Junior Playmate Billiard Tables are available in six sizes, at $7.50, $13.50, $18.50, $37.50, $60.00 and $100.00. (*Prices slightly higher west of Denver and in Canada.*) Each model, irrespective of price, is staunchly made, accurately angled and completely equipped with balls, cues, etc. The $7.50 Model (illustrated) must not be confused with ordinary toy tables. It is sturdily built, portable, with folding legs and complete playing equipment, and available at leading stores every-

where. You will instantly identify it by its rich mahogany finish and the Brunswick Trademark in Gold, which is shown below.

BRUNSWICK JUNIOR PLAYMATE
THE BRUNSWICK-BALKE-COLLENDER CO.

The more expensive tables shown in our catalog, which we will gladly send you on request, can be bought on the deferred payment plan (*only a modest initial payment required*) from the Brunswick branches, located in all principal cities.

THE BRUNSWICK-BALKE-COLLENDER CO. *General Office:* 625 So. Wabash Avenue, *Chicago, Ill.* In Canada: *Toronto*

FAMOUS PARKER GAMES

WINGS
Great Aviation Game

New! Entirely original in play. Immensely popular! Fast action. An exciting, novel game. Fun for all ages. 2, 3, or 4 can play. Price, 75c at DEALERS', or by mail.

PEGITY

A simple, splendid game of skill. Learned in two minutes. Exciting fun to watch or play. Especially recommended. Price $1.25 at DEALERS', or by mail.

PING-PONG
REG. U. S. PATENT OFFICE
PARKER BROTHERS, Inc., *Sole Makers*

There is no better game! Fast, exciting action. Sets from $2 to $20. **Sold by all leading DEALERS',** or by mail. Write for illustrated circular.

PING-PONG *always* bears the brand PING-PONG upon the box, rackets, net and balls, and contains the official Laws of PING-PONG, adopted by the American Association. It is made *only* by Parker Brothers, Inc.

Some Other Famous Parker Games

POLLYANNA, Touring, Hokum, Boy Scouts' Progress Game, Five Wise Birds, Across the Continent, Peg Baseball, Rook, Game of OZ, Lame-Duck, Halma, Pit, Pastime Picture Puzzles, finest Puzzles in the world (send for descriptive list).

THE KNIGHT'S JOURNEY

Especially recommended. A surpassingly beautiful and amusing game based on Fairyland legends of the Middle Ages. Players benefit through the good fairies and must triumph over ogres, witches, and many other obstacles encountered by medieval knights, ere the Fairy Princess is won. Price, $3.25 at DEALERS', or by mail.

PARKER BROTHERS, INC.
SALEM, MASS., NEW YORK, AND LONDON

The Porter Chemical Company, c. 1927

▶ Lionel, 1923

The 1920s was a period of substantial growth for the toy industry with U.S. manufacturers taking the place of European imports as more Americans were able to purchase luxury goods such as toy trains. Lionel was an early leader in toy advertising with lavish sales catalogs and full-page color ads.

Die 1920er waren eine Zeit des Wachstums für die amerikanische Spielzeugindustrie, denn US-Produkte ersetzten die europäische Importware und mehr Amerikaner konnten sich nun Luxusgüter wie Spielzeugeisenbahnen leisten. Lionel war mit seinen aufwendigen Katalogen und ganzseitigen Farbanzeigen führend in der Spielzeugwerbung.

Les années 1920 sont une période de croissance importante pour l'industrie du jouet américaine, qui prend le pas sur les importations européennes alors que de plus en plus d'Américains peuvent s'offrir des produits onéreux comme des trains électriques. Lionel est un pionnier de la publicité pour jouets, avec ses catalogues luxueux et ses encarts pleine page en couleurs.

The Merriest Christmas of All—

Bright and early Christmas morning you and your boy will be running his Lionel Train, enjoying the "thrills" of the World's most fascinating and educational toy.

Lionel Trains and Miniature Railroad Equipment are exact reproductions of those used on America's leading railroad systems.

Lionel locomotives are powerful enough to haul a train of twenty or more cars around curves, through tunnels, over bridges and across switches.

The realistic Lionel equipment includes Crossing Gates that automatically lower as the train approaches and raise as it passes by. Electric Block Signals flash "Danger" and "Clear Track Ahead," while Electric Warning Signals ring at the crossings.

Lionel products have all the up-to-the-minute improvements in modern railroad design and construction. All Lionel Locomotives, Cars and Accessories are of steel construction and practically indestructible.

For 23 years Lionel Electric Trains have been electrically and mechanically perfect—fully guaranteed. They are attractively finished in rich enamels and baked like automobile bodies.

You can see Lionel Trains in operation at the best toy, hardware, electrical, sporting goods and department stores.

Complete Lionel Outfits sell from $5.75 up.

Send for the new 48-page Lionel catalogue—a handsome book showing the complete line in colors. It's Free!

THE LIONEL CORPORATION
Dept. 18, 48-52 East 21st Street, New York City
"Standard of the World" Since 1900

LIONEL ELECTRIC TOY TRAINS
& Multivolt Transformers

► Kingsbury, 1927

►► The Toy Tinkers, 1920

It is no coincidence that Tinker Toys first appeared in 1914 at the tail end of the Second Industrial Revolution. Technology was part of the zeitgeist, which valued innovative thinking, so toys encouraging children to build and create were an easy sell to America's parents.

Es war kein Zufall, dass Tinker Toys 1914 auf den Markt kamen, gegen Ende der zweiten industriellen Revolution. Technikbegeisterung gehörte zum Zeitgeist, und Spielzeug, das Kinder zum kreativen Bauen anregte, fand bei amerikanischen Eltern Anklang.

Rien d'étonnant à ce que Tinker Toys apparaisse en 1914, à la fin de la seconde révolution industrielle. La technologie est inscrite dans l'esprit du temps, qui valorise la pensée novatrice, si bien que les jouets encourageant les enfants à bâtir et créer n'ont aucune peine à séduire leurs parents.

►►►► A. C. Gilbert Company, 1935

John Lloyd Wright, 1925

John Lloyd Wright came up with the idea for Lincoln Logs while working on the Imperial Hotel in Tokyo with his architect father, Frank. When the toy hit shelves, it was advertised as the most American of toys, "A visualization of the romance of Colonial Days," though the prototype was based on his father's design in Japan.

John Lloyd Wright hatte die Idee für Lincoln Logs, während er zusammen mit seinem Vater Frank, dem berühmten Architekten, am Imperial Hotel in Tokio arbeitete. Das Spielzeug wurde als zutiefst amerikanisch beworben – "eine Visualisierung der romantischen Kolonialzeit" – obwohl der Prototyp vom Entwurf seines Vaters in Japan inspiriert war.

John Lloyd Wright a l'idée des Lincoln Logs alors qu'il travaille à la construction de l'Imperial Hotel à Tokyo avec son architecte de père, Frank. Quand le jeu arrive en boutique, il est vendu comme le plus américain des jeux, « une représentation de l'idyllique temps des colonies », alors qu'il s'inspire d'un bâtiment érigé au Japon.

KINGSBURY *MOTOR DRIVEN* TOYS

Kingsbury Passenger Bus No. 788

Looks for all the world like those big ones that run from city to city and town to town all over America. 17-passenger model. Beautifully finished. Rubber balloon type tires. Strong, long-running spring motor. Length 16½ inches. *Price $2.50.

Kingsbury Dump Truck No. 362

This clever toy is hinged so that body may be raised at an angle to dump out load. Finished in natural colors. Rubber tired wheels, bumper and other accessories. Strong spring motor. Length 14 inches. *Price $3.00.

FREE — New Catalog.
Write for It

*Prices slightly higher West of Mississippi and in Canada.

Fastest Car in the World!

Exact copy of the famous Sunbeam Racer that made the world's speed record, 203 miles per hour. Approved and autographed by Major Segrave who drove the Sunbeam. Contains swiftest spring motor ever used in a toy. Length 19 inches. Kingsbury Toy No. 333. *Price $3.00.

Kingsbury Town Car No. 340

Just like Fifth Avenue—Aristocratic! Smart! Big balloon type tired wheels. Spare wheel, trunk, etc. Strong, long-running spring motor. Length 13½ inches. *Price $3.00.

Dreams Come True!

Delightful dreams of joy-bringing toys! Toys like life! Toys that *last!* That's the really important thing. Kingsbury Motor-Driven Toys are built to outlast most every toy that peeps from Christmas stocking or hangs from Christmas tree. Good toy stores all sell them. Prices to fit every pocketbook. Ask at the store where *you* buy toys.

KINGSBURY MANUFACTURING CO.
KEENE, N. H.
In the Foothills of the White Mountains

DEALERS: Kingsbury Toys are always "best sellers." Write for our proposition.

SEND 10c FOR NOVEL ERASER
A real Kingsbury disc wheel, its big balloon tire made of pure, solid Eraser Rubber. 10c. Set of four, 35c.
Kingsbury Mfg. Co., 82 Myrtle St., Keene, N. H.
  I enclose $_____ . Please send me_____erasers.
  Please send me your FREE Catalog..............☐

Name ....
Address..

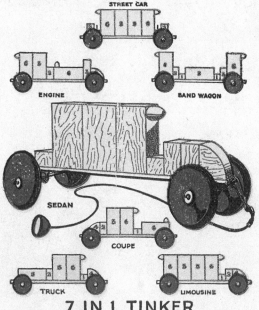

7 IN 1 TINKER

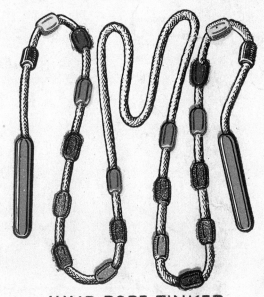

JUMP ROPE TINKER

SIREN TINKER

PONY TINKER

CLOWN TINKER

CHOO-CHOO TINKER

NECKLACE TINKER

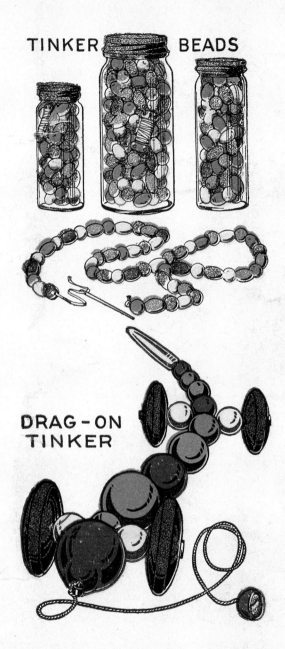

TINKER BEADS

DRAG-ON TINKER

WHIRLY TINKER

FOLLO-
ME
TINKER

TEN-PIN TINKER

TOYS SURVIVE THROUGH THE DEPRESSION BOLSTERED BY COMIC BOOK CHARACTERS AND CELEBRITY ENDORSEMENTS.

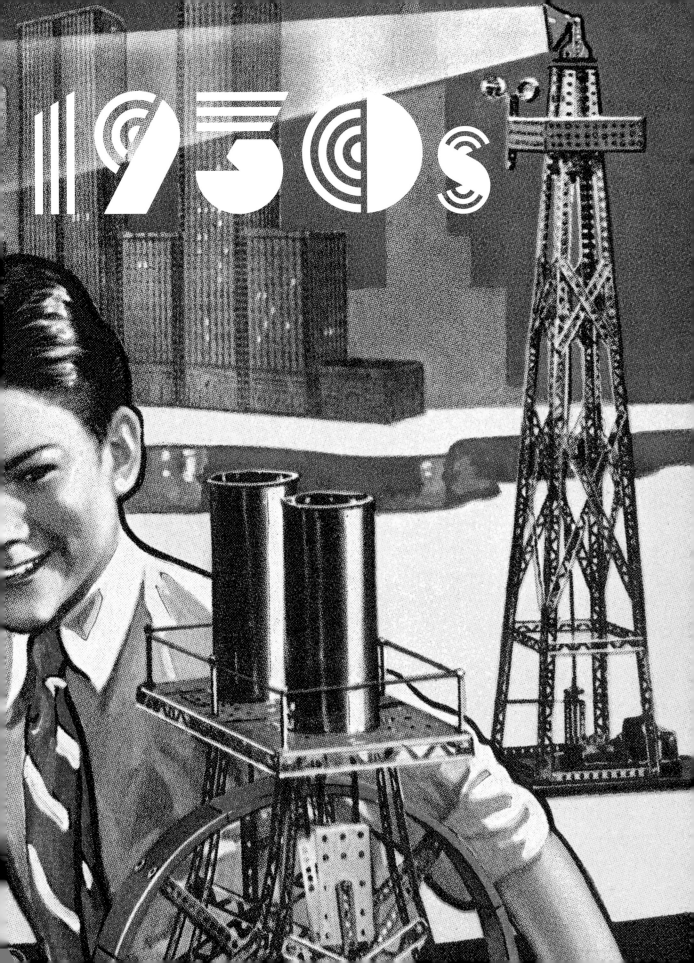

The 1936 Parade of **HUBLEY TOYS**

"They look just like the real ones"

THE HUBLEY MANUFACTURING CO., LANCASTER, PA.

SEE THEM AT THE TOY FAIR

HARD TIMES, GOOD TOYS

UNFORTUNATELY, THE GREAT DEPRESSION WAS NOT THE TITLE OF A TOY OR GAME. It began with the devastating stock market crash of October 1929 and did not officially end until after a battery of New Deal recovery initiatives got people back on their feet by 1939. It was the hard-times-brother-can-you-spare-a-dime era, and the intense burdens of the economic downturn were not borne by adults alone. Children suffered too. The hardest hit went without food and clothes, and, to their psychological detriment, many were denied diversions that enriched childhood and stimulated play.

The toy industry was as vulnerable as any other American industry, perhaps more so. It was a hand-me-down society. Toys may have been integral to mental health but not essential to basic survival. Advertising, while necessary for toy companies

1930

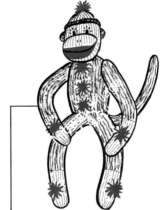

1932

Herm Fisher, Irving Price, and Helen Schelle found Fisher-Price toy company

Herm Fisher, Irving Price und Helen Schelle gründen Fisher-Price

Herm Fisher, Irving Price et Helen Schelle fondent l'entreprise de jouets Fisher-Price

1931

Teacher Ruth Faison Shaw develops finger paint to "let children be children"

Die Lehrerin Ruth Faison Shaw entwickelt eine Fingerfarbe, mit der „Kinder Kinder sein dürfen"

L'institutrice Ruth Faison Shaw invente la peinture à doigts, qui « laisse les enfants être des enfants »

Nelson Knitting Company's "Rockfords" provide basis for iconic sock monkey

Die Nelson Knitting Company aus Rockford macht ihre Sockenaffen zum Kult

Rembourrées, les chaussettes de la Nelson Knitting Company de Rockford deviennent un célèbre singe to promote their wares, was something of an indulgence. Toy companies and stores went out of business. Still, parents did not want their children to sacrifice their Christmas or birthday presents entirely. Shop window displays were, therefore, one means to advertise (if not unintentionally tease the poor). Color and less costly black-and-white comics ads in newspapers were another; they offered tie-ins with certain kid-related products, like Quaker cereal, Ovaltine milk powder, and Aunt Jemima pancake mix, and they were associated with branded comics, radio stars, or film characters like Dick Tracy, Tom Mix, Jack Armstrong, and Buck Rogers. Toys were offered as premiums (and could be ordered by mailing in a coupon—although stamps were not free). These were usually modestly produced and ran the gamut from airplanes, telescopes, periscopes, magnifying rings, decoder rings, and pen knives to a "mystery, 'torpedo' flashlight" that could be redeemed by mom at "your grocer's…while they last." The "while they last" caveat was the most dreaded of phrases. (What if they were all gone by the time mom scraped together enough

1933

Antonio Pasin constructs 45-foot Coaster Boy wagon for the Chicago World's Fair

Antonio Pasin baut einen 13-m-Handkarren für die Weltausstellung in Chicago

Antonio Pasin construit un chariot Coaster Boy de 13 m pour l'Exposition universelle de Chicago

1934

Ideal Novelty and Toy Company announces the Shirley Temple doll

Ideal Novelty und Toy Company künden die Shirley-Temple-Puppe an

L'Ideal Novelty & Toy Company annonce la sortie d'une poupée Shirley Temple

1934

Sales of Mickey Mouse handcar save Lionel from Depression bankruptcy

Der Erfolg der Micky-Maus-Draisine rettet Lionel vor der Pleite

En pleine Dépression, les ventes de la draisine Mickey sauvent Lionel de la faillite money to go shopping?) Five-and-dimes and drugstores offered even cheaper options.

Some products were not impacted by the economy. Those most frequently advertised included Lionel electric trains, Erector sets, and Daisy air rifles, as well as sleds, pedal cars, and bicycles. Then there were the faux-adult playthings like replica typewriters, medical equipment, cash registers, and telephones. Board games by Milton Bradley, Parker Brothers, and Selchow & Righter were also popular for children and adults in the 1930s. Notably, as widespread as the Depression was, not all Americans suffered from it—unemployment started at 25 percent in 1930 and dipped to 15 percent by 1939, so families that never lost or regained their incomes could afford to purchase toys until the next period of austerity—the war.

1935

1937

1938

The Little Orphan Annie decoder ring epitomizes successful product tie-ins

Der Dechiffrier-Ring von Little Orphan Annie belegt die Wirksamkeit von Werbekooperationen

L'anneau décodeur d'Annie la petite orpheline incarne le succès des produits dérivés

Madame Alexander produces first doll based on a licensed character, Scarlett O'Hara

Madame Alexander produziert die erste Puppe, die auf einer Lizenzfigur basiert: Scarlett O'Hara

Madame Alexander produit sa première poupée d'un personnage sous licence, Scarlett O'Hara

William Gruber develops idea for View-Master while visiting caves in Oregon

William Gruber kommt beim Besuch von Höhlen in Oregon die Idee für den Diabetrachter View-Master

William Gruber a l'idée du stéréoscope View-Master en visitant des grottes en Oregon

SCHLECHTE ZEITEN, GUTES SPIELZEUG

Die Spielzeugindustrie übersteht die Weltwirtschaftskrise, indem sie Werbung mit Comicfiguren und Prominenten macht.

Die Spielzeugindustrie war genauso anfällig wie jede andere amerikanische Branche, vielleicht sogar noch anfälliger. Spielzeuge wurden in der Familie weitergereicht. Leider war „The Great Depression" nicht der Name eines Spiels. Alles fing mit dem Börsencrash im Oktober 1929 an und endete erst 1939, nachdem die umfangreichen New-Deal-Maßnahmen der US-Regierung die Menschen wieder aus dem Gröbsten herausgeführt hatten. Die schwere Bürde der Wirtschaftskrise lastete nicht nur auf den Schultern der Erwachsenen, sondern auch die Kinder litten: Die Allerärmsten hatten weder Kleidung noch genug zu essen – von Spielzeug konnten sie nur träumen.

Die Spielzeugindustrie war genauso anfällig wie jede andere amerikanische Branche, vielleicht sogar noch anfälliger. Spielzeuge wurden in der Familie weitergereicht. Die Produkte mochten zwar der Psyche guttun, zum bloßen Überleben waren sie aber nicht nötig. Werbung war für die Unternehmen zwar notwendig, erschien aber wie ein Luxus. Unternehmen gingen pleite und Läden mussten schließen. Trotzdem wollten Eltern nicht, dass ihre Kinder völlig auf Geburtstags- und Weihnachtsgeschenke verzichten mussten. Schaufensterdekoration war ein probates Mittel der Werbung (und weckte so manche unerfüllten Sehnsüchte). Ein anderes waren Comicstrips (farbig oder in preiswerterem Schwarzweiß) in den Zeitungen, die bestimmte kindgerechte Produkte wie Haferflocken von Quaker, Ovaltine-Milchpulver und die Pfannkuchenbackmischung von Aunt Jemima bewarben und mit Markencomics, Radiostars oder Filmfiguren wie Dick Tracy, Tom Mix, Jack Armstrong und Buck Rogers operierten. Spielzeuge waren darin oft als kostenlose Beigaben enthalten (oder konnten durch Einsenden eines Coupons bestellt werden – wobei das Porto allerdings nicht frei war). Dabei handelte es sich um alle möglichen billig produzierten Objekte von Flugzeugen, Teleskopen und Periskopen über Lupen, Dechiffrierringe und Taschenmesser bis hin zu einer „geheimnisvollen ,Torpedo'-Taschenlampe". „Solange der Vorrat reicht" war dabei eine gefürchtete Phrase, denn was, wenn alles schon weg war, wenn Mutti endlich genug Geld zusammengekratzt hatte, um einkaufen zu gehen? Drugstores und „Five and dime"-Stores boten noch billigere Optionen an.

Einige Produkte wurden nicht von der Wirtschaftskrise beeinflusst. Zu den am häufigsten beworbenen gehörten die elektrischen Eisenbahnen von Lionel, Bausätze von Erector und Luftgewehre von Daisy sowie auch Schlitten, Tretautos und Fahrräder. Auch Kinderversionen von Geräten für Erwachsene wie Spielzeugschreibmaschinen, Arztkoffer, Ladenkassen und Telefone sowie Brettspiele von Milton Bradley, Parker Brothers und Selchow & Righter waren in den 1930ern beliebt bei Kindern und Erwachsenen, denn obwohl die Wirtschaftskrise das ganze Land lähmte, litten nicht alle Amerikaner gleichermaßen darunter. Die Arbeitslosenquote lag 1930 bei 25 Prozent und war 1939 auf 15 Prozent abgesunken, Familien, deren Einkommensquellen nie versiegt waren, konnten es sich leisten, Spielzeug zu kaufen – zumindest bis zur nächsten Durststrecke, dem Zweiten Weltkrieg.

▶ Cream of Wheat, 1936

BUCK ROGERS
SOLAR SCOUTS

SECRET CLUB OF THE RADIO

MAUVAIS JOURS, ON JOUE TOUJOURS

Les jouets survivent à la Grande Dépression grâce aux personnages de comics et aux parrainages de célébrités.

L'industrie du jouet est aussi vulnérable que les autres, si ce n'est plus. L'heure est à la récupération et à la transmission plutôt qu'à la consommation. La Grande Dépression n'est malheureusement ni un jeu ni une partie de plaisir. Elle commence avec l'effondrement dévastateur de la Bourse en octobre 1929 et ne s'achève officiellement qu'après l'instauration d'une batterie d'initiatives, le New Deal («nouvelle donne»), qui remet le pays sur pied en 1939. «Les temps sont durs, mon frère», dit le célèbre refrain de l'époque, et les adultes ne sont pas les seuls à subir les violents effets de la crise. Les enfants souffrent aussi. Les plus durement touchés manquent de nourriture et de vêtements et ils sont aussi cruellement privés de la diversion salutaire et formatrice que constitue le jeu.

L'industrie du jouet est aussi vulnérable que les autres, si ce n'est plus. L'heure est à la récupération et à la transmission plutôt qu'à la consommation. Les jouets ont beau être cruciaux pour la santé mentale, ils ne sont pas essentiels à la survie. Dans ce contexte, faire leur promotion est une gageure. Beaucoup de marques et de boutiques mettent la clé sous la porte. Les parents sont pourtant déterminés à ne pas totalement sacrifier le Noël ou l'anniversaire des enfants et les vitrines des magasins deviennent le meilleur moyen de faire de la publicité (quitte à frustrer les pauvres). L'industrie recourt aussi aux encarts dans les comics et dans les journaux, en noir et blanc ou en couleurs quand le budget le permet, qui permettent d'associer le jouet à un produit destiné aux enfants, comme les céréales Quaker, la poudre de lait Ovomaltine ou la pâte à pancakes Aunt Jemima, et à des vedettes sous licence des comics, de la radio et du cinéma comme Dick Tracy, Tom Mix, Jack Armstrong et Buck Rogers. Les jouets sont offerts pour l'achat de produits de première nécessité et peuvent être commandés par correspondance en échange d'un coupon – même si les timbres ne sont pas gratuits. Ils sont généralement de piètre qualité et comptent foison de canifs, télescopes, périscopes, anneaux grossissants ou décodeurs, et la «lampe torche mystère Torpedo», que «les mamans trouveront à l'épicerie, tant qu'il en reste!» – ce dernier avertissement a une sinistre résonance. (Et s'il n'y en avait plus quand maman aura assez d'argent pour faire les courses?) Les «tout à cinq ou dix cents» et les drugstores proposent des options moins chères encore.

Certains produits ne sont pas touchés par les fluctuations de l'économie. Les plus présents dans les publicités sont les trains électriques Lionel, les kits Erector et les carabines à air comprimé Daisy, ainsi que les luges, les voitures à pédales et les vélos. Viennent ensuite les jouets qui imitent des activités adultes, comme les petites machines à écrire, les sacoches de docteur, les caisses enregistreuses et les téléphones. Les jeux de plateau de Milton Bradley, Parker Brothers et Selchow & Righter sont aussi appréciés des enfants que des adultes dans les années 1930. Notons que malgré l'ampleur de la Dépression, tous les Américains n'en ont pas souffert – le taux de chômage, de 25 % en 1930, est descendu à 15 % en 1939, si bien que les ménages qui n'ont jamais perdu leur emploi ou en ont trouvé un peuvent se permettre d'acheter des jouets, jusqu'à la nouvelle phase d'austérité – la guerre.

◀ Halsam, 1936

Get DICK TR
DETECTIVE SECRETS
How to use my Official Detecto-Kit -Dick Tracy
Dick Tracy Secret Formula Q-11

America's Premier Line Stuffed Toys

KNICKERBOCKER TOY CO., Inc.
200 FIFTH AVENUE   LEO L. WEISS, Pres.   NEW YORK, N. Y.

PRINTED IN U·S·A
Kameo-Plymouth Press, Brooklyn, N. Y.

◄ Quaker, c. 1938

► National Fireworks, c. 1937

Knickerbocker Toy Company, 1938

What Fun You Will Have If You Get *this* for Christmas

Can you imagine more fun than this? Make all kinds of funny men and animals — donkeys, monkeys, giraffes, kangaroos, humpty-dumpties, cows, gobblers, soldiers, acrobats, boxers, fat men, tall men. Hundreds of funny things, each one different. Twist and turn them into the funniest shapes and forms you've ever seen. Make animals and have your own circus. Stage a parade of soldiers, a boxing bout, an acrobatic act. All you need is a set of Krazy-Ikes. Then the fun begins. A tail here, a head there, an arm or two, and oh! yes, a couple of legs, and you have a Krazy-Ike. And another

and another. It's so easy, too. Just push the pieces of wood together and pull them apart when you don't want them that way any more. Play with it for weeks and weeks and still there is lots more fun because there is almost no end to the things you can make. Picture pages included with Krazy-Ikes show some of the things you can make. Of course, you will build your own, too. Have loads and loads of fun. Just whisper to dad and mother that you want a set of Krazy-Ikes for Christmas. Costs only $1. If your dealer can't supply you use coupon below.

KRAZY-IKES

TRADE MARK REG. U.S. PAT. OFF.

1000 in 1 Builder Toy

$1

(Denver & West $1.15)

$3.50

Complete with battery and 15 cards. (Denver and West $3.75).

Maybe You Will Get This, Too!

It's the famous Knapp Electric Questioner. This grand toy knows wonderful, unusual things that you want to know—things about the world a million years ago—and the strange world under the sea—the amazing things seen under a microscope—about wild animals and flowers and the flags of nations and heaps of other thrilling things. And— *think of it!*—it tells you all it knows by a mysterious buzzing sound that answers your

questions correctly. You have never had such a wonderful toy. Each of the 15 cards that come with Knapp Electric Questioner is a thrilling game in itself. And you can keep adding other sets of cards and get fun from this toy for years. Operates with simple flashlight battery, included. Ask for a Knapp Electric Questioner for Christmas. Costs only $3.50. If your dealer can't supply you use coupon below.

KNAPP ELECTRIC QUESTIONER

KNAPP TOYS

KNAPP ELECTRIC (Div. P. R. Mallory & Co., Inc.), 3029 E. Washington Street, Indianapolis, Ind.

NOTE: Use this coupon if your dealer can't supply you

KNAPP ELECTRIC (Div. of P. R. Mallory & Co., Inc.), Dept. J-11
3029 E. Washington St., Indianapolis, Ind.

☐ Send Set of Krazy-Ikes, $1 ($1.15 Denver & West).
☐ Send Knapp Electric Questioner $3.50 ($3.75 Denver & West).
☐ Money enclosed.　　　　☐ I'll pay postman.
☐ Send Free Booklet of Knapp Toys.

Name..

Address..

◄ Knapp, 1930

"Can you imagine more fun than this?" Krazy-Ikes, the "1000 in 1 Builder Toy" was a not-too-distant relative to Tinker Toys and Erector — toys that spurred creative thinking and endless amusement. For only $1, it was a sensible purchase for Depression-era families who needed to stretch every dollar.

„Mehr Spaß geht nicht!" Krazy-Ikes bot „1000 Bauspielzeuge in einem" und war ein nicht allzu entfernter Verwandter von Tinker Toys und Erector – ein Spielzeug, das die kindliche Kreativität anregte und unendlichen Spaß brachte. Und das Beste für von der Wirtschaftskrise gebeutelte Familien: Es kostete nur 1 Dollar.

« Que pourrait-il y avoir de plus amusant ? » Krazy-Ikes, « 1000 jeux de construction en 1 », est un parent de Tinker Toys et du kit Erector, qui encourage aussi la créativité et la réflexion pour des heures de jeu. Vendu seulement 1 dollar, c'est un achat raisonnable pour les familles frappées par la crise.

Holgate Brothers Company, 1930

MAGIC BUILDERS!

Is your child daily asking "Mother, *now* what can I do"? Answer that question permanently with a set of our Magic Builders Blocks. Designed by a group of our leading nursery school and kindergarten teachers after actual observance of the needs and wishes of children. Our MAGIC BUILDERS are different from anything hitherto available.

These blocks are made of clear, attractive hardwood. They are larger than the usual blocks and may be piled easily by the smallest hands. The range of designs which can be built from a standard set is almost limitless and make it suitable for children of all ages, either at home or in school.

With each Set is included a sturdy hardwood box on wheels. This box is extra large allowing the child to replace the blocks at random without careful packing.

Actual tests of the approved set show children to be fascinated with these blocks to the exclusion of other toys. Their large size and the correct design of the different pieces gives the child an exceptional opportunity to develop mental planning and muscular control.

Don't you owe your child this chance to develop mind and muscle in perfect balance?

Fill in the coupon below to receive full description and prices of this essential toy of childhood.

HOLGATE BROTHERS
COMPANY
KANE, PA.

HOLGATE BROTHERS COMPANY
Kane, Pennsylvania
Please send me, without cost or obligation, prices and descriptive circulars of the Magic Builders.

Name ....
Address ....
City .... State ....

Quaker Oats, 1935

▶ *The Household Magazine*, 1930

The word *Eskimo* is generally known to describe native inhabitants of Alaska and the Arctic, though the term is considered derogatory by many of those same people. In 1930, *The Household Magazine* was blissfully unaware of the negative connotations when it offered this Eskimo Doll as a premium for subscribing.

Die Ureinwohner von Alaska oder der Arktis wurden in der Regel als Eskimos bezeichnet, viele von ihnen empfinden den Begriff jedoch heutzutage als abwertend. Von diesem sprachlichen Minenfeld wusste die Zeitschrift *The Household Magazine* allerdings noch nichts, als sie 1930 eine Eskimopuppe als Abo-Prämie anbot.

Le mot Eskimo a longtemps qualifié les habitants autochtones de l'Alaska et de l'Arctique, et nombre de ces peuples refusaient cette dénomination. En 1930, *The Household Magazine* ignore ces connotations péjoratives lorsqu'il offre une poupée eskimo pour chaque abonnement.

A New Playmate—
ESKIMO DOLL
for the Little Folks

With Christmas just around the corner, Santa Claus has a big surprise this year for the children—a surprise that will bring more hours of real pleasure for the little folks than any gift The Household Magazine has offered during the Holiday Season.

This Eskimo Doll is dressed in a warm, snug suit of brushed wool, with cap to match. It will sit up—stand up—or go to bed—whatever you want it to do. Being made of good, unbreakable material it will withstand the hardest knocks and falls. See how it holds out its chubby arms. You can almost hear it saying, "I am starting out from Eskimo Land, and I am looking for some little child to give me a happy home."

Along with this Eskimo Doll will come an ornamental Christmas Tree in colors, with a jolly Santa Claus standing by its side. You can put the tree and Santa Claus on the table Christmas Day, or you can place it by the Eskimo Doll for its first Christmas Tree.

Here's the Way to Get This Eskimo Doll and Christmas Tree

It won't cost you a cent to get this darling Eskimo Doll and ornamental Christmas Tree. We will send both the Doll and Tree to every boy and girl who sends us two one-year subscriptions to The Household Magazine at 50 cents each—just $1.00 in subscriptions. At the bottom of this page you will find a coupon on which to write the names and addresses of your subscribers. Mail the coupon to The Household Magazine, Topeka, Kansas, with a $1.00 bill, money order or check. Be sure to write your own name and address on the bottom line of the coupon, so we will know where to mail the Doll and Christmas Tree.

Mothers—You Can Help

This darling Eskimo Doll and Christmas Tree won't cost you a penny, and they will bring hours of fun to every child. If you wish to make two children happy, we will send you two dolls and two trees for $2.00 worth of subscriptions.

Eskimo Dolly with Eskimo charms
Comes swiftly, comes surely
Right into your arms,
Carried warmly and safely
On Santa Claus' back
And sent by The Household
In Santa Claus' pack.

TRAIL BLAZER ★ SLEDS

Second Growth White Ash Tops

Concave shoe bites in like a sharp skate. New square foot where knee attaches stands on runners relieving strain.

$1.45

Watch Him Turn!
Compare Ward's "TRAIL BLAZER" With the Very Best—None Excepted!

Every boy knows there are two kinds of sleds for sale—one a rather cheap line; the other, known from coast to coast as the best, selling for about three times the price. We believe our "Trail Blazer" Sleds are the equal in quality of this best line—and we can save you nearly half! "Trail Blazer" Sleds incorporate these features: (1) Tops of second growth selected white ash such as baseball bats are made of—half again as thick as on cheaper line of sleds. (2) Varnished with two coats special spar varnish—sun-proof, water-proof, cold-proof; very glossy top decorated with colorful picture. (3) Runners are carbon steel heated to overcome brittleness and to avoid breakage in use. Note the manner in which knees are attached to runners—the weight is no longer supported by the rivet. (4) Steel front hinged at first knee allowing greater flexibility. (5) Speed boat lines. Let us send you a "Trail Blazer" and you be the judge! Only 32 and 36-inch mailable. All Larger Sizes Shipped Not Prepaid.

Shaped Like a Speedboat

"Trail Blazer" distance is due to its Speedboat lines. When you throw yourself on sled, the angle of the top changes downward motion of your weight into FORWARD PUSH.

With Single Steering Bar

448 G 1760—Length 32 in. 4 knees. We Pay Postage		$1.45
448 G 1761—Lgth. 36 in. 4 knees. We Pay Postage		1.75
148 G 1762—Lgth. 40 in. 4 knees. Ship. wt. 10 lbs.		2.19

With Double Steering Bar

148 G 1763—Lgth. 45 in. 4 knees. Ship. wt. 13 lbs.		$2.59
148 G 1764—Lgth. 56 in. 6 knees. Ship. wt. 14 lbs.		2.95

SHOOTING STAR

95¢

All maple tops, varnished. Speedboat lines; resembles "Trail Blazer" Sleds. The best low priced sleds on the market. Concave steel runners; steel front rail hinged for steering. The 32 and 36-in. sizes are mailable. Larger Shipped Not Prepaid.

With Single Steering Bar

448 G 1723—Length 32 in.; width 11½ in.; height 6 in. Four knees. Postpaid		95¢
448 G 1724—Length 36 in.; width 12½ in.; height 6 in. Four knees. Postpaid		$1.29
148 G 1730—Length 40 in. width 12½ in.; Ht. 6 in. Four knees. Ship. wt. 10 lbs.		$1.42

With Double Steering Bar

148 G 1728—Length 45 in.; width 14½ in.; Ht. 6 in. 4 knees. Ship. wt. 13 lbs.		$1.79
148 G 1726—Length 56 in.; width 14½ in.; ht. 6 in. Six knees. Ship. wt. 14 lbs.		$2.39

$2.79

Triple Motor Airplanes
20-Gauge Auto Body Steel

PROVED CARRYING STRENGTH 200 POUNDS. An exact miniature! Very latest Cabin design with windows. Passenger space and pilot's cockpit. Glossy baked-on enamel. Three propellers revolve—just pull it along and hear the motors hum! We Pay Postage.

Large Tri-Motor Plane 28 inches long with 24-in. wing spread by 9½ inches high. Steel wheels—rubber tires.
448 G 1213—$2.79

Small Tri-Motor Plane 20 inches long with 18 in. wing spread by 6¼ inches high. Steel wheels.
48 G 1232—$1.00

$1.89

TESTED!
Will Hold 200 Pounds

19-Gauge Steel

20½-Inch Dump Truck of auto body steel. A tremendous value! A good action toy for creative minds! Baked-on enamel in vivid blue with red trim and bright stripings of gold. Turn crank at side to dump bed. The 3½-in. wheels have rubber tires molded on steel base—cannot pull out. Size 20½ by 7 by 8¼ inches high.
448 G 1221—We Pay Postage.............. $1.89

$2.15

20-Gauge Steel Airplanes

SO STRONG—a man can easily sit on this large Airplane and coast down hill! Lines of a real plane. Very latest Cabin design with windows. High gloss finish. This toy with revolving propeller and motor-hum is sure to please. Motor hums as it is pulled along the floor.

Large Steel Airplane 28 inches long with 24-in. wing spread by 10 inches high. Steel wheels—rubber tires.
448 G 1227—Postpaid $2.15

Small Steel Airplane 22 inches long with 20-in. wing spread by 7¼ inches high. Steel wheels.
48 G 1229—Postpaid $1.22

$4.69

White Dump Truck
Our Finest 20-Gauge Steel

Extra strong, made of automobile steel with reinforced chassis. Will hold 300 pounds. Miniature of a real White Auto Truck in fact this toy was supervised by the White Auto Truck Company themselves. It's the finest reproduction we have ever seen. Steering wheel in cab turns front wheels. 4-inch steel disc wheels have detachable rubber tires with bead tread. Positive worm gear slow action dump raises just like big trucks. Enameled black with red wheels and frame. End gate in back of bed opens and lowers with chain. Truck size: 26 by 8¼ by 10½ inches high to top of cab. Size of Dumping Bed: 15 by 8¼ by 2¼ in. deep. We Pay Postage.
448 G 1227.................... $4.69

Your Choice $1.00 Each

"Structo" Steam Shovel
24-Gauge Steel

Digs dirt like a real steam shovel. Place cab in any position on turntable. Turn crank—chain and wood drum raises and lowers bucket and automatic trip drops the load. Riveted together. Size 16¼ by 5¾ by 13 in. high.
48 G 1219—Postpaid.........$1.00

Police Patrol
24-Gauge Steel

Clangety CLANG! Just like a real Patrol. Large Packard type hood; well designed body with inside seats. Rear step and hand rails. No sharp edges. Enameled blue, colorfully trimmed. Brass hub caps. Size 16½ by 5½ by 7 inches in height.
48 G 1236—Postpaid.........$1.00

"Structo" Dump Truck
24-Gauge Steel

Splendidly constructed. Beautifully finished baked-on enamel. Every boy wants at least one Dump Truck. Use it with sand outdoors or with blocks on the floor. Pulling lever throws dump. Size 18 by 5¾ by 6 inches in height. Bed is 6 by 9¼ in. Smooth—no rough edges.
48 G 1230—Postpaid.........$1.00

$1.45

Zeppelin
28-Gauge Steel Supports 100 Lbs.

Over 2 Feet Long. Plenty of thrill and satisfaction in owning this toy! It is so impressive it will appeal to any child. Shaped to correct proportions. Strong enough for a small boy to ride—it will support 100 lbs. Modeled after the Graf Zeppelin, with passenger gondola beneath. Supported on three wheels. Size 26 by 6 by 7 inches high. Aluminum finish with red, white and blue trim. Two propellers on front gondola revolve making a noise like a motor when Zeppelin is pulled along the floor. We Pay Postage.
448 G 1224.................... $1.45

Big, Strong Locomotive
24-Gauge Steel

A boy's favorite toy is a Locomotive! Durably enameled in gay colors. Piston moves when pulled along floor. Massive boiler, roomy cab and tender. It will be sure to please . . . it's such a well made toy! Size 20 by 5 by 5½ in. high.
48 G 1235—Postpaid.........$1.00

Fire Hose and Ladder
20-Gauge Steel

Fully equipped with hose reel and 32 inches of rubber hose with nozzle. Two extension hose. Two ladders, sidelights, bumper, bell and chemical tank, step on rear. Enameled bright colors. Size 16½ by 4½ by 5¼ in. high.
48 G 1233—Postpaid.........$1.00

Wrecking Car
24-Gauge Steel

Pretend you're a garage man with this strong Service Truck made of heavy sheet steel. No sharp edges. Complete even to the headlights and wrecker with windlass and chain. Crane can be taken off to make truck. Enameled. Size 19½ by 6¼ in. high to top of cab.
48 G 1237—We Pay Postage...$1.00

Lincoln Logs, 1937

▶ Lionel, 1931

Two years after the stock market crashed, Lionel was having its worst year ever. You wouldn't guess it based on a colorful advertisement with a celebrity endorsement – "Lionel Trains are just like mine" – but the company was headed toward bankruptcy, which would change in a few years with the help of a certain mouse named Mickey.

Zwei Jahre nach dem Börsencrash verzeichnete die Firma Lionel ihr schlechtestes Geschäftsjahr seit Bestehen und steuerte mit Volldampf auf den Bankrott zu, was man angesichts der Werbung mit prominenter Unterstützung – „Lionel-Züge sind genau wie meine", sagt Eisenbahningenieur S. E. Godshall – nicht vermuten würde. Ein paar Jahre später wendete sich das Blatt dank der Hilfe einer gewissen Maus namens Micky.

Deux ans après le krach boursier, Lionel vit sa pire année; une situation critique que dissimulent plutôt bien cette publicité haute en couleur et la vedette qui assure : « Les trains Lionel sont comme les miens. » La société sera sauvée de la faillite par un certain Mickey Mouse quelques années plus tard.

Ask Dad

o buy you a LIONEL TRAIN

"the trains .. that railroad men buy for their boys!"

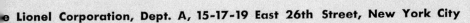

EVERY boy has dreamed of owning a Lionel Train—with bridges, and nels, semaphores and switches and those things that go to make up a l railroad.

Now is your chance! Go to Dad and him that you want a Lionel Electric ain for Christmas. Lionel trains are commended by many famous railroad gineers—because they are so real, so e to life, so swift, so strong.

What fun you are going to have with your Lionel! What beautiful trains they are—like real railroads in everything but size.

Lionel railroading is thrilling fun. Your Christmas, this year, will be an exciting one if Dad will get you a Lionel Electric Railroad.

Sit down and write for your FREE copy of the new 52-page full color Lionel Railroad Planning Book and Catalog.

e Lionel Corporation, Dept. A, 15-17-19 East 26th Street, New York City

See Lionel Trains demonstrated at your local Department, Toy, Hardware, Sporting Goods and Electrical Goods store. Lionel Trains priced as low as $5.95.

S. E. Godshall, famous engineer of the "Pennsylvania Limited," says: "Lionel Trains are just like mine—every boy should own a Lionel. It will help him to learn the principles of railroading."

S. E. Godshall

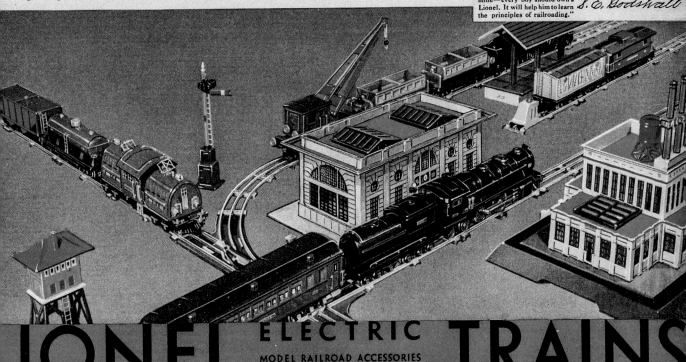

IONEL ELECTRIC TRAINS
MODEL RAILROAD ACCESSORIES
MULTIVOLT TRANSFORMERS

A. C. Gilbert Company, 1938

▶ General Mills, 1939

Despite its intrepid name – the Mystery, "Torpedo" Flashlight – General Mills insisted this premium was not a toy but a practical bedside tool that could be obtained by purchasing two boxes of Wheaties, which were "light as snowflakes" and "as alluring to a childish imagination as French confection."

Trotz ihres draufgängerischen Namens – Mystery „Torpedo"-Taschenlampe – bestand die Firma General Mills darauf, dass diese Prämie kein Spielzeug, sondern ein praktisches Nachttischutensil sei. Um sie zu bekommen, musste man zwei Packungen Wheaties kaufen, die angeblich „leicht wie Schneeflocken" und für Kinder „so verlockend wie französische Pralinen" waren.

Malgré son nom, la lampe torche Mystère « Torpedo » n'est pas un jouet, insiste General Mills, mais un parfait accessoire de table de chevet. Pour l'obtenir il suffit d'acheter deux boîtes de Wheaties, « légers comme des flocons de neige » et « aussi attrayantes pour les enfants que les pralines françaises ».

Free

AT YOUR GROCER'S ...WHILE THEY LAST

Illustration shows flashlight larger than actual size. **ACTUAL MEASUREMENT:** 4 INCHES LONG. Comes in 3 beautiful colors:—(a) Congo Red (b) Hongkong Blue (c) Midnight Black. Look for display at dealer's today.

Ideal for Finding Small Objects

Wide-Angle Beam For Larger Objects

Just the Thing For Auto Repairs

Handy Bedside Emergency Light

Mother: Accept This Brand-New

Jack Armstrong
MYSTERY, "TORPEDO" FLASHLIGHT

for your child, free with purchase of 2 packages of WHEATIES

—the delicious whole wheat breakfast cereal that children simply adore

Not a toy. Comes completely equipped with genuine Tung-sol bulb and Marathon battery, made to U. S. Bureau of Standards specifications. Barrel is streamlined, with concealed "mystery" switch.

TO OBTAIN FLASHLIGHT, DO THIS:

Simply Go to Your Grocer and Purchase Two Packages of Wheaties at the Regular Price and Receive Flashlight, Complete with Battery, FREE of Extra Charge. Offer Good Only While They Last. So Act at Once!

MOTHERS:—Here's a chance to delight your child with a Jack Armstrong "MYSTERY" FLASHLIGHT, entirely free of extra charge. Not a toy—but a sturdy, 4 inch all-purpose flashlight, with a *concealed* operating principle that's sure to intrigue the curiosity of any youngster, girl or boy!

These unusual flashlights—finished in genuine, rust-resisting Terne plate with simulated alligator barrel—are now *free* at your grocer's. They are given solely to induce you to start serving Wheaties, the delicious breakfast cereal that offers still *another* way of delighting your child.

For Wheaties are whole wheat in a form that children simply adore. Light as snow-flakes—toasted to a crispy, golden brown—as alluring to the childish imagination as a French confection. And made *doubly* delicious with malt flavoring.

But that's not all. Whole wheat—as embodied in Wheaties—furnishes an excellent supply of the largest need of the diet, food energy. In fact, it is richer in amino compounds, essential to the building of muscle tissue, than such cereals as either corn or rice.

Limited Offer—So Hurry

So take advantage of this free flashlight offer without fail. Get Wheaties and see how their magic taste ends breakfast table coaxing and arguing. See how your child "goes" for them—eats them up—and asks for *more!*

Look for the Wheaties display featuring free flashlights, at your grocer's. And remember that this special offer holds good only as long as dealers' stocks last.

To avoid disappointment—why not order your two packages of Wheaties right NOW—and make *certain* of securing one of these unusual FREE gifts for *your* child!

"Breakfast of Champions" is a reg. trade mark of General Mills

GENERAL MILLS, INC., MINNEAPOLIS, MINN.

Your Child Will Love This

"Breakfast of Champions"

Wheaties with fruit, sugar and plenty of milk or cream

Copr. 1939, General Mills, Inc.

Now Alice has this nifty
ZEPHYR AUTOMOBILE

"What boy or girl 3 to 6 years of age wouldn't be good all year to get this fine, streamlined auto?" asks Alice. "A big car—42½ inches long, 17½ inches wide, its steel body is enameled in a beautiful new shade of brown, trimmed in orange. Fast, too—that's because the 10-inch double-disc steel wheels run on roller bearings. They have ¾ in. rubber tires and large hub caps. Fully equipped like Dad's car—streamlined windshield, radiator ornament, front bumper, French bulb horn and headlights (non-electric). Pedals adjust to your leg reach. You'll be the envy of your friends with this modern car."

$11.95

42½ INS. LONG

No. BR156

"I'm so glad I was good"

$6.75

No. BR157

33½ INS. LONG

Here's a snappy, speedy
ROADSTER

Other cars will have to take your dust as you speed along in this flashy green roadster with ivory trim. It's the ideal low-priced car for any tot 2 to 4 years old. 33½ ins. long, 17 ins. wide. Latest artillery-type 8-inch disc steel wheels have large beaded hub caps and rubber tires. Has as radiator ornament and long dummy headlights. Body of sturdy steel to give many miles of happy motoring.

BALL BEARINGS IN ALL WHEELS

No. BR158

New Style Handle Bars!
TUBULAR VELOCIPEDES

12-IN. SIZE $8.95

16-IN. SIZE $9.95

20-IN. SIZE $10.95

The newest thing on wheels—and the finest. Note the new underslung handle bars that make steering easier. Heavy 1¼-inch electric welded tubular frame will "take it" for years. All wheels run on ball bearings and have bicycle-type spokes and 1-inch rubber tires. Pedals and saddle also the kind used on bicycles. Fender on front wheel. Large rear platform. Beautiful colored enamel finish.

Billy and Ruth 33

WOLVERINE TOY FAMILY
"Sandy Andy" "Sunny Andy" "Sunny Suzy"

NEW

Drum Major

New, ingenious musical toy. Drummer actually plays stirring march-rhythms. Each note clearly accented. Operated by strong motor with new action principle. Height, 13¾ in.

No. 39N236
Each
$1.42

Arnold's Educational Chimes

NEW

Trains children in first steps of instrumental play. Endorsed by educators. Features *Three Tone System* used in leading schools. Scores for sixteen easy-to-follow tunes, along with mallet, included. Length, 8¼ in.
No. 39N237—Each—$1.34

The Little Gardener

Practical flower-planting set for indoors and outdoors. Contains 6 flower pots; 6 saucers; 6 packages of tested seeds; sprinkling can and shovel. Four-color box. 18¾ x 13½ in.
No. 25N137—Each—$1.34

The DE LUXE LITTLE GARDENER contains 12 flower pots; 12 saucers; 12 pkgs. of tested seeds; sprinkling can; shovel; hoe; rake; pail; can of fertilizer; sieve.
No. 25N138—Each—$2.68

Improved

Pull-and-Ring Street Car

The leader in pull-along toys. Bell rings clearly when car is moved. Trolley pole added. Heavy gauge metal. 13¾ in. long.
No. 39N238—Each—$1.34

NEW

Pull-and-Ring Ferry Boat

Splendid toy for the "younger youngsters". When pulled over sidewalk or floor, bell rings continuously and walking beam goes up and down. Length, 13½ in.
No. 39N240—Each—$1.34

NEW

Spot Shot

New type marble action game. When pushed down, trigger ejects marbles which whirl around surface of disc till they settle into numbered holes or drop through center opening. Points scored by adding numbers of filled holes. Automatic re-loading. All metal. Handsomely lithographed. Length, 13½ in.
No. 50N175—Each—68c

Zilotone

Music master plays on keys, duplicating action of real Xylophonist. Tone is clear, melodious. Strong motor. Sound produced by records. 3 records included. 9 in. long.
No. 39N75—Each—$2.90

Bowler Andy Mill

Marbles in chute cause windmill to revolve and car move up and down. Strong, 8 steel marbles. 21 in. high.
No. 39N232—Each—$1.42

Bizzy Andy Trip Hammer

Trip hammer effect. 6 marbles. 10½ in. high.
No. 39N231
Each
68c

Kiddie Kampers

6 Boy and Girl Scouts in camp activities. Action controlled by strong motor.
No. 39N233—Each—$1.20

Sandy Andy Merry Miller

Novel sand toy with humorous twist. As the wheel, carrying sand, revolves, Merry Miller tries to get around corner of house. Can of sand included. All set up. 12 in. high.
No. 39N241—Each—$1.20

Sandy Andy Incline

Automatic sand toy of speed and pep. Car races up and down chute as long as hopper contains sand. Can of white sand included. Display box forms tray. Height, 14¾ in.
No. 39N230—Each—$1.34
Smaller size, without engineer, is 11 in. high.
No. 39N229—Each—72c

Fleet Flyer

Remarkable action toy. Plane runs out of hangar along upper incline, then drops to lower track. Then rolls back into hangar for another trip. Strong motor. 25½ in. long.
No. 39N234—Each—$1.30

◄ Billy and Ruth, 1939

Wolverine, 1933

► Cream of Wheat, 1936

EQUIPMENT

HOW TO GET YOUR OFFICIAL BUCK ROGERS OUTFIT....

EVERY real Solar Scout gets as much official equipment as he can. It's easy! Save the green triangles from the top of Cream of Wheat packages your mother and her friends buy. Send them with the small amount of money indicated to Cream of Wheat, Dept. BR, Minneapolis, Minn.

NOTE:—Items at the prices shown are not available in Canada or outside continental U. S. Write us for Canadian prices on specific items wanted. Offers as shown in this booklet, of merchandise sent for Cream of Wheat package tops and money are void in all states whose laws prohibit such an offer or require a license therefor. We reserve the right at any time to reject an order and to refund the money sent. Not redeemable through speculators or any person other than the receiving consumer.

You may send, postal or express money order. These are the safest and most satisfactory means of transmitting money. However, we will accept coin or stamps, but when sending these be sure they are carefully wrapped and the envelope securely sealed.

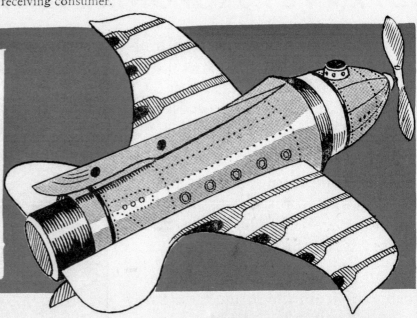

SPACE SHIP
THAT FLIES
Yes, it really flies! The newest, fastest addition to Buck Rogers' fighting fleet! Nearly 12", long. Anyone can build it! Parts of light balsa wood, with special wire and wing fabric, red, blue and yellow paint, glue, complete assembly plans and special landing gear furnished. Also high-pitch propeller and rubberband motor.
1 C. of W. top and 25c.

REPELLER RAY RING

Simulated gold, with Buck Rogers in his space ship molded into top. Special repeller ray lens set into side of space ship. May be used as seal on all secret club documents and correspondence.
1 C. of W. top and 10c.

GIRL'S
PENDANT AND CHAIN

Just like Wilma wears! Beautiful simulated gold, on a heavy gold-plated chain with spring clasp. Shows Wilma and the star and crescent design that is the good luck symbol of Solar Scouts.
1 C. of W. top and 15c.

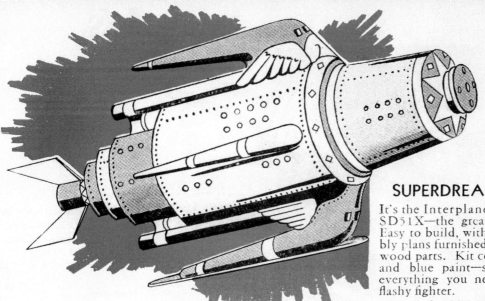

SUPERDREADNOUGHT

It's the Interplanetary Space Ship SD51X—the greatest of them all! Easy to build, with the secret assembly plans furnished. 6½" long. Balsa wood parts. Kit contains red, white and blue paint—sandpaper—glue—everything you need to build this flashy fighter.

1 C. of W. top and 15c.

LEAD FIGURINES

Real likenesses of Buck and other 25th Century characters. Molded in lead... with movable arms! Finished in three brilliant colors. Average height 2¼ inches. Following figurines available: Buck Rogers ...Dr. Huer...Ardala... Robot...Wilma...Killer Kane.

Each 1 top and 10c.
Set of six for 3 C. of W. tops and 50c.

OFFICIAL SOLAR SCOUT KNIFE

Handle is of ray-resisting white bone-like material. Picture of Buck navigating his space ship stamped on each side in blue. Big 2⅛ in. cutting blade. Also combination tool blade, with screw adjuster.

1 C. of W. Top and 25c.

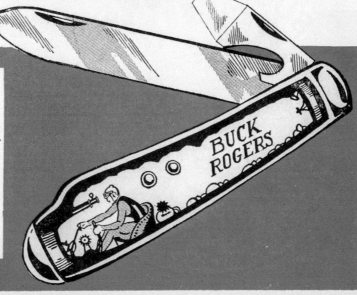

Speed-AMAZING PERFORMANCE
~and See What You Save!

QUALITY FEATURES

Make Both the
Hawthorne De Luxe (below)
and Hawthorne Speed Models
(at left on opposite page)
High in Quality

(1) Beautiful low racy lines. (2) Baked on enamel finish, beautifully trimmed and hairline striped. (3) Giant strength frame of 18-gauge seamless steel tubing. Frame has 1-inch drop at seatpost for riders with inseams 27 to 36 inches from crotch to heel. (4) Ball bearings used throughout-front hub, crankshaft, coaster brake, steering head and pedals. (5) Practically unbreakable high carbon steel crank and crankshaft. (6) Nickeled ball-bearing pedals with big, 4-surface rubber treads. (7) New Departure Model C multiple disc coaster brake. Considered one of the finest brakes on the market. (8) Deep center Motor-bike metal mudguards. (9) High grade front hub. (10) Spokes: finest steel piano wire Cadmium plated. (11) Motorcycle truss fork-rods chromium Plated. (12) Rims: Choice of Lobdell cement type armored rims, rock maple incased in chromium-plated steel or enameled all-steel clincher type rims. (13) Broad base parking stand. (14) Braced 20-inch handlebars with flexible rubber motobike grips. (15) Troxel bucket style saddle colored to match frame. (16) Chromium finished The hardest, brightest and most permanent plating ever known for resisting tarnish and rust. Chromium is applied over nickel and nickel over copper, making a triple protective coat. Chromium is whiter and has a more brilliant luster than nickel and it's harder than the finest steel

Y OUR HAWTHORNE—It's off like a flash on the quick get-away. It leaps like a living thing when you ask it for a quick pick-up. On the long, steady run it rolls along almost as though it furnished its own power. The Hawthornes have richly earned their nation-wide reputation for speed, sturdiness, easy-running qualities.

Buy Your Bike *Now*—Prices Are *Lower!*

FIVE beautiful Hawthorne Models shown on this and opposite page—and we've cut prices on every last one to make it easier for you to own the Hawthorne of your choice! All models are braced like a motorcycle for strength, power and endurance—with chromium finish brighter than burnished silver and harder than chilled steel. Baked-on enamel in a choice of snappy color combinations with beautiful hairline striping. New Departure Coaster Brakes for quick, positive control.

The Hawthorne Motobikes are made in two models—the Speed model at left on opposite page and the De Luxe model below. Both have all the 16 quality features shown at left, the only difference between them being the color choices and the extra equipment on the De Luxe model that every boy covets and which he attaches to his bicycle from time to time. When he selects a De Luxe Hawthorne he gets this equipment all at once —it includes:

1—A new Flyer Delta Headlight with battery case and auto type switch—and a snappy colored military visor that shoots the light straight ahead!

2—An action getting Auto Type Horn that "Clears the road!"

3—A strong Package Carrier—handy and useful.

4—Streamlined Tank Toolcase with coaster brake wrench.

5—A brilliant, flashing Red Jewel Reflector on rear mudguard.

AND IN ADDITION there's the extra mileage you get in the Riverside Trail Blazer Tires—big husky, live rubber tires with a handsome black thread and snappy white rubber sidewalls! The Riverside Trail Blazer is a higher grade tire than the Riverside Giant Stud used on the Hawthorne Speed Model Bike.

Robert Vehorn Wins 700-Mile Non-Stop Endurance Race With His Hawthorne

"120 hours continuous running and not a bobble," said Robert Vehorn. His Hawthorne De Luxe Model, ridden by himself and three team-mates, won the 700-mile, non-stop endurance race for the Indiana championship. Before the race his Hawthorne had already covered more than 5,000 miles on his newspaper route and now it is still mechanically almost as good as new. What more could *anyone* ask from a bicycle, no matter what its cost?

GUARANTEE
We Guarantee to Replace
Free of Charge any part of a Hawthorne Bicycle which proves defective in material, workmanship or construction. We also guarantee that if after you receive and try the Hawthorne you do not believe it is the greatest value you can buy anywhere, or if for any reason you are not perfectly satisfied after riding it you may send it back and we will refund all you have paid, including transportation charges both ways.

JEWEL REFLECTOR

THE SPIRIT OF PROGRESS — WARD'S QUALITY SYMBOL

$32.95 CASH PRICE

$5.00 DOWN

All Bicycles carried in Stock at Kansas City, Saint Paul and Oklahoma City. Send your order to the house nearest to you.

HAWTHORNE De Luxe Model—*Fully Equipped*

Send your order in the regular way—all cash or a payment of only $5.00 down. Pay the balance in small monthly payments. For easy payments use Order Blank in back of catalogue. Boys under 21 years must have parent or guardian sign easy payment order blank. Headlight battery not included—order battery number 60 G 3543 on Page 324. Actual weight fully equipped, 42 pounds. Shipped Not Prepaid. Ship. wt. 67 pounds. Estimated Total Freight Charges for 150 miles $1.14; 300 mi. $1 80; 500 mi. $2.69; 750 mi. $3.11; 1000 mi. $4.47. Express rates about one-half more.

With Lobdell Chromium-Plated Cement Type Rims and Riverside Trail Blazer Cement Type Tires		With All Steel Clincher Type Rims and Riverside Trail Blazer Clincher Tires	
160 G 3044—Indian Orange and Black.		160 G 3047—Indian Orange and Black.	
Cash Price....$32.95	Easy Payment Price....$36.25	Cash Price....$35.95	Easy Payment Price....$39.55
160 G 3045—Royal Packard Blue and White.		160 G 3048—Royal Packard Blue and White.	
Cash Price....$32.95	Easy Payment Price....$36.25	Cash Price....$35.95	Easy Payment Price....$39.55
Easy Payments—$5 Down and $5 a month.		Easy Payments—$5 Down and $5 a month.	

RIVERSIDE TRAIL BLAZER

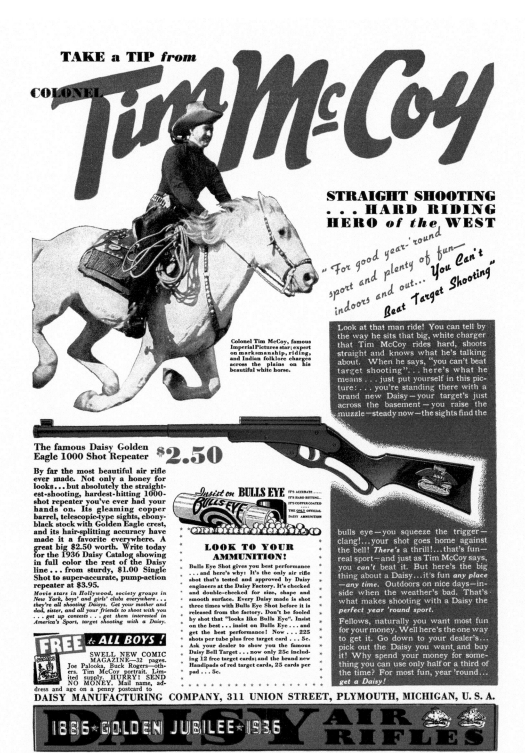

TAKE a TIP from

COLONEL Tim McCoy

**STRAIGHT SHOOTING
. . . HARD RIDING
HERO *of the* WEST**

"For good year-'round sport and plenty of fun—indoors and out... **You Can't Beat Target Shooting"**

Colonel Tim McCoy, famous Imperial Pictures star; expert on marksmanship, riding, and Indian folklore charges across the plains on his beautiful white horse.

Look at that man ride! You can tell by the way he sits that big, white charger that Tim McCoy rides hard, shoots straight and knows what he's talking about. When he says, "you can't beat target shooting"... here's what he means... just put yourself in this picture:... you're standing there with a brand new Daisy — your target's just across the basement — you raise the muzzle — steady now — the sights find the

The famous Daisy Golden Eagle 1000 Shot Repeater **$2.50**

By far the most beautiful air rifle ever made. Not only a honey for looks...but absolutely the straightest-shooting, hardest-hitting 1000-shot repeater you've ever had your hands on. Its gleaming copper barrel, telescopic-type sights, ebony-black stock with Golden Eagle crest, and its hair-splitting accuracy have made it a favorite everywhere. A great big $2.50 worth. Write today for the 1936 Daisy Catalog showing in full color the rest of the Daisy line... from sturdy, $1.00 Single Shot to super-accurate, pump-action repeater at $3.95.

Movie stars in Hollywood, society groups in New York, boys' and girls' clubs everywhere . . . they're all shooting Daisys. Get your mother and dad, sister, and all your friends to shoot with you . . . get up contests . . . get them interested in America's Sport, target shooting with a Daisy.

Insist on **BULLS EYE**   IT'S ACCURATE.....
IT'S HARD HITTING..
IT'S COPPER COATED
THE ONLY OFFICIAL DAISY AMMUNITION

**LOOK TO YOUR
AMMUNITION!**

Bulls Eye Shot gives you best performance . . . and here's why: It's the only air rifle shot that's tested and approved by Daisy engineers at the Daisy Factory. It's checked and double-checked for size, shape and smooth surface. Every Daisy made is shot three times with Bulls Eye Shot before it is released from the factory. Don't be fooled by shot that "looks like Bulls Eye". Insist on the best . . . insist on Bulls Eye . . . and get the best performance! Now . . . 225 shots per tube plus free target card . . . 5c. Ask your dealer to show you the famous Daisy Bell Target . . . now only 25c including 12 free target cards; and the brand new Handipads of red target cards, 25 cards per pad . . . 5c.

FREE *to* **ALL BOYS !**
SWELL NEW COMIC MAGAZINE—32 pages. Joe Palooka, Buck Rogers—others. Tim McCoy portrait. Limited supply. HURRY! SEND NO MONEY. Mail name, address and age on a penny postcard to

bulls eye — you squeeze the trigger — clang!...your shot goes home against the bell! *There's* a thrill!...that's fun — real sport — and just as Tim McCoy says, you *can't* beat it. But here's the big thing about a Daisy...it's fun *any place* — *any time.* Outdoors on nice days — inside when the weather's bad. That's what makes shooting with a Daisy the *perfect year 'round sport.*

Fellows, naturally you want most fun for your money. Well here's the one way to get it. Go down to your dealer's... pick out the Daisy you want and buy it! Why spend your money for something you can use only half or a third of the time? For most fun, year 'round... *get a Daisy!*

DAISY MANUFACTURING COMPANY, 311 UNION STREET, PLYMOUTH, MICHIGAN, U. S. A.

DAISY AIR RIFLES
1886 * GOLDEN JUBILEE * 1936

◄ Hawthorne Bicycle, 1930

Daisy Manufacturing Company, 1936

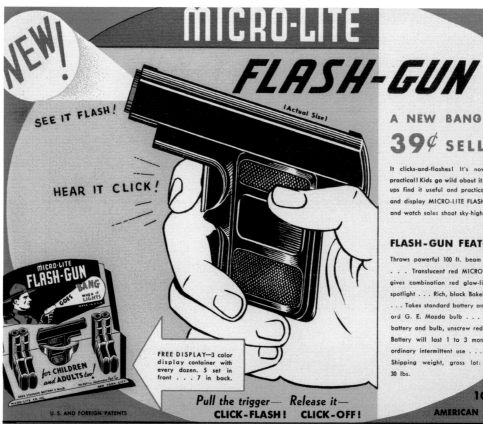

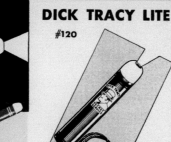

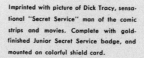
Micro-Lite, 1938

▶ Miner's, 1938

PAINTING SETS

Ethel likes these special Billy and Ruth

$1.00   No. BR87

"Just look!" says Ethel. A set like real artists use. Airplane-type suitcase box. When opened, there are 3 trays in which your painting materials fit and the back becomes a sketchboard. 18 cups, 6 cakes and 3 bottles of paint of different colors, wood palette, brush, 2 water dishes, 7 crayons, protractor, ruler, compass & drawings to color."

AIRPLANE-TYPE SUITCASE BOX

50c

No. BR88

Ethel was telling her friends about this fine painting set. "You can take it with you wherever you go, for it is all in a fine airplane-type suitcase box with snap lock and handle. You'll soon learn to draw and paint fine pictures—instructions and color hint sheet, also outline pictures to color are included. The back of suitcase box opens up to make a sketchboard on which to draw. Palette, brush, 6 cups and 6 cakes of paint of different colors, 6 crayons, 2 water dishes give you all the materials you need to become an artist.

AS A DESK

It's New! SLATE ART

A new idea in painting and drawing for you young artists. There's a dandy 8½"x12½" wood-framed, natural slate with white reverse side. Plenty of artists' materials—6 bottles water color, 6 sticks of chalk, 6 crayons, a brush, 2 water pans and stencils.

$1.00

No. BR90

You can see, Louise likes her new . . .

DESK BLACKBOARD
With HOBBY SEAT

Louise thanked Ruth for picking such a fine blackboard. "Gee, it even has a seat," she exclaimed. "And there are 14 panels in six colors on the moving chart. Just let down the blackboard and you have a fine desk. Chalk and eraser, too."

$2.95

38¼ INS. HIGH
17¾ INS. WIDE

No. BR89

They come in Six lovely colors in modern design

They are arranged in beautiful "Alice in Wonderland" Boxes

Alice gives children the
Golden Key to Table Manners

in these gay tea-party
sets of Richelain . . . .

"At this moment the door of the house opened, and a large plate came skimming out, straight at the Footman's head: it just grazed his nose, and *broke to pieces* against one of the trees behind him." (From *Alice's Adventures in Wonderland*.)*

"What a shame," said Alice, ignoring the Footman's alarm and stooping to pick up the fragments. "Such a pretty plate, too. Now, wouldn't it be wonderful if only someone would invent tea things which would not break easily. They would save such a lot of worry for mothers and spankings for children!"

* * *

Now, just fancy. Here's Alice's wish come true at last in gay little tea-party sets of Play-Proof Richelain cups, saucers, sugar bowls, cream pitchers, and all made of this marvelous new material which is lighter but much stronger than glass or china. Dishes to delight the eye and thrill the heart of any child!

These little dream sets of Richelain are made in a rainbow of lovely colors—blue, green, yellow, cream, orchid and red. They are styled in the most modern manner by one of the country's foremost designers, who

* *By permission of The Macmillan Company: Publishers*

originally designed them for his own children! Each set is a complete tea service for four and is arranged in a beautiful "Alice in Wonderland" tea-caddy box!

This box is simply scrumptious! On the cover there's a picture of Alice herself surrounded by her quaint Wonderland companions that children love so well. The King, and The Duchess; the Mad Hatter and March Hare; Tweedledee and Tweedledum; the Cheshire Cat, Humpty Dumpty and the Lobster. And inside the cover (Ah! here's something that will please Mother), a set of rules for good table manners, all written in jolly jingle form, by the noted children's author, Dixie Willson—rules that children will love to read and memorize! The kind of teaching that makes a lark of learning!

Can you imagine a more beautiful or practical gift for a child? And what an adorable Christmas present! Little Housekeeper set, $3.00. Little Sister set, $1.50. See them at leading department or toy stores—or write to THE RICHARDSON COMPANY (Lockland) Cincinnati, Ohio. New York Office: Tom McGinty, 200 Fifth Ave.

Richelain is practically unbreakable—"Play-Proof" and non-inflammable

NRA

CHILDREN'S *Toy Tea Sets*
OF "PLAY-PROOF" RICHELAIN

◀ Billy and Ruth, 1939

The Richardson Company, 1933

Tell Santa.. to bring you a SHIRLEY TEMPLE GIFT for Christmas!

BATHROBES, HOUSECOATS
DOLLS & DOLL CLOTHES
DRESSES
TODDLER FROCKS
GLOVES & MITTENS
HANDBAGS, MUFF BAGS
HATS, WITH SCARFS, BERETS
HOSIERY, SOCKS
SLIPPERS
UNDIES & PAJAMAS

Look for the Authentic Shirley Temple Label or Tag — It is Your Guarantee of Quality!

At leading stores in your city — or write for name of nearest dealer, mentioning items wanted.

THE MAKERS OF SHIRLEY TEMPLE LICENSED PRODUCTS • 55 WEST 42nd STREET, NEW YORK, N. Y.

Shirley Temple Licensed Products, 1937

Shirley Temple rose to stardom in the middle of the Great Depression. Such was her popularity that in 1938, at age 9, she was the seventh-highest paid person in the U.S. Half of this income came from licensed products, which included dolls as well as non-toy items such as dresses and hats.

Shirley Temple wurde während der Wirtschaftskrise zum Star. Ihre Popularität war so enorm, dass sie 1938, im Alter von neun Jahren, in der Liste der Amerikaner mit dem höchsten Einkommen auf Platz sieben stand. Die Hälfte ihrer Einnahmen stammte von Lizenzprodukten, darunter Puppen sowie Kleider und Hüte.

Shirley Temple accède à la gloire en pleine Grande Dépression. Sa popularité est telle qu'en 1938, à neuf ans, elle est la septième personne la mieux payée aux États-Unis. La moitié de ses revenus provient de ses produits dérivés, notamment des poupées, mais aussi des robes et des chapeaux.

▶ The Brunswick-Balke-Collender Company, 1930

PLAY BILLIARDS

WHAT A Christmas PRESENT!

... AND ONLY $7.50 COMPLETE WITH ALL PLAYING EQUIPMENT

THE Brunswick Junior Playmate Pocket Billiard Table is the best juvenile Christmas investment you can make. Children and grown-ups alike, all love games. In Billiards you have one that affords healthful recreation . . . mental and muscular coordination . . . endless, tireless amusement . . . all-year, all-weather play.

It gives parents added control over the children by making the home more attractive . . . thus keeping them within the family circle during their most formative and impressionable years. Every member of the family will enjoy the game . . . *and Billiards is easy to learn.*

The Junior Playmate is strong . . . sturdily constructed . . . of quality materials. Children won't drop it in a week like a cheap toy but will play on it for years . . .

Five other sizes, $13.50, $18.50, $37.50, $60.00 and $100.00 (prices slightly higher west of Denver and in Canada).

For sale at leading department, hardware and sporting goods stores, everywhere. You'll identify it immediately by its rich mahogany finish and the gold and black Brunswick trade-mark on the rail, which is shown below.

Brunswick
JUNIOR PLAYMATE
MF'D BY
THE BRUNSWICK-BALKE-COLLENDER CO.

A complete line of Junior Playmates and other home tables are shown in "The Home Magnet" catalog, which we will gladly send on request. The more expensive tables can be bought on a deferred payment plan from Brunswick Branches in all principal cities. *Address*

THE BRUNSWICK-BALKE-COLLENDER CO., 631 South Wabash Avenue, Chicago, Illinois. In Canada, Toronto.

Spencer Fireworks, c. 1938

 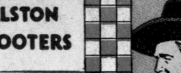

Soft, Cuddly Chums *for* The Little Ones

C531

C534

They win the hearts of Grown-ups too

These stuffed toys are made of long-pile plush and are of the highest grade of domestic manufacture. The cuts really do not do them justice. Mickey Mouse and Twistums, of course, are not of pile plush. We wish we could show you the difference between these items and the cheap stuffed teddy-bears and other toys on the market, but will ask you to take our word and of course, as always with any Needlecraft merchandise, you may return anything that is not up to expectation and have your money instantly refunded.

No. C531. Pussy. She is made of long silky-piled plush, lemon-yellow color, with satin ribbon around her neck. She is 10 inches long, and stands 8 inches high, and has a squeaking voice. **Price each, $1.39.**

No. C532. Mickey Mouse is just like his picture, dressed in red and black sateen, with orange felt shoes and yellow-felt mittens. He is indeed, a gay young man. Mickey Mouse is 12 inches tall to the top of his ears. **Price each, $1.19.**

No. C533. Eskimo Baby. Colored plush clothes this sumptuous Eskimo Cuddly Doll. White mittens and white trim to her bonnet. Red lips, blue eyes and yellow hair give life to this cuddly doll 12½ inches tall, with squeaking voice. **Price each, $1.29.**

No. C534. Scottie is too cute for words. Not so long and silky, but heavy gray-black plush that looks for all the world like a real dog's coat. This is a very high-grade animal. Scottie is 9 inches long, and stands 8½ inches tall, and has a squeaking voice. **Price each, $1.39.**

No. C535. Teddy-Bear. Did you ever see a lovely yellow-plush bear? Here is a new one. Long silky plush, soft stuffing, squeaking voice, 12 inches tall. A perfect Teddy-Bear. **Price each, $1.39.**

No. C536. Twistums is a real bisque doll, with unbreakable head. Body is so jointed that Twistums sits down all the time and twists from the hip. Dressed in romper suit, 9½ inches high, jointed arms, and jointed at hips. You can have a pickaninny or a white baby. Order **black** or **white. Price each, 50 cents.** Send your orders to

NEEDLECRAFT MAGAZINE
Augusta, Maine

C532

C533

C535

C536

◀ Quaker, c. 1938

A cereal advertisement masquerading as a toy ad in the form of a comic strip: Such was the formula to reach young consumers in 1930s. All you had to do to get Dick Tracy's Secret Detecto Kit was convince your parents to buy you Quaker Oats cereal and try to eat two boxes of it.

Eine Werbung für Frühstücksflocken in Comic-Form, die so tut, als würde sie Spielwaren präsentieren: Mit dieser Formel wollte man in den 1930ern junge Konsumenten erreichen. Um Dick Tracys Secret Detecto Kit zu ergattern, musste man nur seine Eltern überreden, Quaker-Oats-Zerealien zu kaufen, und dann zwei Packungen davon verschlingen.

Une BD ? La promotion d'un jouet ? Non, une pub pour des céréales ! C'est la formule magique pour toucher les petits consommateurs des années 1930. Ceux qui veulent le kit détecteur secret de Dick Tracy n'ont qu'à convaincre les parents d'acheter des Quaker Oats et à en manger deux boîtes.

A. C. Gilbert Company, 1935

▶ Lyons Metalcraft, c. 1938

▶▶▶ Mercury Bicycles, 1940

SEE WHAT MIGHTY MECHANICAL MARVELS YOU CAN BUILD WITH
The Great New
ERECTOR

Hello Boys!

LOOK at that giant power plant! You build it yourself with the great new Erector. Piece by piece you erect its massive steel frame. Assemble its enormous fly wheel—pistons—governor. Mount its big, shining boilers. Then you hook up the powerful Erector electric engine and it throbs with action.

That's only one of the many exciting engineering models you can build with Erector. You can make that marvelous magnetic crane. Click the switch on the Erector Engine—pull the control levers and it raises or lowers—swings to the right or left, just as you command. Its magnet is so strong it grabs up steel girders before it touches them.

You can build *all* of the engineering models shown in the picture—and dozens more—with *one* Erector set. Enormous drawbridges that actually open and close. Towering airplane beacon that revolves just like the real ones. All-metal airplane. Dump-trucks. And—with the new Erector Skyscraper Sets—you can build skyscrapers as tall as you are.

You're a full-fledged engineer when you have an Erector—ready to build realistic, engine-driven models of the world's greatest mechanical marvels. There are more wonders — more exciting hours of fun—packed in an Erector Set than anything you can own.

A.C.Gilbert

Ferris Wheel
Built with the No. 7½ Set
Operated with the new Erector Electric Engine.

NEW COLORS MORE PARTS
Easier Model Building
The Great New Erectors are the finest ever made.

Look at this
SENSATIONAL No. 7½ SET
Contains the powerful new Erector Electric Engine. Girders and structural plates finished in red, yellow and blue. Glistening boiler parts. The new snap rivets, gears and other engineering parts for building ferris wheel, magnetic crane, trucks, bridges and over 150 action models. With all these new features, only $10.95. Other sets from $1.00 to $25.00.

See the GILBERT HALL OF SCIENCE
The most stupendous boys' scientific exposition ever created. See the fascinating Gilbert Opto Kits—the mysterious Electric Eye—the Gilbert Chemistry Laboratory—Mysto Magic—the Gilbert Kaster Kit—and dozens of other thrilling sights. Look for these exhibits at your local toy store. Take your Dad along.

FREE—Gilbert Thrills Magazine
32 big pages packed full of exciting pictures and up-to-the-minute scientific information. True stories of how red-blooded boys have won fame and big awards in building Erector models—in making important chemical discoveries—and becoming masters of home craftsmanship. Regular price 25c. Free—combined with color catalog on the Great New Erector—to the first 50,000 boys who mail this coupon.

NEW
The Erector Electric Engine. Not just a motor—but a real engine complete with built-in gears.

NEW
Skyscraper parts. Builds realistic models of Radio City and other famous skyscrapers.

NEW
Big solid steel base plates and giant girders—make possible larger and stronger models.

NEW
Double feature. Snap rivets for speedy building—nuts and bolts for sturdy building.

Mail this Coupon today
Mr. A. C. Gilbert, The A. C. Gilbert Co.
508 Erector Square, New Haven, Conn.
Please send—free—Gilbert Thrills Magazine combined with big color catalog on the Great New Erector.

Name...
Street..
City.. State.............

Mention of "The Youth's Companion Combined With The American Boy" Will Bring Prompt Attention From Advertisers

Get a Letter from Capt. Jack Bursey

Famous British Ace in the World War and now Commander of the Lyonsport Aero Club

COMMANDER BURSEY

Notice that, attached to the Flying Hour Certificate in this box, there is also a *Registration Blank.* PRINT your name and address on the Registration Blank, tear it off, and mail it *now* to the Metalcraft Corporation, St. Louis, Missouri.

Capt. Jack Bursey, Commander, who saw years of real fighting in the Great War and who now in peace time is helping boys like you to learn all about planes and flying, will write you a letter and acknowledge receipt of the Registration Blank. To show his appreciation of your promptness, he is going to send you something else, too — a beautifully printed copy of a wonderful poem called "Slim," that tells the story of Colonel Lindbergh's flight from New York to France and what this meant to the boys of America. When you read it, you'll say it's HE-man reading.

Now, when you've mailed the Registration Blank, you'll still have the Flying Hours Certificate. SAVE THIS. Keep it until you have more certificates. When you have enough certificates to make a total credit of 200 hours or more, mail them to us with your name and address PRINTED on them, and Commander Bursey will make you a full-fledged member and pilot, and will mail you your free winged emblem.

Pilots of the Lyonsport Aero Club at work on their flying field

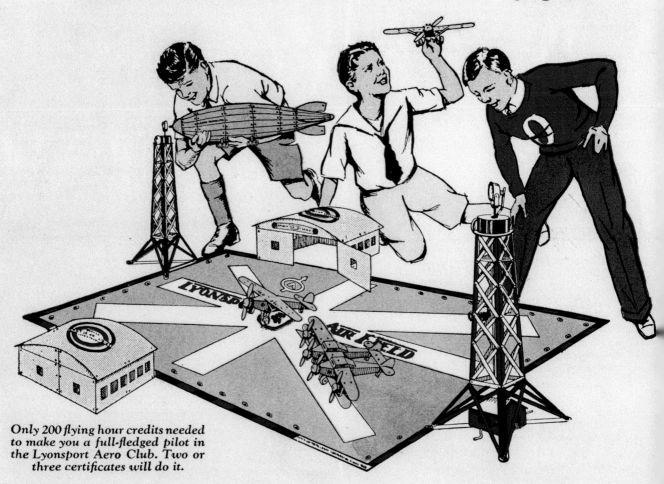

Only 200 flying hour credits needed to make you a full-fledged pilot in the Lyonsport Aero Club. Two or three certificates will do it.

LYONS METALCRAFT
Complete Airport Sets

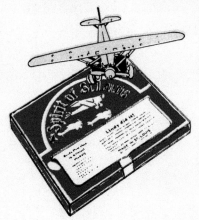

950—*Spirit of St. Louis.* Builds over 10 different planes. Price $1.00. Certificate — 50 flying hours.

951—*Spirit of St. Louis.* Builds over 25 models, including "Spirit of St. Louis." Price $1.50. Certificate—50 flying hours.

952—*Spirit of St. Louis.* Builds over 100 varieties of planes. Price $3.00. Certificate — 100 flying hours.

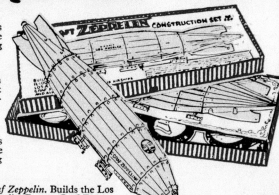

962—*Graf Zeppelin.* Builds the Los Angeles, Italia, R-100, Graf Zeppelin and other famous dirigibles. Models are 28 inches long and very sturdy. Price $5.00. Certificate—150 flying hours.

959—*Combination Beacon Light and Mooring Mast.* It really lights; equipped with bulbs. Price $3.75. Certificate — 100 flying hours.

953—*Spirit of St. Louis.* Builds more than 250 styles of planes. Builds two monoplanes at one time. Price $5.00. Certificate—150 flying hours.

960—*Zeppelin.* Builds over eight different dirigibles; painted red and yellow. Price $1.00. Certificate—50 flying hours.

965—*Lyonsport Air Field.* Set consists of airport printed in colors on durable fibre sheet, 40 x 60 inches; also boy's helmet; also a wonderfully interesting and instructive booklet on air field management. Price $1.00. Certificate—50 flying hours.

961—*Zeppelin.* Builds more than 20 models; light gray and nickel, same colors as many actual Zepps. Price $1.50. Certificate—50 flying hours.

955—*Metalcraft Flyer.* All metal construction set; flies like a real ship; takes off, loops, side slips, stalls, lands, etc. Actually teaches handling of planes. Price $1.00. Certificate—50 flying hours.

958—*Hangar.* Construction set, quickly put together. Price $1.00. Certificate — 50 flying hours.

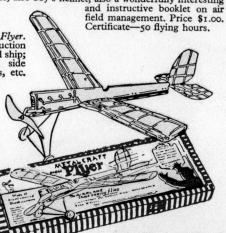

956—*Metalcraft Flyer.* Same as above but comes set up instead of knockdown. Price $1.50. Certificate — 50 flying hours.

A LACK OF HOME-FRONT MATERIALS LEADS TO INNOVATION, WHICH ACCELERATES A POSTWAR BOOM IN SALES.

SERIES 216—STARS
AND STRIPES GAS BALL

ON DISPLAY-by Barr

THE NATION'S FINEST
AND MOST COMPLETE ARRAY
OF RUBBER TOYS!

See the merchandise behind BARR'S
own Centralized Service!

ONE SOURCE FOR EVERY RUBBER TOY NEED

ROOM 507
FIFTH AVENUE BUILDING

ROOM 931
HOTEL McALPIN

Mr. Wm. J. Canary in charge

SERIES 207—FIVE STRIPE
GAS BALL

SERIES 221—STAR
END GAS BALL

SERIES 112—THREE COLOR
SPONGE BALL

SERIES 413—CIRCLE, STAR
EMBOSSED GAS BALL

SERIES 225-136—BOB FELLER
BUCKSKIN BASEBALL

SERIES 104—TWO
COLOR SPONGE BALL

SERIES 231—SKI-HI
GAS BALL

SERIES 225-122—RED
EMBOSSED SPONGE BASEBALL

BEAUTIFUL BALL ASSORTMENTS

Three exceptionally attractive ball assortments are available
namely, JV-40, JV-50, and JV-60. Each assortment is designed as a
deal, which includes one of BARR'S efficient new ball display
racks, as illustrated above.

SERIES 213—CIRCLE
GAS BALL

WARFARE AND TOYFARE

IT WAS A GRIM FIRST HALF DECADE FOR THE ADVERTISING AND MARKETING OF PLAYTHINGS. Following the attack on Pearl Harbor on December 7, 1941, the United States government called for even more draconian austerity measures throughout the toy industry than it had during the Great Depression. The war affected every industry, leading to restrictions on the use of essential materials such as metal and rubber, which were stockpiled for wartime applications. Labor itself was at a premium, too, and innovation was reserved for the war effort. Kids often donated their toys to various material drives, according to *Playthings* magazine, the venerable official trade journal of the toy industry.

In January 1942, less than one month after the U.S. entered the conflict, President Franklin D. Roosevelt established the War

1940

1941

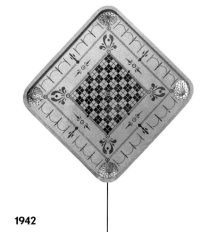

1942

Chemtoy, a Chicago cleaning supply company, popularizes bubble solution

Chemtoy, ein Hersteller von Reinigungsmitteln aus Chicago, macht Seifenblasen populär

Le fabricant de produits de nettoyage Chemtoy commercialise le liquide à faire des bulles

Lewis H. Glaser founds Precision Specialties, later named Revell

Lewis H. Glaser gründet Precision Specialties, das später in Revell umbenannt wird

Lewis H. Glaser fonde Precision Specialties, plus tard rebaptisée Revell

The time-honored game of Carrom is given new form in Nok Hockey

Das altehrwürdige Spiel Carrom kommt in Form von Nok Hockey zu neuen Ehren

L'ancestral carrom est revisité et vendu sous le nom de Nok Hockey

Production Board (WPB) to oversee the necessary conversion of civilian factories into war production facilities. As Tara Winner wrote for the National Museum of Play, the 1942 issue of *Playthings* "documents the toy industry's awareness of the War Production Board and the ways its orders would eventually affect their business." Many of the magazine's editorials and articles focused on how to successfully transform brands and product lines, suggesting that manufacturers incorporate alternatives such as making games and toys using wood. "On March 30, 1942, the WPB issued General Limitation Order L-81 prohibiting the production of toys that contained critical materials (iron, steel, zinc, and rayon) that made up more than 7 percent of their weight. Existing toys with content over that amount could be sold until June 30, 1942." There was little need to advertise these depleted products, but toy manufacturers were indeed challenged over how to make do with the materials at hand, testing their ability to stir children's imaginations — the result of which would then be worthy of spending a few advertising dollars. Among the most obvious themes of the war was the war itself. Military items were

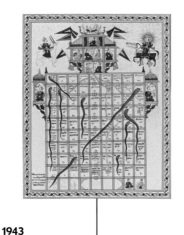

1942

1943

1946

War Production Board places limits on materials used for toys

Die War Production Board rationiert Materialien zur Herstellung von Spielzeug

Le War Production Board rationne les matériaux utilisés par l'industrie du jouet

Milton Bradley releases Chutes and Ladders, a kid-friendly version of an Indian classic

Milton Bradley bringt Chutes and Ladders heraus, die kindgerechte Version eines indischen Brettspiels

Milton Bradley édite Chutes & Ladders, version enfantine d'un jeu traditionnel indien

Li'l Abner and His Dogpatch Band is "the first postwar windup metal toy"

Li'l Abner und seine Dogpatch Band sind „das erste aufziehbare Blechspielzeug der Nachkriegszeit"

Li'l Abner et sa bande de Dogpatch est « le premier jouet mécanique en métal de l'après-guerre » popularized. Lionel Corporation was contracted to produce G.I. compasses, but it also designed a wartime toy freight train made entirely out of heavy-duty paper stock. "It wasn't the same as a Lionel electric train," notes Winner, "but it was the best the company could offer under the circumstances."

After the Allies won the war, America (with its manufacturing capacity still intact) returned to toy production and experienced a surge in sales resulting largely from the baby boom. Advertising did not, however, change overnight. Throughout the postwar '40s, much of the same techniques, including comic strips and character tie-ins, were continued. Kids did not anticipate entirely new, futuristic toy options. The usual prewar novelties of bikes, model planes, and dolls were still abundant, but a new toy fashion for children was found in the burgeoning fascination with the cursed atomic age.

1947

1947

1949

Howdy Doody airs on TV for the first time, kicking off a merchandising juggernaut

Howdy Doody wird zum ersten Mal ausgestrahlt und löst eine wahre Merchandising-Flut aus

La télévision diffuse pour la première fois *Howdy Doody*, une manne commerciale

Tonka, then called Mound Metalcraft, begins shift from garden tools to toys

Tonka (damals noch Mound Metalcraft) verlagert die Produktion von Gartengeräten zu Spielzeug

Tonka, qu'on appelle encore Mound Metalcraft, entame sa transition du jardinage au jeu

Candy Land, created by Eleanor Abbott for kids with polio, is released by Milton Bradley

Das Candy Land von Milton Bradley wurde von Eleanor Abbott für Kinder mit Kinderlähmung erfunden

Candy Land de Milton Bradley est créé par Eleanor Abbott pour les enfants atteints de polio

KRIEG UND SPIELZEUG

Der kriegsbedingte Material-Engpass führt zu Innovationen, die den NachkriegsVerkaufsboom zusätzlich befeuern.

Für Spielzeugwerbung und -marketing waren es keine rosigen Zeiten. Nach dem japanischen Angriff auf Pearl Harbor am 7. Dezember 1941 belegte die US-amerikanische Regierung die Spielzeugindustrie mit noch drakonischeren Einschränkungen als zur Zeit der Wirtschaftskrise. Der Krieg wirkte sich auf sämtliche Industriezweige aus und führte zur Verknappung von so wesentlichen Materialien wie Metall und Gummi, die nun hauptsächlich in der Rüstungsindustrie eingesetzt wurden. Laut *Playthings*, dem offiziellen Handelsblatt der Spielzeugbranche, spendeten Kinder häufig sogar ihre Spielsachen, wenn zum Sammeln bestimmter Wertstoffe aufgerufen wurde.

Im Januar 1942, kurz nach Kriegseintritt der USA, setzte Präsident Franklin D. Roosevelt das War Production Board (WPB) ein, um die notwendige Umwandlung von zivilen Fabriken in Produktionsstätten für Kriegsgerät zu überwachen. Tara Winner schrieb für das National Museum of Play, die 1942er-Ausgabe von *Playthings* dokumentiere, „dass der Spielzeugindustrie bewusst war, wie sehr die Arbeit des War Production Board sich auf ihre Branche auswirken würde". Viele Artikel und Editorials der Zeitschrift behandelten die Frage, wie man Marken und Produktlinien erfolgreich umwandeln könne, und schlugen vor, dass sich die Hersteller auf Alternativmaterial wie Holz verlegen sollten. „Am 30. März 1942 erließ das WPB die General Limitation Order L-81, die die Herstellung von Spielzeug verbot, dessen Gewicht zu über sieben Prozent aus kritischen Wertstoffen (Eisen, Stahl, Zink und Rayon) bestand. Bereits produzierte Spielwaren mit einem höheren Gehalt konnten noch bis zum 30. Juni 1942 abverkauft werden." Viel zu bewerben gab es also nicht, doch die Spielzeughersteller nahmen die Herausforderung an, mit den vorhandenen Materialien auszukommen und die Fantasie der Kinder anzuregen – etwas, das dann die Investition von ein paar Werbedollar wert war. Das naheliegendste Thema in Kriegszeiten war natürlich der Krieg selbst. Die Lionel Corporation erhielt den Auftrag, Kompasse für das Militär zu produzieren, entwarf aber auch einen Spielzeuggüterzug, der vollständig aus Pappe bestand. „Es war zwar nicht dasselbe wie eine richtige Elektroeisenbahn von Lionel", bemerkt Winner, „aber das Beste, was die Firma unter den Umständen anzubieten hatte."

Nachdem die Alliierten den Krieg gewonnen hatten, kurbelten die USA (in den intakten Fabriken) die Spielzeugproduktion wieder an und erlebten, größtenteils dank des Babybooms, einen starken Absatzanstieg. Die Werbung änderte sich dadurch jedoch nicht über Nacht – auch in den späten 1940er-Jahren vertraute man auf altbekannte Formen, darunter Comics und die Einbindung beliebter Figuren. Und auch bei den Spielsachen selbst handelte es sich meist um Bewährtes wie Fahrräder, Modellflugzeuge oder Puppen. Eine neue Marketingstrategie setzte jedoch auf die aufkeimende Begeisterung für das Atomzeitalter.

► Leo Strauss and Murray K. Richstone, 1946

Electric Eye

SHOOTING GALLERY

- SHOOTS ONLY A FLASH OF LIGHT!
- SAFE FOR CHILDREN!
- SWINGING TARGET!
- HOURS OF FUN!
- FOR ALL AGES!
- BUILT TO LAST FOR YEARS!

MANUFACTURED BY

S. F. FRANKLIN, Inc.

127-131 WEST 25th STREET · NEW YORK 1, N. Y.

Phone: CHELSEA 2-4835-6-7

JEUX DE GUERRE ET GUERRE DU JEU

La pénurie nationale de matériaux encourage l'innovation et donne de l'élan aux ventes records de l'après-guerre.

La première moitié de cette décennie est bien sombre pour les créateurs et vendeurs de jouets. Après l'attaque de Pearl Harbor, le 7 décembre 1941, le gouvernement américain impose à l'industrie des mesures d'austérité plus draconiennes encore que pendant la Dépression. La guerre affecte tous les secteurs et exige de restreindre l'emploi de matériaux essentiels aux applications militaires, comme les métaux et le caoutchouc. La main d'œuvre aussi est une denrée rare et l'innovation est réservée à l'effort de guerre. Le magazine *Playthings*, vénérable organe officiel de l'industrie, rapporte que les enfants font don de leurs jouets à des services de collecte.

En janvier 1942, moins d'un mois après l'entrée en guerre des États-Unis, le président Franklin D. Roosevelt instaure le War Production Board (WPB), qu'il charge de superviser la nécessaire conversion des usines civiles en centres de production dédiés à la guerre. Comme l'écrit Tara Winner pour le Musée national du jeu, le *Playthings* de 1942 « montre que l'industrie du jouet avait pris acte des réquisitions du War Production Board et des conséquences qu'elles auraient sur ses affaires ». Ce numéro est composé pour une bonne part d'articles et d'éditoriaux qui évoquent différents moyens de transformer les marques et les collections et suggèrent notamment aux fabricants de recourir à des matériaux alternatifs comme le bois : « Le 30 mars 1942, le WPB a émis l'ordre de restriction générale L-81 qui interdit de produire des jouets contenant des matériaux critiques (fer, acier, zinc et rayonne) dans une quantité supérieure à 7 % de leur masse. Les jouets préexistants ayant une plus forte teneur de ces matériaux pouvaient être vendus jusqu'au 30 juin 1942. » Ces produits au rabais peuvent se passer de publicité, mais fonctionner avec les matériaux disponibles constitue effectivement un défi de taille pour les fabricants, dont la capacité à embraser l'imagination des petits est mise à rude épreuve ; il faut que le produit vaille la peine d'investir un peu dans sa promotion. Parmi les thèmes majeurs de l'époque se trouve bien sûr la guerre. L'équipement militaire se popularise. L'entreprise Lionel est réquisitionnée pour produire les boussoles des G.I., mais elle conçoit aussi des trains de marchandises miniatures en papier renforcé. « Ce n'est pas comme un train électrique Lionel, note Winner, mais c'est le mieux que peut offrir la marque dans ces circonstances. »

Lorsque les Alliés gagnent la guerre, l'Amérique (dont la capacité industrielle est intacte) reprend la production en masse de jouets et voit ses ventes exploser, en grande partie grâce au baby-boom. Toutefois la publicité ne change pas du jour au lendemain. Dans la seconde moitié des années 1940, l'industrie recourt souvent aux mêmes techniques, notamment aux produits dérivés de comics et de personnages célèbres. Les enfants ne s'attendent pas à voir apparaître des jouets futuristes et inédits. Les classiques d'avant-guerre, vélos, maquettes d'avions et poupées abondent encore, mais une nouvelle génération de jouets naît de la fascination naissante de cette génération pour la maudite ère nucléaire.

◄ S. F. Franklin, 1947

♪♪ JUNIOR JUKE WOWS THE KIDS! ♪♪

Lights up and changes colors
as it plays records

PROJECT OF
Bing Crosby
RESEARCH FOUNDATION

Fun to hear, naturally . . . and fun to WATCH, too! Its colored lights win a flurry of attention from everyone. The soft red glow changes as the yellow light flashes on and off!

A New "Junior Juke" Electronic Record Player **$29⁹⁵** Cash
$3.00 Down

B Big value Toy Electric Phonograph. **$7.98**

C "Melody Grand" Piano **$3.59**

D Vinylite Records . . . 3 for 89c

E Juke Box Bank . . . **$4.98**

◀ Dillon-Beck, 1946

Marshall Field and Company, 1943

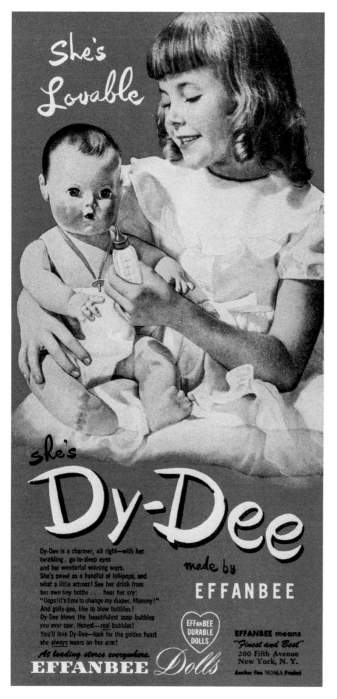

She's
Lovable

she's
Dy-Dee
made by
EFFANBEE

Dy-Dee is a charmer, all right—with her
twinkling, go-to-sleep eyes
and her wonderful winning ways.
She's sweet as a handful of lollipops, and
what a little actress! See her drink from
her own tiny bottle . . . hear her cry:
"Oops! it's time to change my diaper, Mommy!"
And golly-gee, like to blow bubbles?
Dy-Dee blows the beautifulest soap bubbles
you ever saw. Honest—real bubbles!
You'll love Dy-Dee—look for the golden heart
she always wears on her arm!

At leading stores everywhere.

EFFANBEE Dolls

EFFANBEE
DURABLE
DOLLS

EFFANBEE means
"Finest and Best"
200 Fifth Avenue
New York, N. Y.
Another Fine NOMA Product

Noma Electric, 1949

One year before Betsy Wetsy entered
the toy market, Effanbee released
Dy-Dee, a doll that children could feed
and watch wet itself by unlatching a
plug on its bottom. The doll grew more
realistic over time so that by the late
'40s it had moving eyelids and could
blow bubbles, making Dy-Dee "sweet
as a handful of lollipops."

Ein Jahr bevor Betsy Wetsy den Spielzeugmarkt betrat, lancierte Effanbee
schon mit Dy-Dee eine Puppe, die Kinder füttern konnten und die in die
Windeln machte, wenn man unten den
Stöpsel zog. Die Puppe wurde im Laufe
der Jahre immer lebensechter – Ende
der 1940er-Jahre hatte sie bereits
bewegliche Augenlider und konnte
Seifenblasen blasen – und war „so süß
wie eine Handvoll Lutscher".

Un an avant l'arrivée de Betsy Wetsy
sur le marché, Effanbee sort Dy-Dee,
qui mange et fait pipi quand on retire le
bouchon de ses fesses. La poupée
gagne en réalisme au fil du temps ; à la
fin des années 1940, ses paupières se
ferment et, « mignonne comme un bou-
quet de sucettes », elle fait des bulles.

▶ Sears, Roebuck, and Company, 1949

"Jimminy! We can put the animals in their stalls inside the barn"

"Time for work . . . I'll hitch the tractor to the spreader"

Happi-Time Farm; Miniature Dolls

"And the prancingest horses and the wooliest sheep,
And the mooingest cows that the toy farmers keep"

15-piece molded rubber Animal Set

True-to-life miniatures. Long-lasting, smoothly finished, appropriately colored. Set includes horse and 2 colts, cow and 2 calves, hog and 2 little pigs, rooster and four hens and turkey. Size of horse $3\frac{3}{4}$x$3\frac{3}{8}$ inches high . . . others in proportion. All stand alone on solid bases.
49 N 6447—Set of 15 animals, color-enameled. Shpg. wt. 1 lb. 4 oz.........89c

89c

Big HAPPI·TIME Farm with rubber animals
. . . colorful buildings, white fencing, rubber implements

Won't the above "work-a-day" farm scene look attractive under your Christmas tree! Children are enchanted by its bright colors —thrilled by its true-to-life detail. Gives happy hours of play.

$**2**^{98}$ Farm Set

14 realistic farm animals molded from rubber—appropriately colored. Included in farm set are horse and one colt, cow and one calf, hog and two little pigs, collie dog, turkey, rooster and four hens. Horse stands $3\frac{3}{8}$ inches high; is $3\frac{3}{4}$ inches long. All others in proportion. Smoothly finished—wipe clean with damp cloth.

Rubber farm implements. $4\frac{1}{4}$-in. long tractor, with farmer driving. Manure-spreader can be unhitched and left in barn. Both pieces realistically molded and colored.

Sturdy fiberboard buildings. Extra-large 2-wing barn is precision die-cut from heavy fiberboard. Has gables, eaves, even R-V-Lite transparent material to attach over windows. Cut-away in rear roof allows built-in stalls to be used—animals can be taken in and out of barn. See illustration at top of page. Barn measures 19x$12\frac{1}{2}$x $11\frac{3}{4}$ inches. Other buildings are in proportion. Included are silo, water-well, farm house, windmill, doghouse, chicken coop. Fencing adds realism. All pieces, except animals and machines, come flat. Easy to set up—complete instructions. Add this set to your Easy Terms order. See page 243 for information.
79 N 06453—Shipping weight 7 pounds............................Complete set $2.98

General Mills, 1947

At the same time the U.S. government was engaged in a top secret effort toward developing a new supersonic aircraft dubbed the XS-1, General Mills was offering as a premium eight different Jet-Atomic Model Space Ships that promised to "go rocketing through the air like a supersonic streak."

Während die US-Regierung in streng geheimer Mission an der Entwicklung eines neuen Überschallflugzeugs namens XS-1 arbeitete, hatte General Mills als Prämie acht verschiedene Jet-Atomic Model Space Ships im Angebot, die laut Werbung „wie ein Überschallblitz in den Himmel schießen" konnten.

Au moment où le gouvernement américain œuvre en secret à la conception d'un nouvel avion supersonique baptisé XS-1, General Mills offre en bonus huit modèles de « vaisseaux spatiaux à réaction atomique » qui « fuseront dans les airs comme un éclair supersonique ».

G and E, 1946

▶ Craftsmen's Guild, 1946

Clark Manufacturing Company, 1945

▶ Parker Johns, 1947

The main selling point for the Dick Tracy Tommy Gun was its similarities to "the real McCoy." For young boys obsessed with the comic strip in which many of the stories ended in a shoot-out, getting their hands on one was the closest they could get to bringing underworld thugs to justice.

Hauptverkaufsargument für das Dick-Tracy-Maschinengewehr war seine Ähnlichkeit mit der echten Waffe. Die jungen Fans der Comics, in denen ziemlich viel herumgeballert wurde, konnten damit zumindest beim Spielen Ganoven zur Strecke bringen.

Le principal argument de vente de la mitraillette Dick Tracy, c'est qu'elle ressemble « à la vraie ». Pour les passionnés du personnage de comics, dont nombre d'aventures finissent par un échange de tirs, posséder cette arme est ce qui se rapproche le plus d'une vie de pourfendeur du crime.

Walter H. Johnson Candy Company, 1948

General Mills, 1946

▶ General Mills, 1945

▶ Nabisco, 1947

◄ F. W. Woolworth Company, 1948

Woolworth rose to prominence in the early 20th century by selling everything for either five or 10 cents. By 1948, the initial concept was no longer possible due to inflation, but the department store continued to initiate novel ideas to sell its products, including a "mid-summer preview of Christmas dolls."

Woolworth wurde Anfang des 20. Jahrhunderts dadurch bekannt, dass alle seine Waren entweder 5 oder 10 Cent kosteten. 1948 war dieses Konzept wegen der Inflation nicht mehr zeitgemäß, aber das Kaufhaus entwickelte weiterhin innovative Verkaufsideen, darunter eine „Mittsommerpreview von Weihnachtspuppen".

Woolworth s'est fait un nom au début du XXe siècle en vendant toutes sortes de gadgets pour 5 ou 10 cents. En 1948, l'inflation empêche le concept initial de perdurer, mais le grand magasin ne manque pas d'idées novatrices pour vendre, comme «l'avant-première estivale des poupées de Noël».

Rig-A-Jig, 1948

New WONDERFUL WAY TO PLAY!

FURNITURE

DESIGNS

AIRPLANES

RABBITS

REINDEER & SLEIGH

DOLLS

GIRL & BUGGY

STEAM SHOVELS

TRAINS

RIG-A-JIG
The WONDER TOY from HOLLYWOOD

FAMILY FUN! TOYS! . . . a wonderland of them . . . create them by the hundreds, yourself—planes, cars, trucks, doll furniture, animals, people. See them come to life at your fingertips. Rig-A-Jig, the box of toyland surprises is here! Remarkable, different building game, perfect play partner that turns idle moments into magnificent FUN.

Think of ALL THE THINGS YOU CAN BUILD! . . . then take up the tantalizing assortment of 7 bright-colored geometric shapes— the Red Circles, Yellow Triangles, Purple Ovals, Green Oblongs, Orange Hexagons, Brown Diamonds, and Blue Squares. Link them together. Watch colorful, lifelike miniatures, beautiful designs, patterns, simple or complex, take shape before your eyes.

CAN'T WEAR OUT! NOT PAPER - NOT CARDBOARD! Every piece is non-toxic, and unbreakable. Made of tough fibre-plastic. Can be joined thousands of times, and in endless variations. Each assembled construction is solid and firm, ready to take apart instantly, easily.

GRAND EDUCATIONAL GIFT for YOUNGSTERS

Exercises every faculty of free imagination, creative skill, finger dexterity, space visualization. All basic aptitudes that guidance experts and child psychologists know lead to future success and a healthy, well-adjusted adult. Rig-A-Jig has everything for the lively curiosity and inventiveness of boys and girls!

In Big Bright GIFT BOX - with Full-Color IDEA BOOK

Regular Set
94 Pieces
$1.75

Super-Set
166 Pieces
$2.95

AT DEALERS or SEND THIS COUPON

RIG-A-JIG, Inc.
32 W. Washington • Chicago, Ill.
Gentlemen: Enclosed is $ . . . .
Please send me:
☐ RIG-A-JIG "Regular" at $1.75 ea.
☐ RIG-A-JIG "Super" at $2.95 ea.

NAME
ADDRESS
CITY   STATE

Nabisco, c. 1949

▶ Daisy Manufacturing Company, 1947

WALT DISNEY CARTOON *Characters*

NOW OFFERED
by
CRAFTSMEN'S GUILD
Hollywood, California

THRU SPECIAL ARRANGEMENT WITH

THE WALT DISNEY STUDIOS

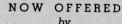

In 35mm *Full Color* Transparencies

. . . Reproduced from the original master films, these slides faithfully embody the exquisite beauty of artistry and color for which Disney Productions have become world renowned. Available in set form, each group of ten slides (except series 1) comprises a complete condensed version of a famous Disney feature picture.

PRODUCED IN 6 SERIES OF 10 SLIDES EACH $2.50 set

Series 2 thru 6 are complete stories—slides are numbered in sequence, and a synopsis of the story is narrated beneath each picture.

1 Famous Disney Characters: Ten specially selected "close-ups" showing 24 leading characters.

2 The Story of Pinocchio: Highlights of the story, including selections from all major scenes.

3 Snow White and the 7 Dwarfs: Snow White, the Prince, the Old Witch & famous Disney Dwarfs.

4 Excerpts from Fantasia: Ostrich Ballet, the Centaurettes, Winged Horses, Ice Fairies—etc., etc.

5 The Story of Bambi: Bambi, the deer, and his lovable forest companions—a *real* children's story.

6 Dumbo: Dumbo, the little elephant with the big ears—and a colorful circus background.

Also available in
COMBINATION SETS
Complete with VIEWER

Complete kits—including the No. 1 Series of slides and a HOLLYWOOD VIEWER, neatly packed in an attractive box $4.95

This is the famous viewer used by thousands of amateur and professional photographers for viewing their color slides. Made of gleaming Tenite, gives extraordinarily crystal-clear magnification. Sold separately at $2.45

MAIL
TELEGRAPH
OR PHONE
Your Order
TODAY

Manufactured Exclusively by

CRAFTSMEN'S GUILD

**1668 NORTH VAN NESS AVENUE
HOLLYWOOD 28, CALIFORNIA**

D. A. Pachter Company, 1944

Constructo Company, 1944

▶ Leatherette Novelty Company, 1944

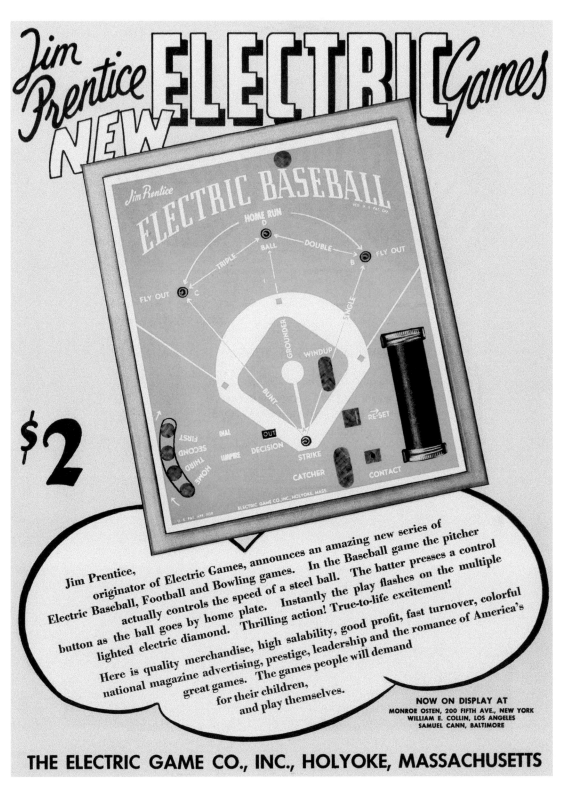

The Electric Game Company, 1946

General Mills, 1947

▶ Parker-Johns, 1948

◄ Northwestern Products, c. 1949

Sears, Roebuck, and Company, 1948

Beloved Kewpie Doll by Rose O'Neill

$1.63

- Molded of sturdy composition . . . has turning-tilting head
- Jointed arms and legs . . . takes many poses . . . stands alone
- Wears cotton sunsuit, rayon socks and imitation leather shoes

This lively little imp with her winning grin, flirtatious painted eyes, and the perky molded lock on her head is bound to win the heart of any girl. She stands 12¾ inches tall. Her pert sunsuit comes in assorted colors. Choose her for a delightful gift . . . her price is pleasingly low.

49 N 3435—Shipping weight 1 lb. 12 oz $1.63

Why not buy Dolls and Toys on Sears Easy Payment plan? See page 243

Universal Toy and Novelty Company, 1944

▶ D. A. Pachter Company, 1944

Presto Slates, 1944

▶ Palo from California, 1944

▶▶ Strathmore Magic Toys, 1944

"Hi, Folks, I'm

PALO

FROM CALIFORNIA

I FELL EM! YOU SELL EM!

"YES, I'm Palo — direct descendant of the pixies who cast the magic spell on the giant Redwood trees! 'Way back, centuries ago, they selected the Redwoods as the ideal trees for toys... brought me to life to convert these giants of the forest into inspired toys for little girls and boys!

"I fell 'em...and do all the work of logging, sawing... creating these profit-making Palos from California. From there on, the fun's all yours —for YOU sell 'em!

"I'll be looking for you at the

AMERICAN TOY FAIR FOR 1944

Room 530 and 532
HOTEL McALPIN

...so tear out this advertisement as a reminder!

"I'm Miss America of 1956
I'm really going places in my Palo Shoefly. You will, too, if you sell them to other little girls—and boys."

"I'm Lolly the Lamb—
I just love to cuddle
I'm cute when I'm clean
Let's not play near the puddle!"

"I'm Robby, the Rooster—
I'm cock o' the walk
I'm such a bright fowl
I can almost talk!"

"I'm Benny, the Bunny
My temperament's sunny
Just see my long ears—
Don't you think they're funny?"

"I'm Porter the Pull Box
The handiest toy
To kiddies a good pal . . .
To mothers—a joy!"

"I'm Freddy the Fawn—
I was born in the hills
I gracefully jumped
Amidst rocks and rills."

"I'm Skippy the Stick Horse—
A peppy young fellow
I trot and I gallop
But my temper is mellow!"

"I'm Carnival, the Toy Chest
A mystery, you know—
You'll see me at my best
At the New York Toy Show!"

PALO
...from California

159 S. Anderson • Los Angeles 33, California

MAGIC Toys

with MAGIC!

...and all the more
...vs! Designed for
...nating fun fea-
...Toys supplies an
...very small cost!

Mickey Mouse MAGIC SLATE

Another 12x18 blackboard with full color pictures of Mickey, Donald and other lovable characters. Full set of 2-color draw-or-trace cards. Alphabets, numbers, games, puzzles, etc., and real Disney Cartoons. in Gift Box, One Dollar.

$1

e COLOR MAGIC!

• Erase

...outfit! Drawing
...as large Magic
...se drawings in
...or, too, right on
... erasing cloth
...ms to clear the
... magic! Special
...k for Crayons,
...rating Stencils.
...an easy habit!
...plete

Jack Sprat
Jack & Jill
Old King Cole
Little Bo-Peep
Little Boy Blue

PAPER SAVER

A marvelous value! 7⅜ x 11⅜ durable Magic Slate and Stylus. Saves pencils and reams of paper! Great for school work, household memos, business, etc. Ideal toy drawing board, too. Only 25c.

25¢

Strathmore Magic Toys at all dealers

...HE STENCILS ARE
...EAT FOR ADDING
...CORATIONS—

NOW, TO MAKE READY FOR A NEW DRAWING JUST RUB THE COLOR OFF, THEN LIFT UP THE FILM... IT'S GONE LIKE MAGIC!

BABY BOOMERS RULE AS TOY
COMPANIES SEE A LUCRATIVE
MIDDLE-CLASS MARKET OF
MAJOR PROPORTIONS AND
TOY SALES SKYROCKET INTO
THE STRATOSPHERE.

1950s

MATTEL

fall 1957

MATTEL, INC. TOYMAKERS®

in this issue:

FASTEST GUN IN THE U.S.A.

New Fanner 50 Becomes Toy Industry's

Fastest Moving Cap Pistol

see page one for story

THE SOUND
OF MONEY

TOY SALES TOTALED $500 MILLION IN 1951 YET THE INDUSTRY SPENT ONLY 5 MILLION ADVERTISING DOLLARS. The toy industry was reluctant to invest money in advertising, believing that playthings were primarily sold at Christmastime, which proved to be a bogus assumption. In the early '50s, as baby boomers were booming, toys were becoming a year-round business, notes *Ad Age*. Incredibly, more toys were sold in the first 10 months of 1950 than in all of 1941 — and why not? The war was won, prosperity reigned, the population increased, and industry flourished.

The second half of the 20th century soon became the modern era of toy advertising. Although before the mid- to late 1950s, toy ads had a carnival quality — more comic book than Madison Avenue — and had not yet attained a sophisticated level or found a sustainable voice — the decade saw major shifts

1952

1953

1955

Mr. Potato Head is invented

Mr. Potato Head wird erfunden

Monsieur Patate est inventé

War of the Worlds play set released in tandem with the film

Das Spielset War of the Worlds erscheint zusammen mit dem Film

Le jeu de plateau La Guerre des mondes sort au même moment que le film

Madame Alexander launches fashionable Cissy line

Madame Alexander lanciert die modische Cissy-Kollektion

Madame Alexander lance sa collection chic Cissy

in demographics and media that were beginning to alter how toys were positioned in the marketplace. Fads such as Wham-O's addictive Hula Hoop and Frisbee, both introduced in 1957; Mattel's 1959 stylish Barbie; and the gymnastic Slinky, invented by Richard James in 1947, grabbed large market shares in the land of postwar plenty.

Television started to make its indelible mark on the culture in general and on Saturday mornings in particular. Kids' shows provided not only a stage for advertising but also a batch of new celebrity and character tie-ins from which to build toy brands. The postwar generation was easily seduced, and parents were poised to voraciously consume. *Ad Age* notes that in 1952, the toy business earned more than $800 million in retail sales with an assist from TV-related merchandise. It was validation for toy manufacturers that products "could be a year-round enterprise." In 1954 Disneyland merchandising went through the proverbial roof thanks to the role models created by *Davy Crockett* and other popular "western" series. TV spawned increased ad spending on screen and print. Toy and game advertising became a profit

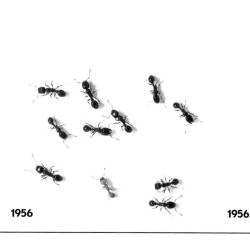

1956

1956

1957

"Uncle" Milton Levine gets idea for ant farm during Fourth of July picnic

„Onkel" Milton Levine hat bei einem Picknick am Independance Day die Idee für seine Ameisenfarm

« L'oncle » Milton Levine imagine sa ferme à fourmis au cours d'un pique-nique du 4 Juillet

Joe McVicker starts marketing his uncle's wallpaper cleaner as Play-Doh

Joe McVicker vermarktet den Tapetenreiniger seines Onkels als Play-Doh (Knetgummi)

Joe McVicker commercialise la gomme à papier peint créée par son oncle sous le nom Play-Doh

Charles Lazarus opens a store exclusively selling toys, calling it Toys "R" Us

Charles Lazarus eröffnet einen Laden nur für Spielwaren namens Toys "R" Us

Charles Lazarus ouvre un magasin qui ne vend que des jouets et l'appelle Toys "R" Us center for some agencies. Toy districts grew in major cities such as New York, and the introduction of a catalog called the Toy Yearbook was made available to a growing number of retailers. Many of the ads and commercials produced in the '50s were created by Friend-Reiss-McGlone, the toy industry's council agency, which aired spots on CBS's most popular kiddie shows, *Winky Dink and You* and *Romper Room*. Ideal Toy Company sponsored the Macy's Thanksgiving Day parade on NBC, which was its biggest national stage to date, and toys soon became the driver of a large segment of America's huge entertainment business.

1958

1958

1959

The Hula-Hoop takes off after appearing on *The Dinah Shore Show*

Der Hula-Hoop-Reifen wird nach zum Renner, nachdem er in der *Dinah Shore Show* zu sehen war

Les ventes de hula hoop s'emballent après un passage dans le *Dinah Shore Show*

The Lego brick first appears

Die ersten Lego-Steine kommen auf den Markt

La briquette Lego fait son apparition

Ruth Handler, co-founder of Mattel, creates Barbie

Ruth Handler, Mitbegründerin von Mattel, erfindet die Barbie

Ruth Handler, cofondatrice de Mattel, crée Barbie

DIE KASSEN KLINGELN

Die Spielzeugindustrie entdeckt die Babyboomer als lukrative Zielgruppe der Mittelschicht. die Spielwarenumsätze schießen in den Himmel.

Obwohl die Umsätze der Spielwarenindustrie 1951 auf 500 Millionen Dollar anwuchsen, gab die Branche nur fünf Millionen Dollar für Werbung aus. Man nahm an, dass Spielzeug hauptsächlich zu Weihnachten verkauft wurde. Das stellte sich als falsch heraus. Mit der Zeit des Babybooms Anfang der 1950er-Jahre entwickelten sich Spielwaren jedoch ganzjährig zu Verkaufsschlagern, wie die Zeitschrift *Ad Age* aufführt. In den ersten zehn Monaten des Jahres 1950 wurde mehr Spielzeug verkauft als im ganzen Jahr 1941 – und warum auch nicht? Der Krieg war gewonnen, es herrschte Wohlstand, die Bevölkerung wuchs, und die Wirtschaft boomte.

In der zweiten Hälfte des 20. Jahrhunderts begann das moderne Zeitalter der Spielzeugwerbung. Anfang der 1950er-Jahre war sie jedoch noch nicht besonders anspruchsvoll oder profiliert, mehr Karneval und Comics als Madison Avenue. Innerhalb dieses Jahrzehnts sollten jedoch ein demografischer Wandel sowie eine enorme Veränderung der Medienlandschaft vonstattengehen, die allmählich auch eine Neupositionierung von Spielwaren im Markt mit sich brachten. Trends wie Wham-Os süchtig machende Hula-Hoop-Reifen und Frisbees (beide 1957), Mattels stylische Barbie von 1959 und das bewegliche Slinky (erfunden 1947 von Richard James) eroberten im konsumfreudigen Nachkriegsamerika große Marktanteile. Das Fernsehen begann, der Alltagskultur seinen Stempel aufzudrücken, vor allen samstagsmorgens, wenn Comics und Kindersendungen liefen. Kindersendungen boten nicht nur eine Werbebühne, sondern zeigten auch Promis und beliebte Figuren, aus denen Spielzeugmarken entwickelt werden konnten. Die Nachkriegsgeneration ließ sich leicht verführen, und ihre Eltern waren im Konsumrausch. *Ad Age* schreibt, dass die Spielwarenbranche 1952 auch mithilfe von Artikeln, die an TV-Sendungen gekoppelt waren, über 800 Millionen Dollar Umsatz machte. Spätestens jetzt war klar, dass sich Spielzeug das ganze Jahr über bestens verkaufen ließ. 1954 ging das Merchandising von Disney dank TV-Western-Serien wie *Davy Crockett* durch die sprichwörtliche Decke. Folglich wurde mehr Geld für TV- und auch Printwerbung lockergemacht, für manche Werbeagenturen wurden Spielwaren zu lukrativen Einnahmequellen. In großen Städten wie New York bildeten sich ganze Spielwarenviertel und der Katalog *Toy Yearbook* erreichte immer mehr Einzelhändler. Viele der Werbeanzeigen und -spots der 1950er im Bereich Spielwaren wurden von der Agentur Friend-Reiss-McGlone produziert, die den Verband der Spielzeugindustrie beriet und in den beliebtesten Kindershows von CBS, *Winky Dink and You* und *Romper Room*, Werbespots platzierte. Die Ideal Toy Company sponserte Macys Thanksgiving-Parade auf NBC – ihre bisher größte Werbeplattform – und Spielwaren entwickelten sich zu einem der Zugpferde von Amerikas gewaltiger Unterhaltungsindustrie.

► Standard Toykraft Products, 1958

...from out of this world!

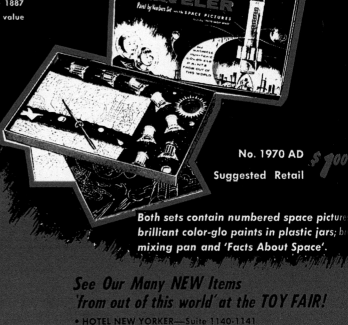

MONOPOLY — *Parker Brothers' trade-mark name for its real estate trading game.* Money, tokens, houses, hotels and various title and other cards enable you to trade in real estate or utilities, secure mortgages and accumulate money, etc. Monopoly is the most popular of the world's great standard family games.

MONNAIE SONNANTE ET TRÉBUCHANTE

Les baby-boomers règnent, les fabricants de jouets enjôlent le juteux nouveau marché des classes moyennes et les ventes de jouets s'envolent dans la stratosphère.

Les ventes de jouets totalisent 500 millions de dollars en 1951, pourtant l'industrie n'a dépensé que 5 millions en publicité. L'industrie du jeu rechigne à investir davantage dans la promotion de ses produits, convaincue que les jouets se vendent surtout avant Noël – mais elle se trompe. Au début des années 1950, les baby-boomers pullulent et les jouets deviennent un marché porteur toute l'année, note *Ad Age*. Il se vend davantage de jouets pendant les dix premiers mois de 1950 qu'au cours de toute l'année 1941, mais est-ce si étonnant ? La guerre est gagnée, le pays est prospère, la population croît et l'industrie se développe.

La seconde moitié du XXᵉ siècle voit la publicité pour les jouets entrer dans la modernité. Bien qu'au début des années 1950 les pubs évoquent encore une ambiance de kermesse – plus proche des comics que de Madison Avenue – et que les annonceurs n'aient encore établi ni image de marque ni stratégie durable, l'explosion de la démographie et des médias que connaît cette décennie commencent à modifier le positionnement du jouet sur le marché. Les tocades addictives comme le hula hoop et le frisbee de Wham-O apparaissent tous deux en 1957. L'élégante Barbie créée par Mattel en 1959 et l'athlétique Slinky inventé par Richard James en 1947 s'octroient de larges parts de marché au pays de cocagne qu'est l'Amérique d'après-guerre. La télévision commence à imprimer sa marque indélébile sur la culture en général et les samedis matins en particulier. Les programmes pour la jeunesse sont une tribune publicitaire et une source aussi inépuisable que rentable de nouveaux héros que les marques de jouets s'approprient. La génération de l'après-guerre est facile à séduire et les parents sont tout disposés à consommer sans retenue. *Ad Age* note qu'en 1952 l'industrie du jouet a engrangé plus de 800 millions de dollars de chiffre d'affaires, en grande partie grâce aux produits associés à la télévision. Ce succès convainc les fabricants que leurs jouets se vendent tout au long de l'année. En 1954, les ventes de produits dérivés Disney crèvent le fameux plafond grâce au statut d'icône acquis par Davy Crockett et les héros d'autres feuilletons « western ». La télévision engendre une croissance des dépenses publicitaires, sur le petit écran comme dans la presse. Les campagnes pour les jouets et jeux deviennent une source de profit pour certaines agences. Dans les grandes villes, New York en tête, des quartiers dédiés au jouet se développent et l'Almanach du jouet (*Toy Yearbook*), sorte de catalogue annuel, est proposé dans un nombre croissant de boutiques. Une bonne partie des publicités produites dans les années 1950 sont l'œuvre de Friend-Reiss-McGlone, l'agence de communication officieuse de l'industrie du jouet, qui diffuse ses spots dans les émissions pour enfants les plus populaires de CBS comme *Winky Dink and You* et *Romper Room*. L'Ideal Toy Company s'offre sa première heure de gloire nationale en sponsorisant la parade de Thanksgiving de Macy's retransmise sur NBC, et le jouet devient bientôt la force motrice d'un large segment de la tentaculaire industrie américaine du divertissement.

◀ Parker Brothers, 1952

SUPERMAN

WRIST WATCHES
FOR BOYS AND GIRLS

DE LUXE—Expansion Bracelet Model. Chrome Plated case; stainless steel back.

No. 290   Retail **$5.95** plus tax

Dealers **$4.00** ea.

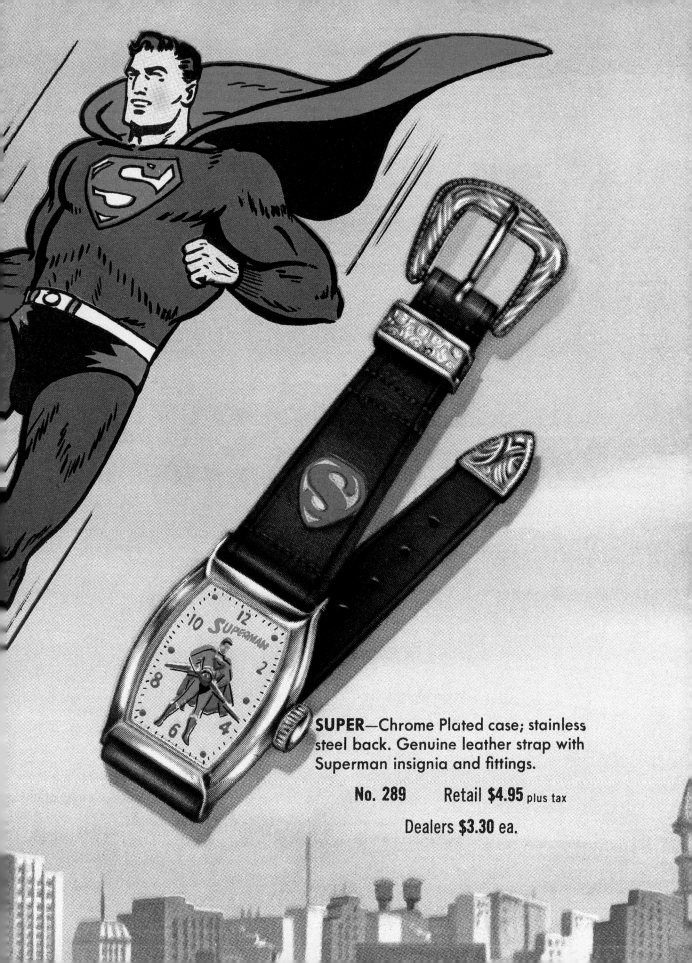

SUPER—Chrome Plated case; stainless steel back. Genuine leather strap with Superman insignia and fittings.

No. 289   Retail **$4.95** plus tax

Dealers **$3.30** ea.

2 OUT OF 3 CHILDREN IN AMERICA

WILL
WEAR
BENAY-ALBEE
HATS
IN
1958*

SEE WHY AT THE TOY SHOW..HOTEL NEW YORKER..ROOM 1126, 200 FIFTH AVE...ROOM 1118

ask your jobber for Tru-Vue

the World's foremost
3-Dimension Line SELLS
IN VOLUME THE YEAR
AROUND BECAUSE...

1. Tru-Vue Features These Stars of Movieland and TV. . . . .
   MICKEY MOUSE • THE LONE RANGER
   ROY ROGERS • WILD BILL HICKOK
   WOODY WOODPECKER • ROBIN HOOD
   BUGS BUNNY • DONALD DUCK
   WALT DISNEY'S ZORRO
   And a Host of Other Children's Favorites

2. Tru-Vue is The Lowest Priced Quality 3-Dimension Line.

3. Tru-Vue customers return to your toy counters again and again for new picture stories.

4. Tru-Vue is a perfect toy for Birthdays, Shut-in days, Christmas, travel with children.

5. Tru-Vue is nationally advertised on TV, in women's magazines: PARENTS', LADIES HOME JOURNAL.

THE NEXT TIME YOUR JOBBER
REPRESENTATIVE CALLS, ASK HIM TO
PUT YOU IN BUSINESS WITH TRU-VUE

BUDGET VIEWER
Suggested
Retail... $1.98

DELUXE
LIGHTED
VIEWER
Suggested
Retail........$3.49
(less batteries)

GIFT SET
Suggested Retail... $2.98

SINGLE PICTURE STORIES
3-D and Color... 35c

3-STORY ALBUMS
3-D and Color... 98c

To make a little girl happy...

PICK HER GIFT FROM THE
Thayer®
WONDERLAND

THAYER Folding Doll Carriages are lovely, too. They fold just like a big carriage in which babies ride. There's a fine model for *every* budget, too!

THAYER Doll Strollers are authentic doll-size versions of famous Thayer strollers for real babies.

THAYER Musical Doll Crib plays a lullaby for daughter's favorite doll. New and different!

THAYER Miniature Doll Furniture is an exact replica of real furniture. Even the mirror is real glass!

She'll be enchanted with the lovely Thayer Doll Coach, "just like a real baby's!" There are dozens of other wonderful play things ...for *boys* as well as girls...in the Thayer Wonderland at your favorite store. Thayer, famous for baby carriages and juvenile furniture, also makes the finest and most complete line of *doll* vehicles and play furniture.

Send 10¢ to Thayer, Inc., Dept. L-8, Gardner, Mass. for your daughter's copy of "SALLY LOU AND MINERVA, HER DOLL." She'll love it!

THAYER Doll Hi-Chair is a doll sized model of a de luxe upholstered baby hi-chair.

THAYER Desk and Bookcase Ensemble beautifully furnishes a room for a *boy* or girl. As sturdy as fine adult furniture. A thrilling gift, and practical, too!

And here's a
Special Christmas Thrill
EXCLUSIVE WITH
Thayer®
RUDOLPH
THE RED-NOSED REINDEER

"Rudolph" Musical Rocker —When rocked, plays that gay little Christmas tune. Nothing to wind! Fits any child from two to ten.

"Rudolph" Table and Chair Set — With gay reproductions of that famous reindeer with the red nose. Built to the standards of finest adult furniture. Wonderful for play, practical for meals, for study.

Thayer, 1950

▶ Noma Electric, 1950

Nosco Plastics, 1950

▶ Playskool, 1952

Leading the parade in back-to-school safety-- AMF ROADMASTER!

School days are here again, and that's a time when parents like to feel that their youngsters are riding the safest possible bikes. And when it comes to safety—AMF Roadmaster Bicycles lead the parade, thanks to AMF engineering and Roadmaster experience.

Here you see the AMF Roadmaster Luxury Liner—America's finer fully-equipped bike—with all its famous features and exclusive extras.

And for the smaller fry, here's the AMF Roadmaster 20″ De Luxe with most of the features of big brother's bike! SAF-T-RIDER attachment keeps him balanced while he's learning.

See the full line of exciting AMF Roadmasters today. At your AMF Roadmaster Dealer's and fine stores everywhere.

Roadometer automatically measures and records the miles you ride from 1/10 mile up to 10,000 miles.

AMF ROADMASTER LUXURY LINER
...America's finer fully-equipped bike!

SAFER, STRONGER electronically-welded frame.
MORE PROTECTION with safety bumper bars (front and rear).
SMOOTHER RIDE with shockmaster coil-spring fork.
BETTER VISIBILITY at night with searchbeam headlight.
ELECTRIC HORN right in the tank.
MEASURES THE MILES with exclusive Roadmaster Roadometer.

AMF ROADMASTER 20″ DE LUXE— *young America's safe-riding favorite!* **SAF-T-RIDER** attachment (optional) • real headlight • streamlined rocket tank • rear reflector • chain guard • wide-base chrome rims • coaster brake

FREE FUN FOR BOYS AND GIRLS! Get your AMF Roadmaster booklet "Let's Go On A Bike Hike." Helpful hints on map-reading, exciting bike hike ideas and games. Write AMF Roadmaster, Dept. L-53-8, West 117th St. & Berea Road, Cleveland 7, Ohio.

amf **products** ARE BETTER...*by design*
AMERICAN MACHINE & FOUNDRY COMPANY

Roadmaster ®

For 1950-Mattel has the Secret

JACK-IN-THE-MUSIC-BOX

A new "surprise" version of an old favorite toy. The Music plays "Pop Goes the Weasel." POP goes the Top—UP jumps "Mr. Jolly Tune," the clown, with ruffled, polka dot suit and perky hat with feather, and UP go your sales on Mattel Music Maker Toys!

Sturdily constructed, with brilliantly colored lithographed decor designed with rare imagination by Bob Routledge. Metal reinforced box, housing Mattel's patented Music Box. Priced for volume sales. No. 438.

Suggested Retail

$1 98 Packed 2 doz. to carton. Shipping wt. approx. 31 lbs. 5⅜" x 5⅜" x 6¾".

Patent Pending

TIPPY CLOWN
"Mr. Jolly Tune"
Suggested Retail
98c

Push me down and I'll bounce right back up again. Turn the crank and I'll play you a jolly tune. That's why I'm known as "Mr. Jolly Tune." I've a fat, funny face and I'm so simple to play. A wonderful toy for the younger music lovers... No. 426.

Patent Pending

Packed 2 doz. to carton. Shipping wt. approx. 18 lbs. 6" high.

Rm. 610 & 614 Hotel McAlpin

Mattel Creations

8436 WARNER DRIVE • CULVER CITY, CALIFORNIA

Mattel Creations, 1950

▶ The Rushton Company, 1956

Take Another Look!

IT'S
A
WONDERFUL
TOY . . .
IT'S

IDEAL

I AM ROBERT THE ROBOT
The Mechanical Man
Drive me, steer me,
Wherever you can!

Ideal's Robert the Robot

Ideal's Talking Police Car

Ideal Toy, 1955

Harmonic Reed, 1955

General Mills, 1951

► A. C. Gilbert and Company, 1957

HAVE FUN...

...building exciting action models with world-famous
ERECTOR SETS

Build a sturdy steel ferris wheel, an oil drilling rig, a magnetic crane, and other thrilling models. Design your own models or build those suggested in the "How to Make 'Em" book that comes with your set. No other construction toy has all the great Erector features.

No. 8½ Erector Set includes 16 lbs. of precision steel parts, powerful electric motor, electric lights and magnet, all in big steel chest. **$27**⁵⁰*

Others from $2.50* *Slightly higher Denver and West.

...performing laboratory experiments with
GILBERT CHEMISTRY SETS

Now Gilbert offers the finest, most complete chemistry sets ever made. Perform chemical tests, original experiments, glass blowing and chemical magic. Great fun, and it helps prepare you for later school courses.

No. 15 Chemistry Set has equipment for hundreds of exciting experiments. Six steel shelves full of chemicals. Two test-tube racks. Balance. Alcohol lamp. **$15**⁹⁵* Others from $2.95*

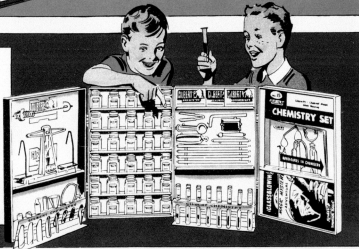

...hatching real shrimp, watching them grow with new
GILBERT MICROSCOPE SETS

See nature in action with these laboratory-type microscope sets. You can even see live birth and growth, as tiny shrimp pass through various life phases before your eyes. As much fun as it is educational.

Hatch real shrimp eggs, see them swim after a few hours, with this new No. 22 Gilbert Microscope Set. Steel cabinet has 4-turret microscope —NEW design—complete lab equipment. Magnifies up to 750 power! **$21**⁵⁰* Others from $5.50*

GILBERT HALL OF SCIENCE, Dept. 111
Erector Square, New Haven 6, Conn.

Please send full-color catalog that illustrates and tells about Gilbert Erector, Chemistry and Microscope Sets.

Name _____

Address _____

City _____ Zone ____ State _____

SEND FOR **FREE CATALOG** TODAY

BOYS! GIRLS! GET THIS AMAZING
"10-IN-1" ELECTRIC TRAIL-KIT!

- Spare Lens Storage (Doubles as Secret Compartment)

- Police Signal Whistle
- Magnetic Compass
- Accurate Sundial

- Focusing 2-Plus Power Telescope
- Magnifying Glass

© S.P.O.Y., Inc.

- Spring-Type Fastener Clip

- Official Sgt. Preston Seal

- Precision-Fitted Parts Separate Here

- Code-Button Switch for Flash Code Signaling

- Actual size approx. 6 in.

- Ball-point pen
- Push Code-Button and Pen Glows for Night Writing

- Powerful Flashlight complete with battery and bulb

PUFFED WHEAT

PUFFED RICE

Muffets SHREDDED WHEAT

GET ONE OF THESE
QUAKER CEREAL PACKAGES

SEND FOR THIS ELECTRIC
"10-IN-1" SGT. PRESTON

TRAIL-KIT

COMPLETE WITH BATTERY

ONLY 50¢ AND QUAKER BOXTOP

SEND NOW for this amazing pen-shaped kit that includes 10 special, useful devices . . . yet fits together into a compact, plastic kit designed to go wherever you go. Just send a boxtop from one of the Quaker Cereal packages shown above and ONLY 50¢. Your money back if you are not satisfied.

ROY ROGERS

KING OF THE COWBOYS

WRIST WATCHES FOR BOYS

Many Happy Trails
Roy Rogers + Trigger

DELUXE OBLONG—Expansion Bracelet. Chrome Plated Slim Case. Stainless Steel back.
No. 291   Retail $5.95 plus tax
Dealers $4.00 ea.

10 KT. ROLLED GOLD Deluxe Case. Round dial. Stainless Steel Back. Genuine leather western strap and fittings.
No. 256   Retail $5.95 plus tax
Dealers $4.00 ea.

DE LUXE EXPANSION With Plaque, Chrome Plated Case. Round dial. Stainless Steel back, Stainless Steel expansion bracelet. Signature of ROY ROGERS and TRIGGER engraved on plaque.
No. 211   Retail $6.95 plus tax
Dealers $4.63 ea.

THIN ROUND — Chrome Plated case. Stainless Steel back. Genuine leather Western strap and fittings.
No. 160
Retail $4.95 plus tax
Dealers $3.30 ea.

QUEEN OF THE WEST

Dale Evans

WRIST WATCHES FOR GIRLS

Roy + Dale
ON N.B.C. TV
COAST TO COAST

DE LUXE —Expansion Bracelet. Smart oblong dial. Chrome Plated slim case. Stainless Steel back.
No. 292
Retail $5.95 plus tax
Dealers $4.00 ea.

SLIM ROUND—Chrome Plated Case. Stainless Steel back. Smart round dial. Genuine leather western strap and fittings.
No. 186   Retail $4.95 plus tax
Dealers $3.30 ea.

DE LUXE EXPANSION ROUND — Chrome Plated slim case. Stainless steel back. Smart round dial. Stainless Steel expansion bracelet.
No. 193   Retail $6.95 plus tax
Dealers $4.63 ea.

DE LUXE 10 KT. ROLLED GOLD—Slim case. Stainless steel back. Smart round dial. Genuine leather western strap and fittings.
No. 257
Retail $5.95 plus tax
Dealers $4.00 ea.

Roy Rogers
DOUBLE R BAR RANCH

ROY ROGERS **ANIMATED** ALARM CLOCKS

ROY ROGERS and TRIGGER actually gallop with each tick. Dependable 40 hour alarm clock with full color Western scene. Attractively styled metal case available in: Sky Blue, Saddle Tan, Cactus Green, Desert Sand.
No. R47   Retail $3.95 plus tax
Dealers $2.65 ea.

Bradley TIME

◄ Quaker, 1958

E. Ingraham Company, 1955

Roberts Manufacturing Company, 1955

▶ Lindberg Products, 1957

Ideal Toy Corporation's Golden Age of Toys

"KISSING PINK" REVLON DOLL (above left) Dressed with pearl earrings and necklace. Crisp crinoline slip under dress. 18", $11.95; 20", $15.95; 23", $19.95.

"QUEEN OF DIAMONDS" REVLON DOLL (center) exquisitely dressed with real fur stole, rhinestone earrings, necklace and ring! 18" tall, $15.95; 20", $19.95; 23", $24.95.

"CHERRIES A LA MODE" REVLON DOLL . . . (above right) "Wash 'n Wear" nylon dress, crinoline slip, smart hat, pearl earrings and necklace complete this lovely lady's outfit. 18" tall, $13.95; 20", $17.95; 23", $21.95.

Revlon dolls by **IDEAL**

These beautiful dolls all have full-formed teen-age figures; bend from the waist, and pirouette on nylon-stockinged legs in high-heeled shoes. Their "Magic Touch" skin can be bathed and powdered; their lovely rooted Saran hair can be washed and waved. All are beautifully dressed in high fashion style with smart personal jewelry.

It's fun to mother
BETSY WETSY

America's favorite crying and wetting doll! She drinks, sleeps, cries real tears and wets! Betsy's soft vinyl body can be bathed, powdered, lotioned; her rooted Saran hair can be combed, shampooed and waved! Every little girl wants Betsy Wetsy, so durably made she will be her favorite doll for years.

BETSY WETSY (Above) with molded hair has layette including: dress, bonnet, slip, shirt, diaper, pins, bottle, nipple, wash cloth, soap and puffs. 11½" $5.98; 13½" $7.98; 16" $9.98.

DELUXE BETSY WETSY (Above) with soft vinyl head and rooted hair. In carrying case with dress, bonnet, shirt, diaper, puffs, bottle, nipple, clothespins, soap. 11½" $8.98; 13½" $10.98; 16" $13.95.

DELUXE BETSY WETSY IN STURDY SUITCASE (Right) containing: pretty dress, bonnet, slip, shirt, diaper, rubber panties, booties, bottle, pins, soap, puffs. Size: 11½" $10.98; 13½" $12.95; 16" $15.95.

She's a wonderful doll, she's IDEAL

"Flight-tested" by famous spacemen...4 helmets you

- cardboard, paper plate
- mailing tubes
- rubber tubing
- clothesline, wood strips
- plastic cheesebox
- fasteners, acetate

OFF in the Space Patrol Experimental Laboratory, Commander Buzz Corry and his comrades have developed new equipment—a Guard Helmet (left) and a Desert Crash Helmet. They'll be on the Space Patrol Shows, August 1, over ABC Radio and TV Networks. For down-to-earth wear we present these discoveries in cosmic headgear.

- colander, corset stay
- plastic cheesebox, spring
- spool, acetate, rubber tubing
- angle irons, can, clothesline
- felt, faucet spray, fasteners
- wire, bolts, paper clip

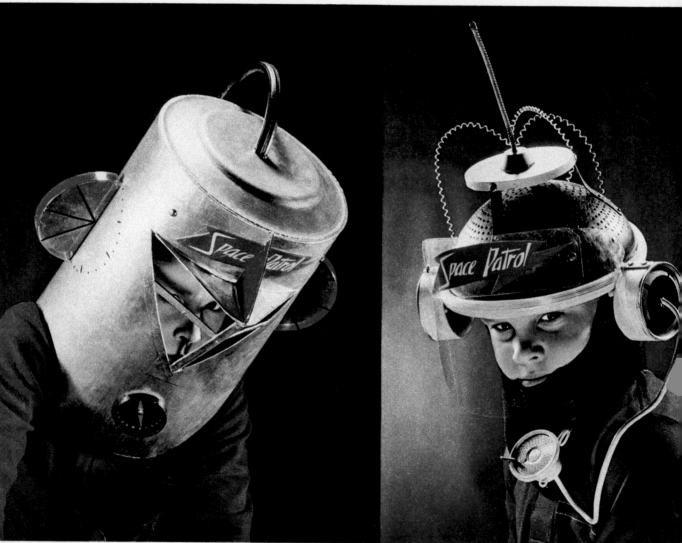

PHOTOGRAPHS BY BEN CALVO, WOMAN'S DAY STUDIO

To be properly stratospheric, cut out one of these official insignia to identify your helmet

can make from household odds and ends

CAPTAIN Video spacemen helped make the very helmets pictured below. Straight from the rocket ship *Galaxy* come these authentic designs. Earthlings who want to play along with the Video rangers on their travels in space can don either of these Emergency Helmets. They're just like space equipment worn on the Captain Video TV show over the Du Mont Network.

CAPTAIN VIDEO
EMERGENCY HELMET

For making, see How To Section, page 105

SEE HOW TO SECTION

A Bigger than ever!
$4.99

Hoist Plastic
bales of hay

Litter carrier
slides on rail

Rear view—open
backed big hayloft

B $4.94

C $3.98

D $5.97

Montgomery Ward, 1955

▶ Louis Marx and Company, 1959

..with BEN HUR

132-piece Set
$7⁹⁸

217-piece Set
$12⁹⁸

Official Sets . . carefully detailed, historically accurate

A vast panorama of the Roman Empire as it was in the time of the Caesars unfolds before your eyes in almost unbelievable detail. Here is the slave market where prisoners are sold on the block . . there the Arena where gladiators meet each other in mortal combat, and the Galleries, before which Ben Hur raced his chariot to victory. **The Galleries:** 18¼x3¼x8½ inches high . . with graceful columns rising above . . here sit the spectators with the Emperor and Empress, watching Ben Hur race. Four Roman chariots, pulled by four horses each, with harness and drivers. 66 figures include Emperor and Empress, gladiators, slaves, charioteers, and Roman citizens. **The Amphitheater:** 16x4x6½ inches high. Within its arena are gladiators with sword and shield, fighting a lion and a tiger which have been released through sliding cage doors. **The Slave Market and Bazaar:** stand with canopy cover has several slaves chained for the auctions. Bazaar food stall is canopy covered, has food containers with molded plastic food . . this bazaar is the hub of the forum, center of Roman life. Other accessories include a tent, portrait busts, lion, tiger, catapult, baskets, fountain, cart, couch, etc.

79 N 05985—132-Piece Set. All items molded to scale in 3-dimensional plastic. Wt. 5 lbs............$7.98

79 N 05974—Giant 217-Piece Ben Hur Play Set . . . a real spectacular! Includes everything in the set above *plus* 4 extra chariots, extra 16 horses and 4 drivers; 40 Romans; two extra tents, braziers, tables, hassocks, lamps, chests, urns, and hookahs. Also includes 2 extra working catapults. Wt. 7 lbs............$12.98

Ben Hur Sword and Shield Set

Patterned after weapons used by gladiators 2000 years ago in their battles for wealth and fame in the great arenas of Rome and Antioch. Two metal shields, 12 inches in diameter. Two 18-inch swords with flexible plastic blades . . two metal scabbards.
49 N 2481—Shipping weight 3 pounds.....$2.89

Build realistic scale models of th

◀ Revell, 1956

▶ Lionel, 1954

Lionel, 1958

One of the best ways
Men get to know Each Other...

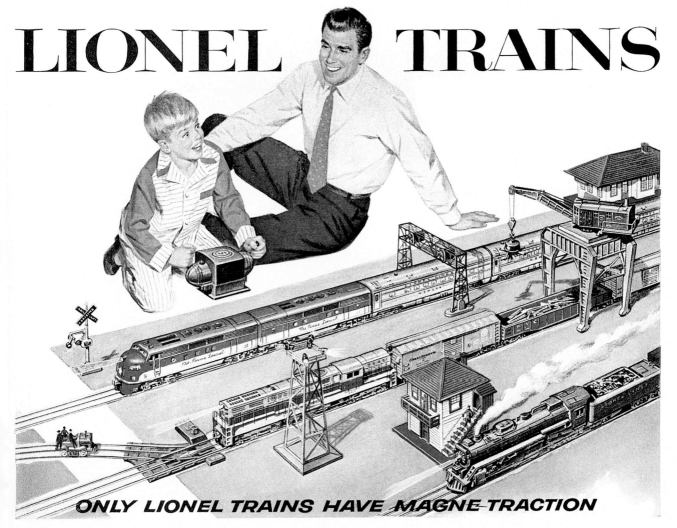

Start a new comradeship this Christmas, with your boy and
LIONEL TRAINS. Share with him the matchless thrills of railroading . . .
and the deep satisfaction of building a bigger and better railroad. Stop in at
your Lionel Dealer's *right away* for a complete choice of Lionel sets.
See *Magne-Traction* at work . . . the exclusive feature that makes Lionel locos
go faster, pull more cars, climb steep grades. Pick the accessories that
will add exciting action all along your right of way. You can buy a complete
set of LIONEL TRAINS for as little as $19.95! Get started *now!*

For details
of all Lionel Trains
and Accessories,
see the great new
Lionel 1954 Catalog.
Your dealer has it!

LIONEL TRAINS

ONLY LIONEL TRAINS HAVE MAGNE-TRACTION

◄ Tastee-Freez Stores, 1956

Montgomery Ward, 1955

G $20.98
cash
$2.50 down
Phonograph
and 10 Records

H $13.49
Phonograph
and 10 Records

D $10.49
Phonograph only
$12.49
With 10 Records
and Rack

E $7.29
Phonograph only
$9.29
With 10 Records
and Rack

F $17.49
Phonograph only
$19.49
With 10 Records
and Rack

CHRISTMAS SPECIAL

Take advantage of these combinations! You save when you buy
phonographs D E F with 10 all-time favorite children's records
and rack. If sold separately, records and rack alone would be $3.98

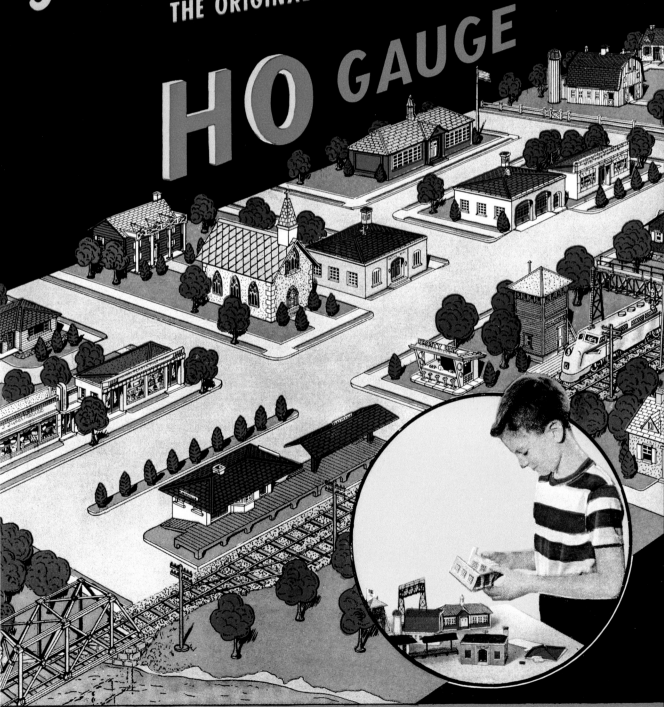

MINIATURE
Plasticville, U.S.A.
THE ORIGINAL PLASTIC VILLAGE

HO GAUGE

Manufactured by **BACHMANN BROS., INC.** *Established 1833* **PHILADELPHIA 24, U.S.A.**

◀ Radio Comics, c. 1959

Parker Brothers, 1952

SORRY — *Parker Brothers' trade-mark name for its slide pursuit game.* A different game in which movement of the pieces is controlled by the draw and play of cards. Skill and chance are combined in ideal proportions and the tail ender always has a chance to win. Sorry is gaining steadily in popularity because of its quick climaxes and interesting play. Rules for point SORRY included.

DAVY CROCKETT PLAYTOGS

K Polly Crockett Hat $1.69

L Davy Crockett Hat $1.69

M Knit Cotton Shirt $1.75 ea. in lots of 2

P Cotton Suede Jacket $4.98

N 2-piece Suit $5.98

R Cotton Flannel Shirt Less than $1.63 each in lots of 2

S 4-piece Slack set $4.98

T Leather Belt 98c

Montgomery Ward, 1955

▶ Transogram, 1955

9⁹⁵

3-DIMENSIONAL 12 INCH GLOBE WITH WORLD-O-FUN BOOK

A scientific "first." A dramatic innovation in globe making and the world can be seen in 3 dimensions! Detailed topographical features. By Replogle.

Ask for 17SW1

9⁹⁸

ELECTRONIC RADAR CIVIL DEFENSE STATION

Flashing lights determine whether or not planes on radarscope are friends or foe. Civil Defense worker plots course of planes on map, warns other cities of possible danger. Complete operator's manual with Morse Code and other CD information. Less batteries. By Product Miniature.

Ask for 17SW2

5⁹⁸

1956 CHEVROLET 4-DOOR HARDTOP

Features remote control and power steering. Car goes forward or backward. Powerful miniature motor powered by flashlight batteries (not included). Another motor turns car left or right by turning miniature steering wheel. By Product Miniature.

Ask for 17SW3

5⁹⁸

HI-WAY HYDRAULIC DUMP TRUCK

Just like those used by state highway departments. Real hydraulic lifting mechanism dumps load and two sides drop down for sanding. Tail-gate has two position regulator for straight dumping or spreading. Rugged, heavy. 13 inches long. By Tonka Toys.

Ask for 17SW4

Tonka Toys
MOUND, MINNESOTA

8⁹⁸

SUBURBAN PUMPER with real hydrant

It shoots a continuous stream of water supplied by its own, operating hydrant connected to garden hose. Removable ladder and two 6 inch rubber hydrant-connecting hoses. 40 inch fire hose wound on reel. By Tonka Toys.

Ask for 17SW5

◀ Nalbands Children's Department Store, 1956

Soldiers, c. 1957

The 1950s saw the rise of "slum," dirt-cheap plastic toys that were mass-produced thanks to a new screw-injection molding process. Children who read comic books were prime targets for companies that sold large quantities of toys — "126 pieces of soldiers and commandos" — for an absurdly low sum.

In den 1950ern kam sogenannte Slum-Ware auf, spottbilliges Plastikspielzeug, das dank eines neuen Spritzgussverfahrens in großen Mengen produziert wurde. Kinder, die Comics lasen, waren die Hauptzielgruppe für Hersteller, die eine große Anzahl von Spielfiguren – z. B. „126 Soldaten und Kommandos" – für eine absurd niedrige Summe feilboten.

Les années 1950 voient apparaître les bidules en plastique produits en masse grâce aux nouveaux procédés de moulage par injection. Les jeunes lecteurs de comics sont les premières cibles des marques qui proposent un grand nombre de pièces – « 126 soldats et commandos » – pour une somme ridicule.

GILBERT NUCLEAR PHYSICS

ATOM

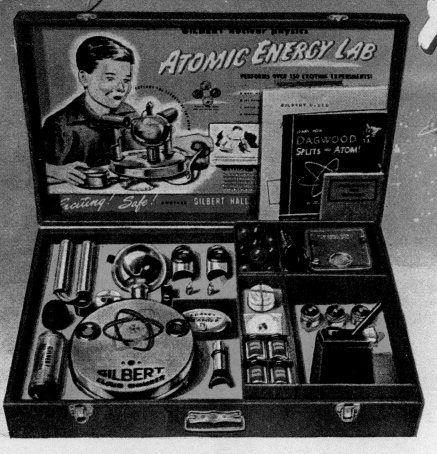

No. U-238 ATOMIC ENERGY LAB

Includes Geiger Counter, Gilbert Cloud Chamber, Electroscope, Spinthariscope, Neutron and Proton Spheres for making Nuclear models, Alpha, Beta and Gamma radiation sources, plus Uranium-bearing ores. Also packed with Lab are "Prospecting for Uranium," "Gilbert Atomic Energy Instruction Booklet." Sturdy attractive hinged chest, plus an illustrated full-color booklet explaining atomic energy in easy-to-understand fashion. Size of Set 25" x 16½" x 5".

Price, $49.50.   Denver and West, $51.00.

GILBERT CLOU[...]
(Included with Ato[...]

Enables you actually to SEE the [...]
alpha particles which travel a[...]
Action is fantastic and awe-in[...]
terrific velocities create delicate, [...]
to watch. The closest approach [...]
Atom. You see sights impossible [...]
Assembly Kit includes Dri-Ele[...]
Compression Bulb, Viewing Ch[...]
Tubing, Wire, and radioactive [...]

NUCLEA[...]
(Included with [...]

Make your own Nucle[...]
Spheres! Aids in unders[...]
tons and Neutrons whi[...]
nating to put together. I[...]

HELIUM

LITHIUM - 6

IC ENERGY LAB

DEVELOPED WITH COUNTRY'S LEADING ATOMIC ENERGY SCIENTISTS!

products ever to
Science! Not just
scientific instru-
engineers with
ith this complete
lore the mysteri-
— with complete

safety! Each one of the instruments in the Gilbert U-238 Atomic Energy Lab actually performs the same feats as professional instruments which cost up to hundreds of dollars! One of the Gilbert instruments alone, the Geiger Counter, enables you to prospect for Uranium — maybe win a Government bonus of $10,000.00.

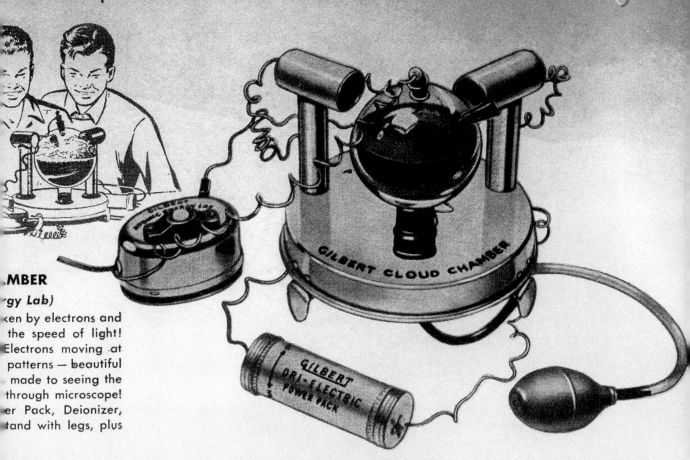

MBER

gy Lab)

ken by electrons and
the speed of light!
Electrons moving at
patterns — beautiful
made to seeing the
through microscope!
Pack, Deionizer,
tand with legs, plus

ERES

nergy Lab)

with these colored
arrangement of Pro-
up the Atom. Fasci-
instructions included.

For months Gilbert engineers worked with America's top Nuclear Physicists and instrument makers, in order to make the Atomic Energy Lab ACCURATE, SAFE and COMPLETE.

◄◄ A. C. Gilbert and Company, 1950

◄ Payton Products, 1958

Kusan, 1958

▶ Post Cereals, 1952

BOYS and GIRLS!

We've pictured all these Roy Rogers and Dale Evans things on these pages just so you can show Mom and Dad exactly what you want for Christmas. Look over each item carefully and then let the folks know which ones you like best. Each item is a guaranteed value and has been personally selected by Roy and Dale.

Roy Rogers Western Shirts

Handsomely tailored, two color with embroidery, slash pockets and wide, western cuffs... Sanforized, vat dyed broadcloth.

Both styles in assorted color combinations. Sizes 4-12... about $2.98

Made by Bob Roy
New York, N.Y.

Authentic Cowboy Boots

Long lasting, quality boots just like Roy Rogers and Dale Evans wear. Pictured is Roy's own Thunderbird design that he wears on TV...choice of several color combinations...$12.95

The Dale Evans Boot is available in red, blue or green. $9.95
Other Roy Rogers and Dale Evans boots. Choice of colors $9.95

Made by Ranger Boot Co., Terrell, Texas

Roy Rogers Trick Lasso for Young Cowhands

It now glows in the dark! For children 4 to 14 ...on sale at all leading stores 98¢

Also Roy Rogers Horse Shoe Pitching Set
A ten piece in-door, out-door all year 'round set made of hard rubber... $1.49

Made by Knox-Reese Mfg., Philadelphia, Penn.

Inflated Plastic "Trigger"

It's lots of fun riding this bouyant "Trigger"...in swimming or on the floor at home...he floats, rolls, bounces, whistles. Plenty sturdy, too... carries up to 175 pounds.

Collapsible —easy to pack... colors as illustrated. $2.00

Made by Dartmore Brooklyn, N.Y.

Gloves Make Great Gifts

Gauntlet Style Fabric Glove Roy and Trigger decal on leatherette cuff. Colors: Brown, Black, Green, Burgundy. Sizes: S, M, L....79¢ pr.

Gauntlet Grain Leather Glove Roy and Trigger decal on fringed leatherette cuff... lined or unlined. Colors: Black, Brown. Sizes: 5, 6, 7, 8 $1.95 pr.

Short Cuff Glove of high grade horsehide... RR metal signature and brand. Colors: Palomino, Chestnut, Black. Sizes: 5, 6, 7, 8... $2.95 pr.

Made by Illinois Glove Champaign, Ill.

Roy Rogers Rider Jeans

You fellows will really go for these Roy Rogers blue jeans styled for long hours in the saddle. Mother will go for the rugged wearing features and top quality materials. Sizes 4-12 about $2.49

Matching Rider Coat—a Roy Rogers authentic—full cut for real comfort— sizes 4-12 about $2.49

Made by Blue Ridge Lynchburg, Virginia

Ride High, Wide and Handsome

Satin Tie, metal cuff slide... about 69¢
Satin Kerchief with hand-screened design, about $1.00
Suedette Bolero—Red, Royal, Buff— sizes S, M, L...about $1.95

Made by Western Art Mfg. Co., Denver, Colo.

Authentic Roy Rogers Double Holster Sets

Exactly like Roy wears on TV and in movies. Topgrain cowhide with embossed hand-tooled effect—wooden bullets around the belt—RR name in embossed letters.

Another style holster set from Roy Rogers collection features criss-cross lacing around the belt and holsters. Double R-Bar Brand metal conchas decorate gun pockets.

Deluxe Double Holster Set complete with two simulated bone-handle guns. $10.95

Double Holster Set of topgrain cowhide, complete with two cross hatch handled guns. $7.95

Made by Classy Prod. New York, N.Y.

These and many more Roy Rogers and Dale Evans single and double holster sets from 98¢ up.

"Trigger"...the Buck-a-way Bronco

Sensational new hobby-horse that actually gallops across the room. Your small "Buckaroos" will love the realistic ride. Sturdily built—safe—with rubber tires to protect furniture. Folds compactly for storage.

24¼" high $13.98

Made by N. D. Cass Athol, Mass.

Western Style Sox

Roy Rogers spun cotton blazer socks— Nylon reinforced heel and toe, assorted colors. Sizes 6-10½

Dale Evans cuffed anklets—mercerized cotton. Sizes 5-8½, assorted colors, all white. 4 prs. to pkg. about $1.00

Made by Chester Roth New York, N.Y.

Roy and Dale "T" Shirts

Sturdy knit, reinforced shoulder seams, shape-retaining neck bands. "T" Shirts, sizes 2-12, about 69¢

Long-sleeved Sweatshirt sizes 2-12, about $1.39

Made by Norwich Norwich N.Y.

For Cowboys and

Colorful Roy R____ Dale Evans outfit____ resistant rayon ____ black, brown a____ copen and ____

Sizes: 2-____ $10.0____

Los Ange____

Roy Rogers Rodeo Game

Four games in one ... Bronc Busting • Trick Riding • Calf Roping • Bull Dogging... fast action, easy to play and understand.

2 to 4 contestants play at one time ... fun and excitement for the whole family. $1.50

Made by Rogden Chicago, Ill.

Roy Rogers Cowboy Band Set

Make music 'round the campfire with this set of not one or two, but six toy band instruments: clarinet, trombone, saxophone, clarion, banjo, leader's baton.

Play cowboy music outdoors—these instruments really blow, toot and strum. Complete set $2.00

Made by Spec-Top-Colors Brooklyn, N.Y.

Roy Rogers Tent

It's fun playing outdoors in your own Roy Rogers Tent. Big, roomy (69"x 69"), 5' center—4' walls. Mother and Dad will see the value, you'll have the fun.

Umbrella Tent in Desert Tan—$11.95
Roy Rogers Tepee in light green (4'6"x 4'6" on 5' pole) $7.35

Made by Hettrick Toledo, Ohio

For Wet Weather Wear

Roy Rogers waterproof boots... pullover style with full color action picture on leg of each boot. Youngsters' sizes 3-13 about $3.98
Childs' sizes 5-12 about $3.89
Roy Rogers Canvas Shoes for boys, youths about $3.59

Made by Conve___ Malden, Mass.

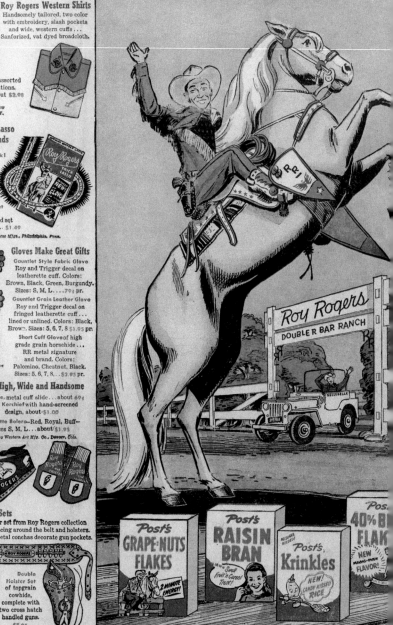

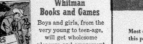

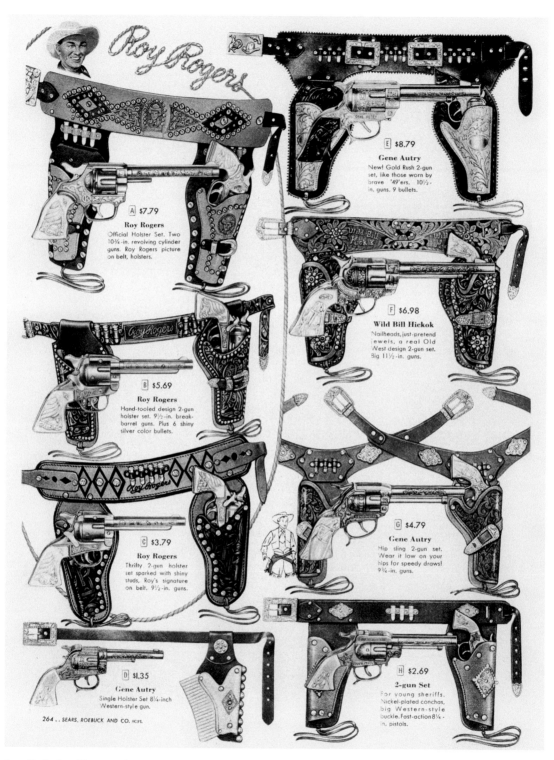

Roy Rogers

A $7.79
Roy Rogers
Official Holster Set. Two
10¾-in. revolving cylinder
guns. Roy Rogers picture
on belt, holsters.

B $5.69
Roy Rogers
Hand-tooled design 2-gun
holster set. 9½-in. break-
barrel guns. Plus 6 shiny
silver color bullets.

C $3.79
Roy Rogers
Thrifty 2-gun holster
set sparked with shiny
studs, Roy's signature
on belt. 9½-in. guns.

D $1.35
Gene Autry
Single Holster Set 8¼-inch
Western-style gun.

E $8.79
Gene Autry
New! Gold Rush 2-gun
set, like those worn by
brave '49'ers. 10½-
in. guns. 9 bullets.

F $6.98
Wild Bill Hickok
Nailheads, just-pretend
jewels, a real Old
West design 2-gun set.
Big 11½-in. guns.

G $4.79
Gene Autry
Hip sling 2-gun set.
Wear it low on your
hips for speedy draws!
9¾-in. guns.

H $2.69
2-gun Set
For young sheriffs.
Nickel-plated conchas,
big Western-style
buckle. Fast-action 8¼-
in. pistols.

264 .. SEARS, ROEBUCK AND CO. SCPL

Sears, Roebuck, and Company, 1955

► Sears, Roebuck, and Company, 1956

It's SEARS for the biggest roundup of Roy Rogers gifts

You'll find it's fun to shop for Roy's famous "Double-R-Bar" brand western-styled togs, toys and fixin's at Sears. There's a full corral of gifts—many pioneered by Roy and Sears together—with a *complete* selection of styles, colors and sizes, for your active young cowboys. For easy, one-stop western shopping, make Sears Stores or the Sears Christmas Catalog your Roy Rogers gift headquarters!

This Big Brother is mighty proud of his colorful Roy Rogers washable western shirt ($2.98), genuine felt hat with adjustable chin-cord ($1.98), and tailored cavalry twill frontier pants ($4.98). The official Roy Rogers double holster set ($6.98) with those comfortable "Double-R-Bar" Brand boots ($9.95), plus a sturdy 1-in. steerhide belt ($1.00) will make him the envy of all the neighborhood cowboys!

And the Young Bronco-Buster is set for any roundup in his truly western rodeo hat ($1.98), trim-fitting Roy Rogers flannel shirt ($2.98) and genuine suede leather jacket ($12.98). His tough denim jeans ($2.29) and Roy Rogers cowboy boots ($8.50) are built for rugged, bull-doggin' wear. And the 1-in. leather belt ($1.00), double holster set ($3.98), sturdy cowhide gloves ($1.98) are sure hits with this youngster.

SEARS ROEBUCK AND CO.

Buy your genuine Roy Rogers gifts at Sears Retail Stores, Sears Catalog Sales Offices, and through the Sears Christmas Catalog—also at Simpsons-Sears Limited in Canada. Prices in Canada will vary in some instances.

It's easy to buy at Sears . . .
Pay cash or enjoy the convenience of Sears *Easy Payment Plan* on purchases of $20 or more. Use Sears *Credit Purchase Coupon Books* like cash. Many Sears retail stores now offer Sears *Revolving Charge Accounts.*

Roy Rogers Watch for Boys—
$4.95 plus 10% excise tax

Dale Evans Watch for Girls—
$4.95 plus 10% excise tax

Roy Rogers "Double-R-Bar"
Ranch Set—$3.98

Roy Rogers Leather
Slippers—$2.98

Roy Rogers Knit
Pajamas—$2.49

SATISFACTION GUARANTEED OR YOUR MONEY BACK

ORIGINAL SLINKY $1.00

SLINKY SOLDIERS $2.00

SLINKY SEAL $1.00

SLINKY HANDCAR $2.00

SLINKY SPIRAL $1.00

SLINKY DOG $2.00

Insist on

Slinky® Toys

AT YOUR NEAREST TOY COUNTER

JAMES INDUSTRIES, PAOLI, PA.

SLINKY WORM   •   SLINKY TRAIN   •   SLINKY JUNIOR   •   SLINKY EYES   •   SLINKY BUCKO

◀ James Industries, 1957

Slinky inventor Richard James spent much of the 1940s spearheading a grassroots campaign to convince people how great his simple, unassuming toy was. By the 1950s, it was a national phenomenon, which led to a series of spin-off toys including the Slinky Dog, an idea submitted by Slinky fan Helen Malsed.

Richard James, der Erfinder des Slinky, verbrachte einen Großteil der 1940er-Jahre damit, die Menschen davon zu überzeugen, wie großartig sein verblüffend schlichtes Objekt war. In den 50ern wurde Slinky dann zu einem nationalen Phänomen und generierte eine ganze Reihe von Spin-off-Spielzeugen, darunter auch den Slinky Dog (eine Idee, die Slinky-Fan Helen Malsed eingereicht hatte).

Richard James, l'inventeur du Slinky, a passé une bonne partie des années 1940 à expliquer aux gens combien sa trouvaille, si simple, était géniale. Dix ans plus tard, son ressort est un phénomène national, qui connaît diverses déclinaisons dont le Slinky Dog, une idée soumise à James par Helen Malsed.

Silly Putty, 1958

▶ Remco, 1955

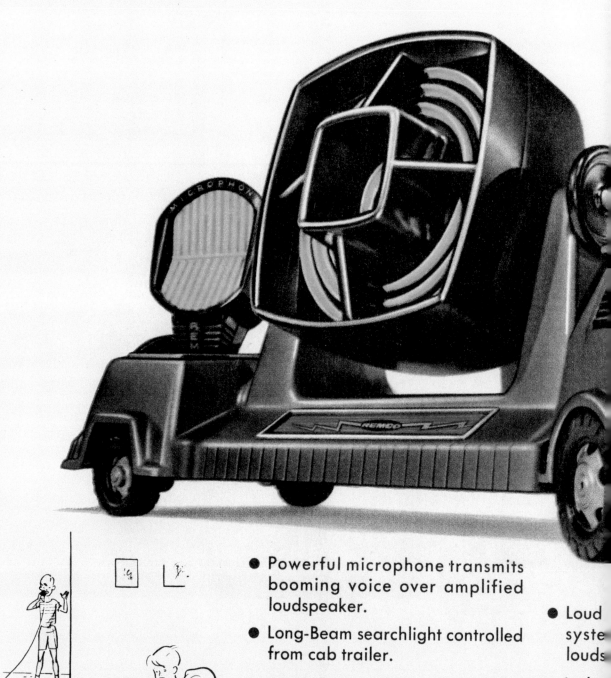

- Powerful microphone transmits booming voice over amplified loudspeaker.

- Long-Beam searchlight controlled from cab trailer.

- Big 2-foot trailer type 6-wheel mobile unit.

- Electronic switches . . . operates amplified signal system and re-volving searchlight beam from cab panel.

- Loud
  syste
  louds

- Inclu
  to op

REMCO INDUSTRIES Inc.

PERMANEN

MOBILE LOUDSPEAKER
and SIGNAL SYSTEM

-toned buzzer signal
. amplified through
r.

batteries, wire, ready

$9⁹⁵ retail

#104, 3 Color Corrugated Package
dual Display Pedestal with each unit
ig—4 to carton
ng Weight 16 lbs.

W ROOM: 200 5TH AVE., N. Y. C.

CTORY AND SALES: 113 N. 13TH ST., NEWARK, N. J.

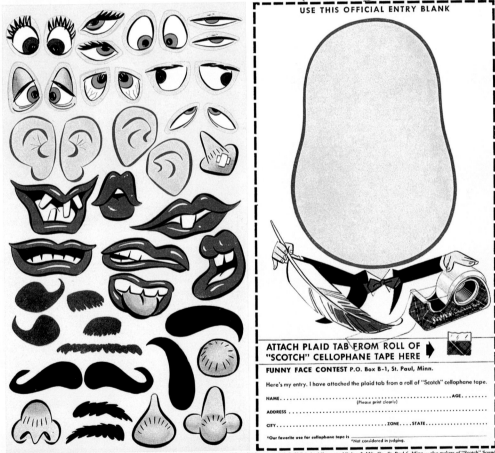

America's Favorite
GIANT INFLATED *PLAYMATES*

Doughboy

FORTI-PLYED

- FORTI-PLYED* VINYLITE PLASTICS
- GUARANTEED NON-LEAKING
- METAL VALVES
- HEAVY CONSTRUCTION
- TWO INFLATABLE RINGS
- MAINTENANCE KITS

FIVE WONDERFUL WADING POOLS

Right: Doughboy's Giant DeLuxe Pool. Gaily
decorated bottom. 7 ft. diameter,
250 gallon capacity ! . . . . . #1570
Above: DeLuxe Pool. 5½ ft., 125 gal. . #1555
Not Illustrated: DeLuxe Pool. Decorated
bottom. 4 ft. 50 gal. . . #1554
Also not illustrated, two pools without
decorated bottoms.
4 ft., 50 gal. . . . . . #1574
40 in., 30 gal. . . . . . #1573

Doughboy, 1950

CHAMP

There's a whole family of these sparring mates who take everything a youngster will give them and bounce back for more! BIG CHAMP is 50 inches high. Retail $5.00 (No. 1568). CHAMP is 40 inches high. Retail $3.50 (No. 1567). LITTLE CHAMP is 30 inches high. Retail $2.00 (No. 1566).

TRIGGER

Roy Rogers' horse TRIGGER is the pride and joy of all young buckaroos—a bronc that really bucks. 24 inches high and 34 inches long. Retail $3.00 (No. 1558). And there's his dekick BOUNCER for the smaller fry. 22 inches high 22 inches long at $2.00 (No. 1557)

Nosco's HOT'SEE HOT ROD

2 GREAT TOYS IN 1

Nosco's original Hot-See with hopped-up friction motor is two great toys in one. Clear plastic chassis permits full view of colorful moving parts in engine. Pistons move up and down, both fan and gears turn, crankshaft goes around, creating interesting action and great educational value. Body is easily removed by pulling out license tag.

Hot-See, the original, educational hot rod with "see-action" engine is bound for a great reception from parents. Children, fascinated by the colorful action of moving parts in engine, quickly learn the basic principles of an engine while having fun at the same time. The double play value of Hot-See attracts both roadster and hot rod enthusiasts . . . as a roadster, Hot-See is the sportiest car in the field . . . as a hot rod, it's a thunderbolt. Supercharge your toy department . . . order and display Hot-See, the new double-take hot rod that sparks sales and accelerates profits.

Catalog No. 6490-Hot-See in three-color protective package promotes profits. Send for Nosco's colorful 1951 catalog . . . your guide to greater toy sales.

Size: 10¼" long, 5" wide, 4¼" high.
Packed 1 dozen to carton. Wt. 17 lbs.
Terms: 2% 10 days, Net 30 days.
F.O.B., Erie, Pa.

Nosco PLASTICS ERIE, PA.

NEW YORK SHOWROOM: 200 FIFTH AVENUE
Address all correspondence to Erie, Pa.

$24. doz.

◀ Sound Spelling Company, 1951

Nosco Plastics, 1951

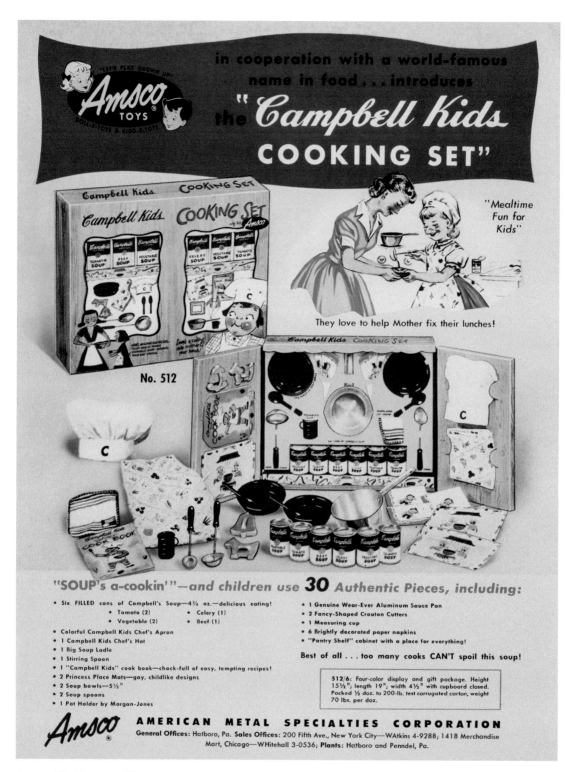

in cooperation with a world-famous
name in food . . . introduces
the "*Campbell Kids*
COOKING SET"

"Mealtime
Fun for
Kids"

They love to help Mother fix their lunches!

No. 512

"SOUP's a-cookin'"—and children use **30** Authentic Pieces, including:

- Six FILLED cans of Campbell's Soup—4¾ oz.—delicious eating!
  - Tomato (2)
  - Vegetable (2)
  - Celery (1)
  - Beef (1)
- Colorful Campbell Kids Chef's Apron
- 1 Campbell Kids Chef's Hat
- 1 Big Soup Ladle
- 1 Stirring Spoon
- 1 "Campbell Kids" cook book—chock-full of easy, tempting recipes!
- 2 Princess Place Mats—gay, childlike designs
- 2 Soup bowls—5½"
- 2 Soup spoons
- 1 Pot Holder by Morgan-Jones

- 1 Genuine Wear-Ever Aluminum Sauce Pan
- 2 Fancy-Shaped Crouton Cutters
- 1 Measuring cup
- 6 Brightly decorated paper napkins
- "Pantry Shelf" cabinet with a place for everything!

Best of all . . . too many cooks CAN'T spoil this soup!

512/6: Four-color display and gift package. Height
15½"; length 19"; width 4½" with cupboard closed.
Packed ½ doz. to 200-lb. test corrugated carton, weight
70 lbs. per doz.

Amsco® **AMERICAN METAL SPECIALTIES CORPORATION**
General Offices: Hatboro, Pa. Sales Offices: 200 Fifth Ave., New York City—WAtkins 4-9288; 1418 Merchandise
Mart, Chicago—WHitehall 3-0536; Plants: Hatboro and Penndel, Pa.

American Metal Specialties, 1954

▶ American Toy Fair, 1955

Helicopters for Industry, 1952

▶ Bell Products Company, 1955

THE NEW JET HELICOPTER

Hiller Hornet

NEW JET HELICOPTER

Complete Scale Model Kit

NEW

NEW

NOW BARBIE® GOES HIGH-FASHION...WITH WIGS!

New! Fashion Queen T.M. **Barbie** #870 *Retail Value: $6.00*

Now you can change her hair color and style as easily as you change her costume! She comes with a beautiful molded hair style and 3 high-fashion wigs—each a different style and color— with a wigstand that holds all 3! Styles are the latest in high-fashion...bubble cut, flip and page boy. There's one perfect for each occasion!

Barbie's Fashion Shop #817 *Retail Value: $7.50*

Her very own Fashion Shop...with a show window mannikin you can dress, a special display counter, curtained stage, dressing room, shelves for hats and bags, a rack for Barbie fashions and even a mirror and chairs for customers! It's easy to assemble, folds up neatly for storage!

Mattel, 1958

BASIC CHARMIN' CHATTY

Futuristic Products, 1953

▶ Nu-Age Products, 1953

Standard Toykraft Products, 1954

▶ Eldon Industries, 1958

THE NEW GAME FOR SIX

its here --- *Deluxe 6* COOTIE

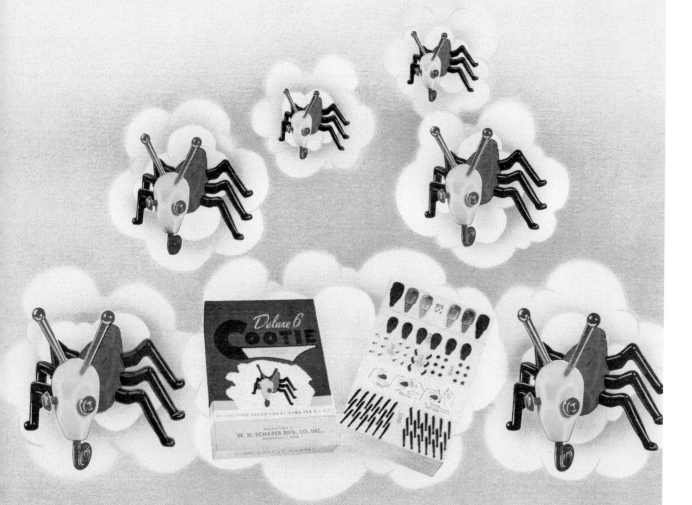

The arrival of the Deluxe "6" Cootie Game was to accommodate a demand for a Party Size Cootie Game. The set consists of six complete Cootie Bugs with a total of 78 gaily colored plastic parts.

Packaged in a beautifully designed box measuring 10" x 13" x 1¾"

FAIR TRADE PRICE
$3.00

PACKED 1 DOZEN
WEIGHT 12 LB.
F.O.B. MINNEAPOLIS

Manufacturers of the record breaking games . . . "Cootie" and "Stadium Checkers"

HIGHLANDER SALES COMPANY

DIVISION OF W. H. SCHAPER MFG. CO., INC.

MINNEAPOLIS 11, MINNESOTA

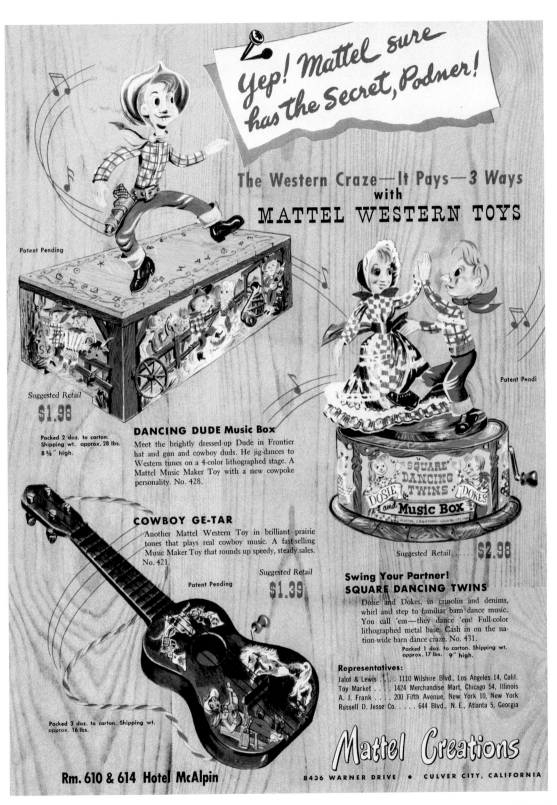

Yep! Mattel sure has the Secret, Podner!

The Western Craze—It Pays—3 Ways
with
MATTEL WESTERN TOYS

Patent Pending

Suggested Retail
$1.98

Packed 2 doz. to carton.
Shipping wt. approx. 28 lbs.
8 ⅜" high.

DANCING DUDE Music Box

Meet the brightly dressed-up Dude in Frontier
hat and gun and cowboy duds. He jig-dances to
Western tunes on a 4-color lithographed stage. A
Mattel Music Maker Toy with a new cowpoke
personality. No. 428.

COWBOY GE-TAR

Another Mattel Western Toy in brilliant prairie
tones that plays real cowboy music. A fast-selling
Music Maker Toy that rounds up speedy, steady sales.
No. 421.

Patent Pending

Suggested Retail
$1.39

Packed 3 doz. to carton. Shipping wt.
approx. 16 lbs.

Patent Pendi

SQUARE DANCING TWINS
DOSIE and DOKES
Music Box

Suggested Retail...... **$2.98**

Swing Your Partner!
SQUARE DANCING TWINS

Dosie and Dokes, in crinolin and denims,
whirl and step to familiar barn dance music.
You call 'em—they dance 'em! Full-color
lithographed metal base. Cash in on the nation-wide barn dance craze. No. 431.

Packed 1 doz. to carton. Shipping wt.
approx. 17 lbs.   9" high.

Representatives:
Jalof & Lewis . . . . 1110 Wilshire Blvd., Los Angeles 14, Calif.
Toy Market . . . 1424 Merchandise Mart, Chicago 54, Illinois
A. J. Frank . . . . 200 Fifth Avenue, New York 10, New York
Russell D. Jesse Co. . . . . 644 Blvd., N. E., Atlanta 5, Georgia

Mattel Creations

8436 WARNER DRIVE • CULVER CITY, CALIFORNIA

Rm. 610 & 614 Hotel McAlpin

◀ Highlander Sales Company, 1953

Mattel, 1950

Walco, 1953

► Hecht's, 1952

Hecht's

IT SPELLS!
IT SUBTRACTS!
IT MULTIPLIES!
IT DIVIDES!

IT TELLS TIME!
IT ADDS!

- Its a Desk
- Its a Peg Table
- Its a Blackboard
- Its a Hammering Set

CARPENTER BENCH, TOOLS, VISE

Little Mr. Fixit is all set with this sturdy maple finish wood bench outfit. With vise that really works, hammer, plane, tri-square, screw driver, chisel, saw, pliers, ruler, sandpaper, nails. 24 x 24½ x 12".

4.98
Add 55c for shipping

Plane
Square
Saw
Pliers
Chisel
Screw Driver
Nails
Sand Paper

Open Monday
Dec. 1st till 9
Open Every
Night, Dec. 4th
thru Dec. 23rd
till 9

99-PC. 5-in-1 KINDERGARTEN SET

Pop a picture or problem in the frame—"Answer Master" spells or solves it. And for tiny tots—blackboard with chalk, eraser . . . 154-hole peg-board, pegs, mallet . . . hammering board, nails, artwood pieces. Hardwood seat.

4.98
Add 55c for shipping

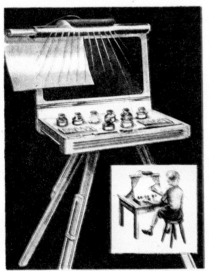

BLACKBOARD & PAINT SET

3-in-1 marvel! Paint outfit with 5 poster paints, palette, brush. Crayon set with paper, snipper. Blackboard with chalk, eraser. Adjustable hardwood easel, 18 x 16 x 48" with light.

4.98
Add 40c for shipping

NURSE UNIFORM & KIT

18 pieces in all! Blue cape, white skirt, durable plastic cap. Black bag with plastic equipment including hot water bottle, wrist watch, eye-ear tester, hypodermic, many more pieces.

2.98
Add 35c for shipping

Doctor Kit & Uniform (inset) 2.98

Also at
Abramson's
another Hecht Co store
Main St at 37th Ave
Flushing, L. I.

De Luxe

1 BOWLING ALLEY   2 SKILL BALL
3 HORSE RACING   4 SHUFFLE BOARD

4-in-1 GIANT-SIZE ALLEY

Bowling, skillball, horse racing, shuffleboard! 52" long strong wood alley, 10 bowling pins, 2 bowling balls, shuffleboard pucks, 4 horses, number spinner.

4.98
Express Collect

"JINGLES" CHIMES
as tots ride this cow pony

Add 40c for shipping **2.98**

Handsome colorful horse of solid wood with strong steel wheels—holds over 200 lbs. Wheels and reins jingle musically as this action toy swoops about indoors and out.

CALL SUNDAY 10 a.m. to 4 p.m. ORegon 5-1000

Come in, Mail Coupon or Phone ORegon 5-1000, Ext. 111

HECHT'S, 55 West 14th St., New York 11, N. Y.

Mail and phone orders filled for 3.01 or more, exclusive of tax. On mail orders, delivery within 2 weeks. Add 3% sales tax for delivery in New York City. On all orders beyond our regular 50-mile delivery area, add shipping charges as noted. On C.O.D. orders, postage and C.O.D. fees collected on delivery. (Send check or money order and save C.O.D. fees.)

Item	Quantity	Price

Print Full Name

Address _____ Apt. _____

City _____ Zone ____ State _____

☐ Check or M.O.   ☐ C.O.D.   Add to My Hecht Account No. _____

MC (71)11-30-52

HECHT'S, 14th St. at 6th Ave., New York 11, N. Y.

Pla-master Play Suits, c. 1955

▶ L. M. Eddy Manufacturing Company, 1955

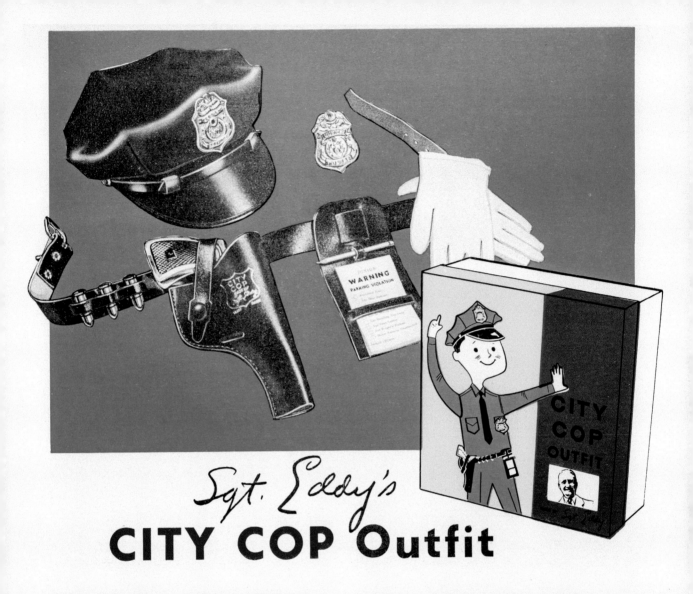

Sgt. Eddy's
CITY COP Outfit

◄ Popsicle, 1952

Jetrail Company, 1956

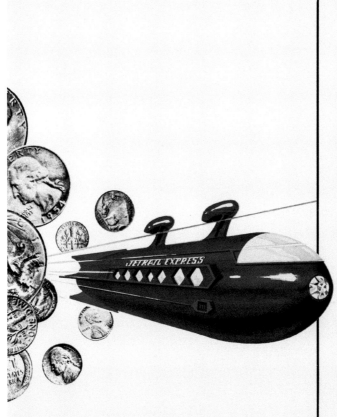

JETRAIL EXPRESS FOR '56!

*Improved design . . .
Exciting new package . . .
Sure-fire sales appeal!*

BATTERY-POWERED . . . attains
scale speeds exceeding 200 MPH

COMPLETELY SAFE . . . no
dangerous electrical connections

SIMPLE CONTROL TOWER . . .
selects fast, slow, and stop

EASILY ASSEMBLED . . . operated
without adult assistance

DURABLE BODY OF HIGH
IMPACT STYRENE

TOPS FOR OUTDOOR PLAY

HIGH VALUE—LOW PRICED FUN

THE TOY MONORAIL
ELECTRIC TRAIN OF TOMORROW

*Double Fun With
Electric Train*

*Fun Outdoors . . .
Easy to Assemble*

*Futuramic Model
Monorail System*

JETRAIL CO.
*1525 Monterey Road,
South Pasadena, California
Phone: PYramid 1-1181*

A SUBSIDIARY OF PHILLIPS AVIATION CO.

Building with BLOCK CITY *
is real family fun... *Through the years!*

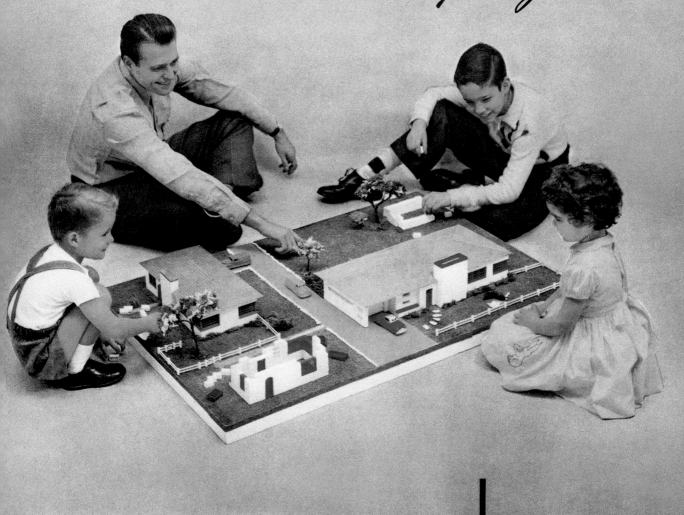

For children, 5 years and up . . . there's nothing like Block City. These stimulating scale model construction toys hold the whole family's interest . . . day after day. They constantly challenge the imagination to create new shapes, new ideas, new ways of self-expression. In the hands of the first grader, the interlocking blocks become a fairy tale tower. With the same molded plastic parts the teen-ager builds a space city on the moon. Block City is for every member of the family . . . and the whole family will love it! 4 BIG SETS — $2.95 TO $15.00.

TRI STATE TOYS

PLASTIC BLOCK CITY, INC.
4225 W. Lake Street, Chicago 24, Illinois • Van Buren 6-6637
NEW YORK: 12 E. 41st Street — MUrray Hill 3-8743

COMMENDED BY THE CONSUMER SERVICE BUREAU OF PARENTS' MAGAZINE AS ADVERTISED THEREIN

*Trade Mark

◀ Plastic Block City, 1955

Remco, 1955

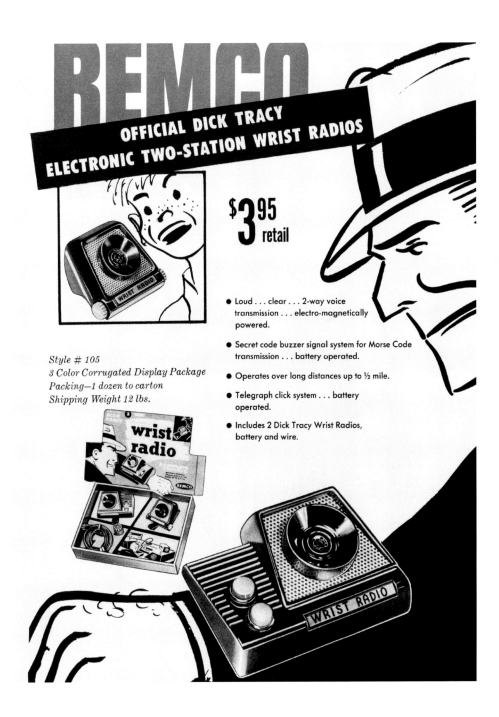

REMCO

OFFICIAL DICK TRACY
ELECTRONIC TWO-STATION WRIST RADIOS

$3⁹⁵ retail

Style # 105
3 Color Corrugated Display Package
Packing—1 dozen to carton
Shipping Weight 12 lbs.

- Loud . . . clear . . . 2-way voice transmission . . . electro-magnetically powered.

- Secret code buzzer signal system for Morse Code transmission . . . battery operated.

- Operates over long distances up to ½ mile.

- Telegraph click system . . . battery operated.

- Includes 2 Dick Tracy Wrist Radios, battery and wire.

Comet Model Hobbycraft, 1959

▶ Ny-Lint Toys, 1958

◄ Knickerbocker Toy Company, 1955

J. Halpern Company, 1959

► Lionel, 1961

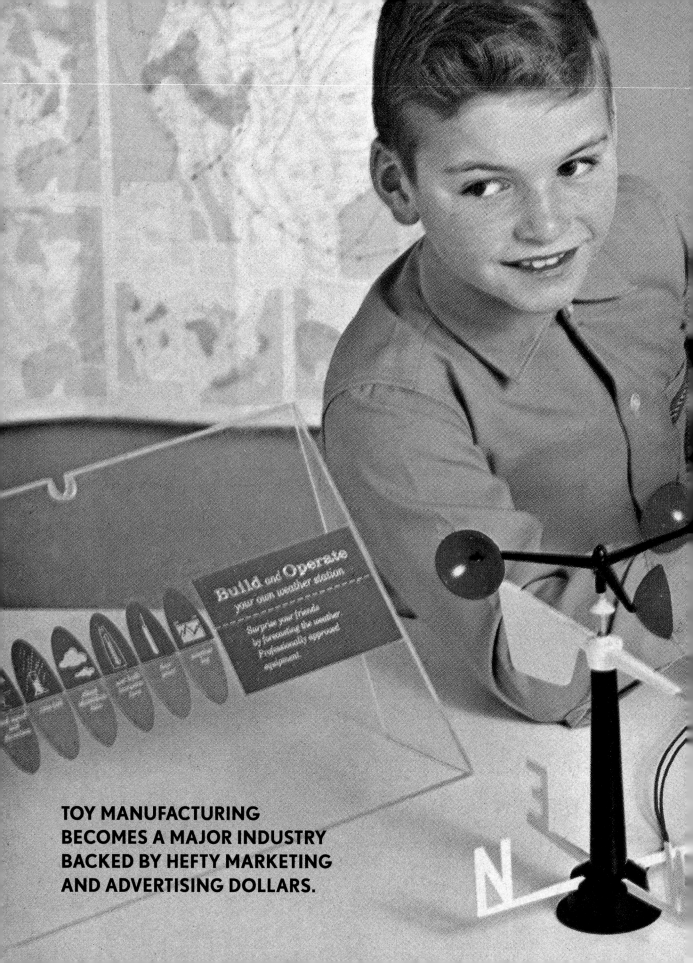

Build and Operate
your own weather station

Surprise your friends
by forecasting the weather.
Professionally approved
equipment.

**TOY MANUFACTURING
BECOMES A MAJOR INDUSTRY
BACKED BY HEFTY MARKETING
AND ADVERTISING DOLLARS.**

1960s

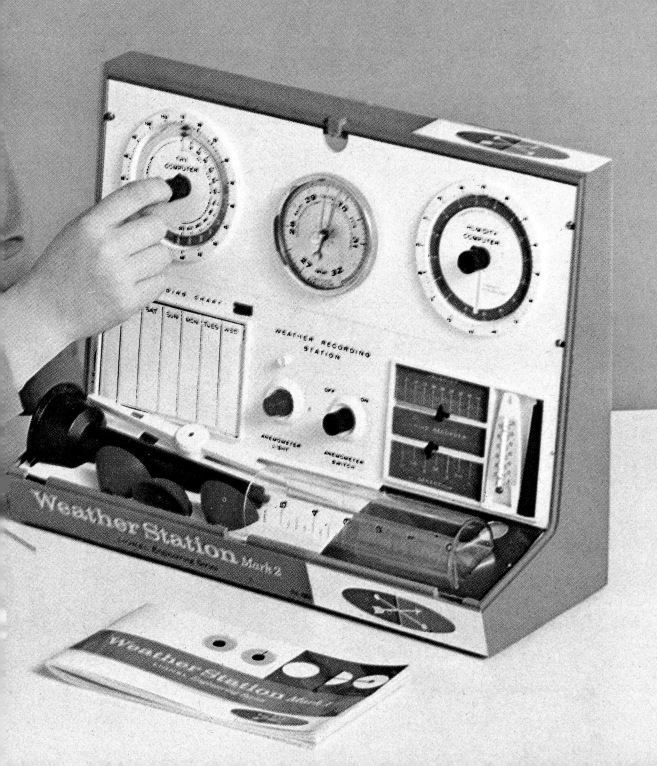

UNGAR 1960

TOY ADS GROW UP

IN THE 1960S TOY ADVERTISEMENTS WERE NO LONGER MERELY KID STUFF. Instead of being passed off to junior creatives at ad agencies, many brands were acknowledged as important media buys and were written and art-directed by veteran creative teams with high levels of imagination and an ability to understand nuance. For the top-of-the-line ads, the actual toys were also more sophisticated in terms of their designs and interactive attributes. Pull the string on Chatty Cathy's back and she repeats one of 11 different phrases, including the hauntingly mechanical, "I love you." The Ken doll, introduced two years after Barbie, was a fully operational (minus a key private part) male companion for the popular doll. And what girl did not want to fix a treat for her own Ken? So, anticipating real romances on the horizon, the Easy-Bake Oven and Suzy Homemaker made edible goodies

1960

1961

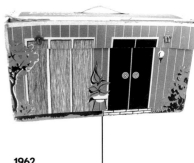

1962

Ohio Art Company releases French invention Etch A Sketch; draws big bucks

Die Ohio Art Company landete mit der Zaubertafel Etch A Sketch, einer französischen Idee, einen Hit

La Ohio Art Company édite Etch A Sketch, l'écran magique inventé en France

Barbie gets a boyfriend, Ken, whom she "met on the set of a commercial"

Barbie lernt ihren Freund Ken „beim Dreh für einen Werbespot" kennen

Barbie a un petit ami, Ken, qu'elle a rencontré « sur le tournage d'une publicité »

Barbie moves into her first Dream House, a one-bedroom made of cardboard

Barbie zieht in ihr erstes Traumhaus ein: ein Einzimmerhaus aus Pappe

Barbie emménage dans sa première Maison de rêve, un deux-pièces en carton to show domestic prowess. For boys and girls, a "toy that makes toys"—the Mattel Thingmaker—was a clever item. And while Ken was courting Barbie, and little girls were learning to bake, G.I. Joe, the masculine equivalent of the feminine role models, was making the world safe for democracy.

Among the hottest toys of the decade, Mattel's 1968 Hot Wheels gave kids the opportunity to approximate the horsepower of such American sports cars as the Camaro, Corvette, Firebird, and Mustang. In fact, to boost its appeal to future consumers, Ford automobile dealers offered a specially priced $12.95 Midget Mustang for children at Christmastime. However, for almost half that price, a "General Sherman" Tank large enough to fit two kids inside was available for the youthful cold warrior. Cheerful Tearful was a doll that cried real tears and smiled, too. Then there was Swingy, the doll that danced to her heart's content. And to show that the toy field did not ignore racial diversity, Mattel produced an African American talking doll. Both Fisher-Price's and Mattel's advertising designs were just as creative as any adult-oriented magazine ads—well photographed

1963

Inspired by New York City pretzel vendors, the Easy-Bake Oven debuts

Der von New Yorker Brezelverkäufern inspirierte Easy-Bake Oven gibt sein Debüt

Inspiré par les vendeurs de bretzels de New York, le four Easy-Bake apparaît

1964

Kids knock their blocks off with Rock'em Sock'em Robots

Kids bauen mit den Robotern des Spiels Rock'em Sock'em Aggressionen ab

Des gosses s'affrontent sur le ring avec leurs robots rouges et bleus Rock'em Sock'em

1964

College student John Spinello invents Operation and sells it to Milton Bradley for $500

Student John Spinello erfindet Doktor Bibber und verkauft es für 500 US-Dollar an Milton Bradley

L'étudiant John Spinello invente le Docteur Maboul et le vend à Milton Bradley pour 500 dollars with smart typography and witty copy. One of Mattel's most striking ads showed four frames of a child working on an all-purpose sawing, sanding, and milling machine followed by a fifth photo of the boy holding up his unscathed hands—the headline read: "Mattel's new toy Power Shop saws and burns and sands real wood (But it doesn't cut real fingers)." Lego building sets were hitting their stride with forts, suburban houses, boats, cars, and trains, among other proto-pixelated options. This was the decade of the racing bicycle: "Sears went to the drag races and came back with a new kind of bike," while Schwinn offered "the ride of a lifetime": a 10-speed Continental. In the realm of car, plane, and boat plastic model kits, Revell was king. And for children who were hooked on dress-up, Sears offered an extensive line of cowboy, spaceman, nurse, and military-themed apparel.

1964

Reyn Guyer creates Twister, then called Pretzel, as shoe polish promotion

Reyn Guyer kreiert Twister (damals noch Pretzel genannt) als PR für Schuhcreme

Reyn Guyer crée le Twister, appelé Pretzel à l'origine, pour vendre du cirage

1965

Barrel of Monkeys is released by Lakeside Toys

Barrel of Monkeys von Lakeside Toys erscheint

Lakeside Toys lance le jeu d'adresse Barrel of Monkeys

1965

The Super Ball drops

Der Flummi titscht auf

La Super Balle fait son premier rebond

DIE SPIELZEUGWERBUNG WIRD ERWACHSEN

Die Produktion von Spielwaren wird zu einem führenden Industriezweig, der sehr viel Geld für Marketing und Werbung ausgibt.

In den 1960er-Jahren war die Spielzeugwerbung längst kein Kinderkram mehr. Anstatt die Kunden aus dieser Sparte den jüngeren Mitarbeitern zu überlassen, betrachteten die Werbeagenturen die Bewerbung vieler Marken nun als lukrative Aufträge, die von erfahrenen Teams mit viel Fantasie und einem Gespür für Nuancen getextet und visualisiert wurden. Die Spielwaren selbst waren, zumindest am oberen Ende der Skala, im Hinblick auf Design und interaktive Attribute nun ebenfalls hochwertiger und raffinierter. Wenn man zum Beispiel an der Schnur in Chatty Cathys Rücken zog, gab sie eine von elf Phrasen zum Besten, darunter auch ein gruselig roboterhaftes „I love you". Die Ken-Figur, die zwei Jahre nach Barbie eingeführt wurde, war ein (von einem entscheidenden männlichen Körperteil abgesehen) voll funktionsfähiger Gefährte für die beliebte Puppe. Und welches Mädchen will nicht für ihren Ken etwas Leckeres kochen? Um kleine Mädchen auf die zukünftige Liebe im wahren Leben vorzubereiten, brachte die Spielzeugindustrie den Easy-Bake Oven und Suzy Homemaker auf den Markt, in denen man richtig backen konnte. Der Mattel Thingmaker – „ein Spielzeug, das Spielzeuge macht" – war für Mädchen und Jungs eine clevere Erfindung. Und während Ken Barbie den Hof machte und kleine Mädchen backen lernten, kämpfte G. I. Joe, die Plastik gewordene Identifikationsfigur für Jungs, für eine gerechte, demokratische Welt.

Zu den begehrtesten Spielzeugen der Dekade gehörten Mattels Hot Wheels von 1968, mit denen schon Minderjährige zu stolzen Besitzern von amerikanischen Sportwagen wie Camaro, Corvette, Firebird und Mustang wurden. Um zukünftige Kunden heranzuziehen, boten Fordhändler zu Weihnachten einen Midget Mustang für schlappe 12,95 Dollar an. Für angehende Kalte Krieger gab es für nur die Hälfte dieses Preises den „General Sherman" – einen Panzer, in dem zwei Kinder Platz fanden. Cheerful Tearful hieß eine Puppe, die echte Tränen vergoss (aber auch lächeln konnte). Dann gab es noch Swingy, die Puppe, die für ihr Leben gern tanzte. Und um auch afroamerikanische Kunden zu ködern, produzierte Mattel eine schwarze Sprechpuppe. Die Werbeanzeigen von Fisher-Price und Mattel waren zu dieser Zeit genauso kreativ wie die Anzeigen für Erwachsenenprodukte – gut fotografiert mit ansprechender Typografie und witzigen Texten. In einer von Mattels auffälligsten Anzeigen waren vier Fotos zu sehen, auf denen ein Junge mit einer Allzweck-Maschine etwas sägt, schmirgelt und fräst, gefolgt von einem fünften Bild, auf dem er seine unversehrten Hände hochhält – die Headline dazu lautete: „Mattels neuer Spielzeug-Power-Shop sägt und flämmt und schmirgelt echtes Holz. (Aber er schneidet keine echten Finger)." Die Bausätze von Lego erklommen in Form von Forts, Einfamilienhäusern, Schiffen, Autos und Zügen neue Bauklötzchenhöhen. Dies war außerdem die Ära des Rennrads: „Sears war beim Dragsterrennen und kam mit einem neuen Fahrradmodell zurück", während Schwinn „das beste Gefährt überhaupt" versprach: ein Continental mit Zehn-Gang-Schaltung. In Sachen Modellbausätze für Autos, Flugzeuge und Schiffe war Revell der Branchenprimus. Und für Kinder, die sich gern verkleideten, bot Sears eine umfangreiche Kollektion an Cowboy-, Astronauten-, Krankenschwester- und militärischen Kostümen an.

▶ Naugahyde, c. 1967

The Nauga is ugly,

This is the Nauga, and he is the greatest. Once a year he sheds his hide for the good of mankind. His hide, happily, is Naugahyde* vinyl fabric. Naugahyde: the prettiest, toughest, most versatile fabric known to man.

It can look like anything. Rich silk. Rough tweed. Shiny plastic. Brocade. Burlap! *Bamboo*, for heaven's sake. Any fabric man has made, Naugahyde can duplicate. (And it lasts about ten times as long.)

One problem. Certain careless, or indiscriminate salespeople think vinyl is vinyl. Uh uh. Don't fall for it. Just-any-old-vinyl is not the same as Naugahyde. We know it, and a few months after you buy it you'll know it, too.

So look for the imaginary Nauga's picture. It hangs on every piece of furniture made with real Naugahyde. If you can't find the Nauga, find another store.

Remember: the Nauga is ugly, but his vinyl hide is beautiful.

*Naugahyde is Uniroyal's registered trademark for its vinyl upholstery fabric.

LA PUB POUR LE JOUET GRANDIT

Le jouet devient une industrie de poids, soutenue par des investissements massifs dans le marketing et les campagnes de publicité.

Dans les années 1960 la publicité pour les jouets n'est plus un truc de gosses. Au lieu d'être laissés aux créatifs junior et aux petites agences, les budgets des grosses marques du secteur sont considérés comme de précieuses prises et souvent confiés à des auteurs et des directeurs artistiques vétérans de la communication promotionnelle dotés d'une imagination fertile et d'un sens aigu de la nuance. Les encarts et réclames haut de gamme promeuvent les produits les plus sophistiqués en termes de design et d'interactivité. Tire sur la cordelette dans le dos de Chatty Cathy et elle prononce une des onze phrases préenregistrées, parmi lesquelles un lancinant « I love you ». La poupée Ken, lancée deux ans après Barbie, est un compagnon parfait (à un petit détail anatomique près) pour la populaire poupée mannequin. Et quelle fille ne veut pas préparer de bons petits plats à son chéri ? Histoire d'anticiper les joies matrimoniales à venir, le four Easy-Bake et le Suzy Homemaker permettent aux filles d'exercer leurs talents culinaires « pour de vrai ». Au rayon unisexe, le Thingmaker de Mattel, « le jouet qui fabrique des jouets », est un choix malin. Pendant que Ken courtise Barbie et que les filles apprennent la pâtisserie, G.I. Joe, le modèle masculin proposé aux garçons, veille à sauvegarder la démocratie.

Parmi les jouets qui font fureur dans les années 1960, les voitures Hot Wheels que Mattel sort en 1968 permettent aux gamins de toucher du doigt la puissance de légendaires bolides américains comme la Camaro, la Corvette, la Firebird ou la Mustang. À Noël, les concessionnaires Ford proposent d'ailleurs pour les enfants une réplique miniature de la Mustang à un prix spécial de 12,95 dollars, histoire de s'attirer les faveurs de futurs clients. Cependant, pour deux fois moins cher, les petits soldats de la guerre froide pouvaient avoir un tank « General Sherman » assez grand pour y tenir à deux. La poupée Cheerful Tearful pleure de vraies larmes mais sourit aussi, Swingy danse à en perdre haleine et pour montrer que l'industrie du jouet n'ignore pas la diversité raciale, Mattel lance une poupée parlante afro-américaine. Les publicités de Fisher-Price et de Mattel sont aussi créatives que les campagnes magazine destinées aux adultes – bien photographiées, avec une typo maline et un texte ciselé. Une des pubs les plus spirituelles de Mattel montre quatre images d'un garçon qui manipule un outil à tout faire, suivies d'une cinquième image où le petit bricoleur montre ses mains intactes sous le slogan : « Le nouveau Power Shop de Mattel scie, brûle et ponce le vrai bois (mais ne coupe pas les vrais doigts) ». Les jeux de construction Lego atteignent leur rythme de croisière avec des forts, des pavillons de banlieue, des bateaux, des voitures et des trains, entre autres créations protopixelaires. C'est aussi la décennie du vélo de course : « Sears a assisté à une course de vitesse et vous a rapporté un nouveau genre de vélo », quand Schwinn promet « la balade d'une vie » sur son Continental à dix vitesses. Revell règne en maître sur le marché des maquettes de voiture, d'avion ou de bateau en plastique. Et pour les enfants qui aiment se déguiser, Sears dispose d'une vaste collection de costumes de cow-boy, d'astronaute, d'infirmière ou de soldat.

◀ E. S. Lowe Company, 1963

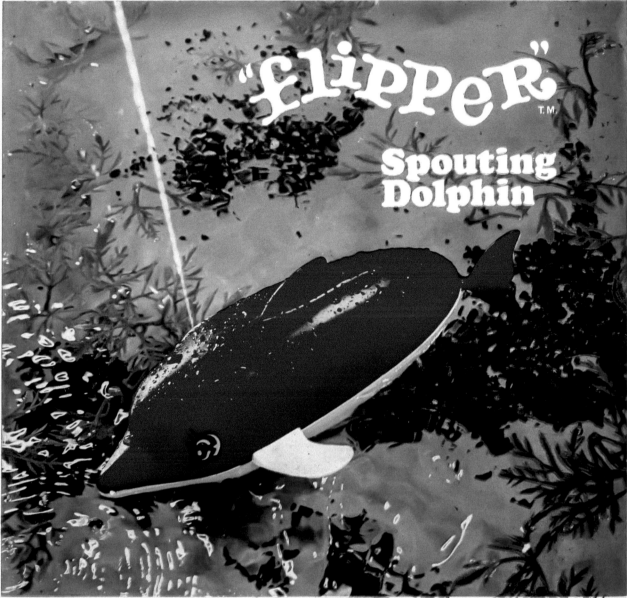

C'MON ALONG...
be a MASTER MODELER, too!

Here's a great new club and you can join up just by building a model! It's called the Master Modelers Club and it's sponsored by Revell, the people who make those authentic Master Modelers hobby kits. It's the kind of club you always wanted because it makes you a real hobby kit expert and even helps you show off your proud collection of models!

It's so easy to join, too. Just walk in to your favorite hobby kit store and ask.

JOIN THE GREAT NEW MASTER MODELERS CLUB TODAY!
You can get an official application inside Master Modelers kits at your nearby Hobby Kit store.

Look what MASTER MODELERS get!

An official, engraved Master Modelers certificate for your wall!

A handsome, personalized Membership Card for your wallet!

Your copy of the Master Modelers Magazine!

A Master Modelers Stamp Album to collect Revell "action" stamps!

...and, to top it off, you even get a chance to qualify as a Revell Design Consultant and plan new hobby kits!

® Revell
Authentic Kits

Gift idea from Texaco–for now, for Christmas!

Big, authentic scale-model service station!

Special Price $350

- Made of rugged plastic, with 18" x 24" metal base • model car • overhead lube bay doors that open and close • car lift that raises and lowers • two pump islands with light poles • two Texaco signs • oil display cabinet • Havoline and PT Anti-Freeze display cans • tire rack with miniature tires • other station equipment.

A delight for any youngster! Order now. Lay it away for Christmas. This toy Texaco Service Station is custom-made by "Buddy-L" — makers of the famous toy Texaco Tank Truck. It will be delivered to your door for the special price of $3.50. Here's all you do. Just drive in to your nearby Texaco Dealer. *Ask for a free coupon.* Mail coupon with check or money order. It's that easy to get this exclusive Texaco Dealer offer — good only in the U.S.A. *Is your car ready for colder-weather driving? When you come in for a coupon, get a Texaco Fall Safe-T check-up!*

Order now...lay away for Christmas. See your Texaco Dealer.

I love you

What could be more fun than a talking doll?

Hardly anything. Because Chatty Cathy® *really* talks! It's true. Just pull the Magic Ring and she might say "Let's play school"...or "May I have a cookie?" ...or perhaps "I love you." Chatty Cathy says 11 different things, and the fascinating part is you never know what she'll say next! Your daughter will love Chatty Cathy, because she can actually converse with her. What's more, Chatty Cathy's life-like rooted hair can be brushed and arranged in different styles. And she has a wonderfully varied collection of beautifully made costume sets to choose from, each perfectly made down to the smallest detail.

For that special gift for that very special little girl...get her Chatty Cathy. She's the most talked about...and talkative doll of the year. You'll find Chatty Cathy wherever toys are sold.

® & © 1962 Mattel, Inc.

Mattel, 1962

Chatty Cathy was one of Mattel's most popular dolls in the 1960s — second only behind Barbie — due to the toy's inventive speaking mechanism, which allowed it to utter phrases like, "I love you." The voice of the early dolls belongs to actress June Foray, who also lent her voice to *The Rocky and Bullwinkle Show*.

Chatty Cathy war in den 1960ern dank eines originellen Sprechmechanismus, mit dem sie Phrasen wie „I love you" sagen konnte, eine von Mattels beliebtesten Puppen – gleich hinter Barbie. Den frühen Puppen lieh Schauspielerin June Foray, die auch in der Comicserie The *Rocky and Bullwinkle Show* zu hören war, ihre Stimme.

Chatty Cathy est une des poupées les plus populaires de Mattel dans les années 1960, juste derrière Barbie, grâce au mécanisme qui lui permet de dire des phrases comme « Je t'aime ». La voix des premières poupées est celle de l'actrice June Foray, qui prête aussi sa voix au *Rocky and Bullwinkle Show*.

▶ Mattel, 1965

Mommy, in the olden days, did you have a Barbie Doll?

Mommy, how do you make a pin curl?

Mommy, do blue shoes go with a green dress?

She'll really learn from you. But Barbie will help. Watch your little girl put together Barbie's Sew-Free costume. Dress Barbie. Style Barbie's Color 'n Curl Fashion Wig.

Dream of tomorrow. It's rewarding for her—and you. No wonder millions of Mommies and little girls all over America and in 30 foreign countries share the delight of Barbie.

"SEW-FREE FASHION FUN" is the trademark of Mattel, Inc. for its DOLL CLOTHES ready to make without sewing. "BARBIE" is the registered trademark of Mattel, Inc. for its TEENAGE DOLL. © 1965 Mattel, Inc

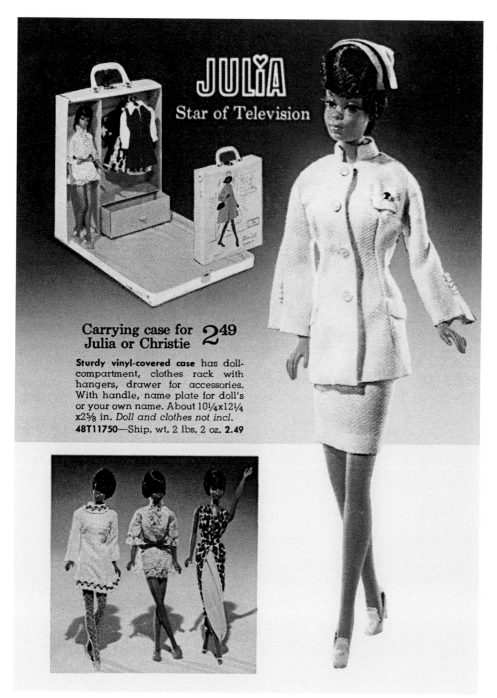

JULIA
Star of Television

Carrying case for 2^{49}
Julia or Christie

Sturdy vinyl-covered case has doll-compartment, clothes rack with hangers, drawer for accessories. With handle, name plate for doll's or your own name. About 10¼x12¼ x2⅝ in. *Doll and clothes not incl.* 48T11750—Ship. wt. 2 lbs. 2 oz. **2.49**

Savannah Productions, 1969

► Revell, 1967

Bring home all the kicks of racing this Christmas with a Revell race set

Revell Rebel "400" Banked Raceway

There's no greater gift for a boy...a car he can race on his own. He'll really race his motor when you bring home a Revell raceway. Especially if he's at that impatient age: Old enough to want a car, but too young to drive one.

He'll get all the thrills of the real thing. He can slam through curves, weave through chicanes, brake hard for turns, go flat out down the straightaway...and really roar around Revell's new banked track! On these steep banked turns, he can hit scale speeds of up to 220 miles an hour. He can race the hot cars, too, like the Mustang 2 + 2, Camaro SS 350,

Ferrari Squalo 555 and Chaparral II. Revell home raceway sets are built to take it...from rugged power packs and controllers, to track that's made to be stepped on. Many have lap counters, so you always know who's winning. All the parts are interchangeable...just keep adding pieces for more and more elaborate layouts. Bring home a Revell. Years from now, he'll still be getting all the kicks of racing at home. So will you. Ten sets to choose from, starting at less than $30.00. Send for free race set catalog to Revell, Inc., 4201 Glencoe Avenue, Venice, California 90292.

Revell

The midnight ride of Paul McBride

It was late and the house slept. Quietly Paul McBride slipped down the stairs where his Wonder Horse waited. His Wonder Horse, gleaming and poised, ready to take him miles in his imagination.

After a ride on the wide open range, a rodeo, a round-up, he'll slip into bed content and smiling. And so to sleep young man . . . to dream about the treasured world of Wonder Horse.

Don't you think your little boy or girl should have a Wonder Horse this Christmas? The sturdy spring frame Wonder Horse is ready to give hours of healthful fun . . . day in and day out, year after year. Wonder Horses are made of long-lasting plastic or soft vinyl that feels like a real pony's coat. And these magnificent horses cost so little . . . give so much fun.

There is a Wonder Horse for every child . . . for every child's imagination. Start your six-month-old (your youngest buckaroo) on the Shoo-Fly, a lively newcomer to the Wonder stables.

Any horse won't do. You must ask for Wonder Horse—at all fine toy and department stores.

Wonder Products from $4.95 to $34.95

 WONDER HORSE® ...A TREASURED PART OF A HAPPY CHILDHOOD

◄ Wonder Products Company, 1966

The Wonder Horse was invented in the late '40s in Arkansas, then known as "the Wonder State." In 1966, the toy was positioned as an essential part of childhood – "Any horse won't do. You must ask for a Wonder Horse" – which transports young buckaroos to the open range, in a quintessentially American ideal.

Das Wonder Horse wurde in den späten 1940ern in Arkansas (damals als „the Wonder State" bekannt) erfunden. 1966 propagierte die Werbung das Schaukelpferd als wesentlichen Bestandteil der Kindheit, um kleine Cowboys in die Prärie, die ultimative amerikanische Landschaft, zu versetzen. Der Slogan dazu: „Begnüge dich nicht mit irgendeinem x-beliebigen Pferd, sondern verlange das Wonder Horse".

Le Wonder Horse a été inventé à la fin des années 1940 dans l'Arkansas, alors surnommé le « Wonder State ». En 1966, il est devenu un morceau d'enfance – « Pas n'importe quel cheval. C'est le Wonder Horse qu'il faut demander » – qui transporte les petits cow-boys dans les vastes plaines du rêve américain.

Mattel, 1965

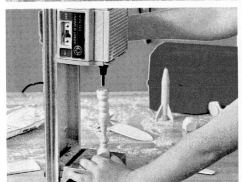 

Mattel's new Toy Power Shop saws and turns and drills and sands real wood.

(But it doesn't cut real fingers!)

Sound incredible? It *is* incredible! Mattel's amazing Power Shop is actually *four* wood-working tools in one! And every one of them is safe enough for a 6-year-old – and tough enough for a 12-year-old!

First of all, the Power Shop is a jig saw with an incredible blade that has no teeth. (Instead, the blade is shaped in a spiral that cuts through wood as hard as pine – but is super-safe for young fingers.) Second, it's a lathe with a safety handle that can't fly off. Third, it turns into a drill press. And fourth, a disc sander!

What's more, the Mattel Power Shop is made of sturdy metal. It runs on regular house current – not batteries. And it works with real wood. So youngsters can make things really *worth* making – like sturdy toys, pipe

racks for Dad, note pad holders.

Everything's included to get your would-be craftsman going: plenty of wood, instructions, patterns, blades, glue, tool bits, drills – over 40 pieces in all. And the Power Shop comes with its own rugged tool box, complete with storage compartments.

In short: here's the kind of constructive, *creative* toy you want for a boy. The kind you can always count on from Mattel.

Surprise your youngster with Mattel's new Power Shop. He'll think it – and *you* – are terrific!

MATTEL
POWER
SHOP
Also available in Canada

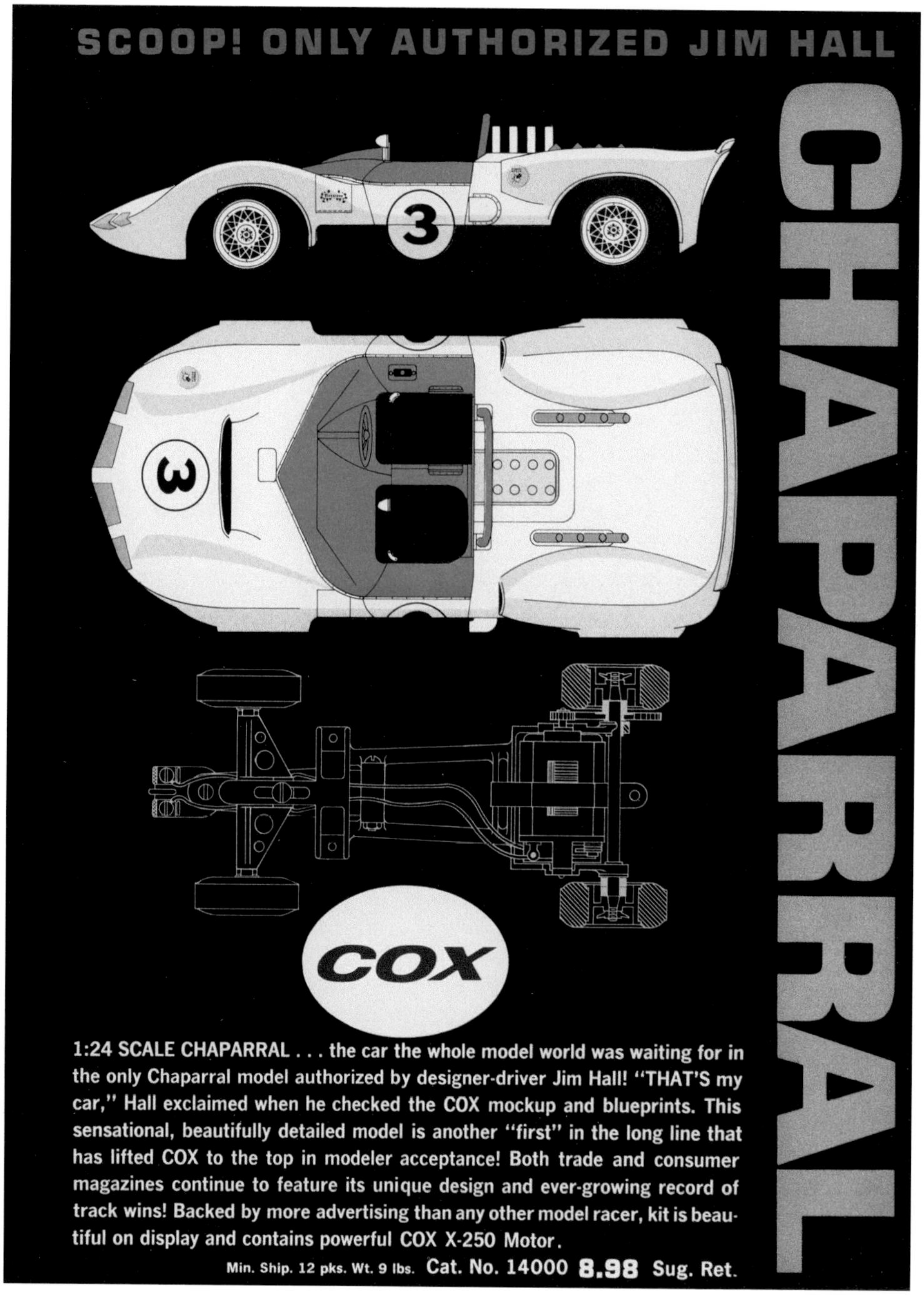

SCOOP! ONLY AUTHORIZED JIM HALL

CHAPARRAL

COX

1:24 SCALE CHAPARRAL . . . the car the whole model world was waiting for in the only Chaparral model authorized by designer-driver Jim Hall! "THAT'S my car," Hall exclaimed when he checked the COX mockup and blueprints. This sensational, beautifully detailed model is another "first" in the long line that has lifted COX to the top in modeler acceptance! Both trade and consumer magazines continue to feature its unique design and ever-growing record of track wins! Backed by more advertising than any other model racer, kit is beautiful on display and contains powerful COX X-250 Motor.

Min. Ship. 12 pks. Wt. 9 lbs. Cat. No. 14000 **8.98** Sug. Ret.

Cox, 1966

▶ American Doll and Toy, 1962

IT'S HERE AT LAST!

Electronic transceiver that sends and receives— it really works!

THE DICK TRACY ⬅2-WAY➡ WRIST RADIO

Exclusive Dick Tracy Wrist Radio! Millions of junior sleuths across the nation will see TV demonstrations of this electronic transceiver that **really works**—sends and receives up to 700 feet. Dick Tracy's greatest link to crime solution is now the clue to big year-round sales! See this fascinating toy at our showroom, March 5-17.

american

AMERICAN DOLL & TOY CORPORATION
1107 Broadway, New York 10, New York

What's new about Francie™

EVERYTHING! Francie is new! She has long, long eyelashes...her very own eyelash brush...a slim teen-age figure – PLUS a whole wardrobe of the most "Mod"ern outfits you've ever seen! Just six of them are shown on this page. She also has *shoulder-length hair* – you can comb, curl and fix it any way you want! What's more, Francie has lifelike bendable legs (like her cousin Barbie®) so you can pose her in all the latest dance steps. Look for Francie – the kookiest, kickiest, happiest, hippest doll of all. She's new from top to toe!

FREE – Wouldn't it be fun to have an autographed picture of Francie for your wall? Just write to Francie, c/o Mattel, Inc., Dept. M, Hawthorne, California.

◀ Mattel, 1966

In the mid-1960s, Mattel wanted to give Barbie a makeover to keep her up to date with youth culture but didn't want to alienate her core audience. Enter Francie, Barbie's younger cousin from England who dressed like a mod, came with an eyelash brush for her long lashes, and had a "slim teenage figure" to boot.

Mitte der 1960er-Jahre wollte Mattel die Barbie zeitgemäßer gestalten und an die Jugendkultur anpassen, ohne dabei die treue Kundschaft zu verprellen. Damit kam die Stunde von Francie, Barbies jüngerer Cousine aus England, die wie ein Mod gekleidet war, eine Bürste für lange Wimpern besaß und darüber hinaus eine „schlanke Teenagerfigur" hatte.

Au milieu des années 1960, Mattel veut offrir un lifting à Barbie sans s'aliéner son cœur de cible. C'est alors qu'entre en scène Francie, la jeune cousine anglaise de Barbie fournie avec une brosse pour épaissir ses longs cils, qui s'habille à la mod et arbore une « silhouette de brindille adolescente ».

Mattel, 1961

Ken™ AND Barbie...
Model Fabulous Fashions For You

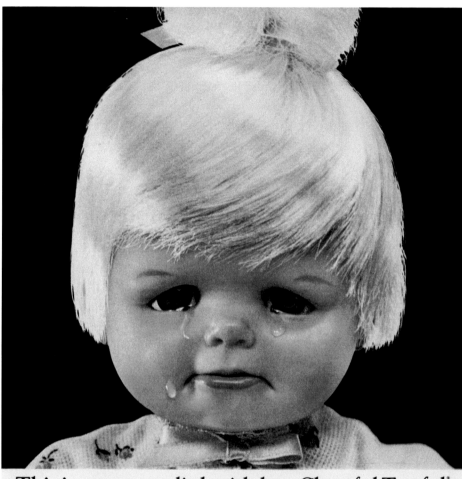

This is one reason little girls love Cheerful Tearful.

This is the other.

The pictures tell the story. They're both the same doll.

Mattel's new Cheerful Tearful can actually *change her expression*. Move her arm up, and her tearful pout turns to a happy smile. Move her arm down, and her smile turns to a pout again. (She even cries *tears.)*

At first, little girls are simply astonished. But in no time, astonishment turns to love. And to endless hours of having fun: taking care of Cheerful Tearful when she's sad, and making her happy again.

On the next few pages, you'll find more new Mattel toys and dolls for Christmas, each one creative, imaginative, and a lot of fun. That's the way we think toys should be.

© 1966 Mattel, Inc.

Most clocks tick. This clock talks!

New from Mattel: A See 'N Say toy that actually teaches youngsters how to tell time!

Is it time your youngsters knew how to tell time? Then it's time you knew about "The Clock Says"! Youngsters simply point the mouse, pull the ring, and the clock recites a rhyme as it teaches them the time.

"The Clock Says" is one more example of the sturdy, creative toys you can count on from Mattel.

These are some others: "The Bee Says" teaches the ABC's. "The Farmer Says" teaches barnyard animal sounds. "Mr. Sound Says"™ teaches everyday sounds. (These See 'N Say™ toys are also available in Canada.)

Look for Mattel pre-school toys. Designed to widen a child's world, and built to last.

THE IDEAL GAME LINE HAS BEEN SPECIFICALLY DESIGNED AND PACKAGED FOR MASS APPEAL TO ALL AGE GROUPS, SELF-SELECTION AND IMPULSE SALES. DISPLAY THE NEW IDEAL GAMES PROMINENTLY AND WATCH YOUR SALES SOAR!

Lego, the toy they won't be tired of by Dec. 26th

Lego isn't just another empty-minded amusement. It challenges children. To think, to build, to create.

They can turn these colorful plastic bricks into almost anything imaginable: skyscrapers, houses, animals. Simple little things like a flower in a pot. Complicated big things like a truck with moving parts. (Lego even has gear and motor sets.) There's no end to what they can make. And that's what keeps them interested in Lego. Long after most Christmas toys are forgotten.

And when you want to add to a child's Lego collection, give an Extra Parts kit.

Choose from 17 Lego sets —for children 3 to 12. As low as $1.50. 205-piece set shown below, about $5.

Lego...the thoughtful toy.

Samsonite Corporation, Toy Division, Denver.

NEW SECRET WEAPON!

Kenner's GUN THAT SHOOTS AROUND THE CORNER

UNBREAKABLE MIRROR SIGHT
geared to pivot automatically

Use as periscope to sight target

Load through **MAGAZINE**

BOLT ACTION
moves next shot to firing position

EASY!
PULL KNOB TO COCK

BARREL PIVOTS IN EITHER DIRECTION

5-SHOT REPEATER
with 10 Soft Sponge Rubber Balls and 3 Targets

AIM and SHOOT without being seen . . .
over and around barricades, from any position, even on your back.
Unbreakable Mirror Sight is geared to pivot automatically with barrel
. . . amazingly accurate!

SELF-SELLING!
BIG SHRINK-WRAPPED DISPLAY BOX

Gun in camouflage colors with 10 soft rubber balls. Bright lithographed corrugated box, 32″ x 9″ x 3½″. 3 Targets —bullseye, tank and lion.

No. 450 **$4.49** Retail

Packed ½ dozen to a case, weight 12½ lbs.

©1966 **KENNER PRODUCTS CO., CINCINNATI, OHIO 45202** • N.Y. Rep. Showrooms: 1412-1424—200 Fifth Avenue

Kenner Products Company, 1966

▶ Mattel, 1969

Muscle cars produced by Detroit automakers captured the imagination of Americans in the 1960s and 1970s. Mattel wisely capitalized on this trend by hiring a top car designer from Chevrolet, Harry Bradley, to work with its in-house toymakers on a line of miniature hot rods called Hot Wheels.

Die Muscle Cars der Detroiter Autohersteller beflügelten in den 1960er- und 1970er-Jahren die Fantasien der Amerikaner. Mattel erkannte die Zeichen der Zeit und engagierte Harry Bradley, einen Topautodesigner von Chevrolet, um zusammen mit den Spielzeugdesignern des Unternehmens eine Serie von heißen Minischlitten namens Hot Wheels zu kreieren.

Les *muscle cars* produites à Détroit font fantasmer les Américains des années 1960 et 1970. Mattel surfe sur cette tendance et engage un designer sénior de Chevrolet, Harry Bradley, pour concevoir avec les créatifs de la marque une collection de bolides miniatures, les Hot Wheels.

Challenge Dad
to a race
in the Hot Wheels® Grand Prix.

You take the McLaren and give Dad the Chaparral.®
Never mind. Let him have the McLaren.
Then line up for a run over the most exciting Hot Wheels set yet.
Mattel's Super-Charger(TM) Grand Prix.
With each Grand Prix set, you get two 2-way Super-Chargers. Each
offers a sizzling power boost on two levels. And each has the
stick-shift speed control.
Each set also contains enough track for two giant courses. Two lap
counters. And four authentic Grand Prix
Hot Wheels cars.
Set up your Hot Wheels
Grand Prix today. Then throw
out the challenge.
See if Dad can stand the pace.

FASTEST METAL CARS IN THE WORLD!

Super-Charger...It Makes The Race.

© 1969 Mattel, Inc.

It's MR. KANDY MAN! (You've seen him on TV)
He's the star of KANDY KiTCHEN!

MAKE MARSHMALLOWS AND GUMDROPS FOR THE WHOLE GANG!

Just pat his hat! Mr. Kandy Man makes candy-making fun. And so safe! He needs no plugs, no bulbs, no batteries. In minutes, you make fat marshmallows and chewy gumdrops. Chocolate, vanilla, cherry and lime! And look at all you get in your Kandy Kitchen set. Colorful Mr. Kandy Man—the master mixer, candy-shaped trays, spatula, measuring spoon and candy mixes. All the fixings for lots of yummy fun. Get Kandy Kitchen, starring Mr. Kandy Man. The whole gang'll love him—and you too!

TRANSOGRAM WHERE THE FUN COMES FROM

50,000,000 Children walk blocks to buy cones and sundaes at the dairy stand

Now! Boys & Girls can make them at home

with *Kenner's*®

FREEZE QUEEN
DAIRY STAND ICE CREAM MACHINE

Great fun to eat, even greater fun to make, this new different way! Make Curly-Top Cones, Sundaes, Milk Shakes, Sherbets, Sodas. Three delicious flavors: vanilla, chocolate, orange; Chocolate and Butterscotch toppings. Easy! No ice to crush. No crank to turn. Put pre-frozen canister into machine; add Freeze-Queen mix; push mixing handle a few times…makes delicious FREEZE-QUEENS in about 10 minutes. Refills available. Or use Mom's ingredients to make ice cream the modern Freeze-Queen way.

MAKES ALL THESE DAIRY STAND TREATS AND MANY MORE!

LOCAL
SATURATION
TV
IN 65
MAJOR MARKETS

Let your tyke take off.

On Playskool's new Tyke Plane.

There's never been anything like it. Takes tykes from two to four years old on let's-pretend flights. Not sky-high, but in your child's imagination as it's rolled around the floor. Then Tyke Plane does ground duty as a TV bench, snack table, game surface and place to crayon and paint. Get a Playskool Tyke Plane for your preschooler today. It's the youngest way to fly. Visit the Play and Learn Center of your favorite store. You'll see our Playskool Tyke Bike, Tyke Tractor, Tyke Pack Horse and Tyke Musical Scooter: a whole new world of free-wheeling fun. Playing is learning with Playskool. Write for our free booklet, Playtools to Shape a Child's World.

Tyke Tractor
(2 to 5 years)

Tyke Pack
Horse
(2 to 4 years)

Tyke
Musical
Scooter
(1 to 3
years)

Tyke Bike
(1 to 3
years)

PLAYSKOOL®

Playskool, Inc. Division of Milton Bradley Company
3720 North Kedzie Avenue, Chicago, Ill. 60618   Dept. GH-99

FISHER-PRICE & THEIR HAND-ME-DOWN TOYS.

Not such a very long time ago, toys were different from the way they are now. They weren't novelties. They were sensible and sturdy but they were also beautiful, and they had heart.

That's the kind of toys Fisher-Price still makes. They aren't designed just for a season, but to last through a whole childhood, and another childhood, and a childhood after that.

They're safe, for one thing. Careful eyes make sure that every edge is smoothed down, every inch of color is fast, wheels and cogs are firmly attached. And children can learn a lot from our toys about cows and ducklings and music and the nice things of life.

Have a look at our whole big Fisher-Price line of toys made to be handed down. They'll take you back to when toyland was a happier place.

James Bond and Oddjob meet again!

11-inch action figures complete with fabric clothes

Secret Agent 007 actually swings out right arm to shoot cap-firing pistol...kicks out knife-wielding foot.

Oddjob throws his steel-rimmed top hat...executes a deadly karate stroke.

Cap-firing gun stores inside case

James Bond *plus* weapons attaché case

$6⁹⁹

You want action . . you get action with this authentic model of Sean Connery as James Bond. Available only at Sears.

007 is licensed to "rub out" evil villains. Just press his right arm down . . *Crack!* Fast reflex aims gun and shoots a bullet-sounding cap (not incl.). Push his right leg back . . *Swish!* Sudden kick springs out harmless knife.

Detailed jointed plastic. Dressed in business suit with shirt, tie. Pack away gun in secret pocket or plastic attaché case.
49 N 5981—Shipping wt. 1 lb.. . .$6.99

Extra Outfits for James Bond
$2⁹⁹ to $3⁹⁹

007 must dress right when he's on different assignments. Impeccably tailored fabrics. You'll find his size only at Sears. No figures. Shipping weight each 8 ounces.

49 N 5986—**Summer Formal**. Tuxedo coat and pants, shirt, bow tie $3.99

49 N 5985—**Sports Outfit**. Casual knit shirt, slacks. Telescopic rifle $2.99

49 N 5984—**Commander Outfit**. Navy dress jacket, trousers, shirt, tie . . .$3.99

Oddjob . . Goldfinger's fearsome handyman

$6⁹⁹

"Perhaps the most dangerous animal on the face of the earth," James Bond said in awe. "Be especially wary if he removes his hat." Oddjob gleefully obeys orders. Push his right arm in towards body . . *Whang!* He flings his hat sideways like a boomerang. Pull his left arm up . . *Whack!* His forearm chops downward like an axe. Authentically detailed just like the movie version. Plastic figure comes dressed in a cutaway formal suit with rigid plastic hat.
49 N 5982—Shipping weight 1 lb.. . . . .$6.99

"Charge it" if you wish

492 SEARS

James Bond 007

Featuring an authentic model of his customized

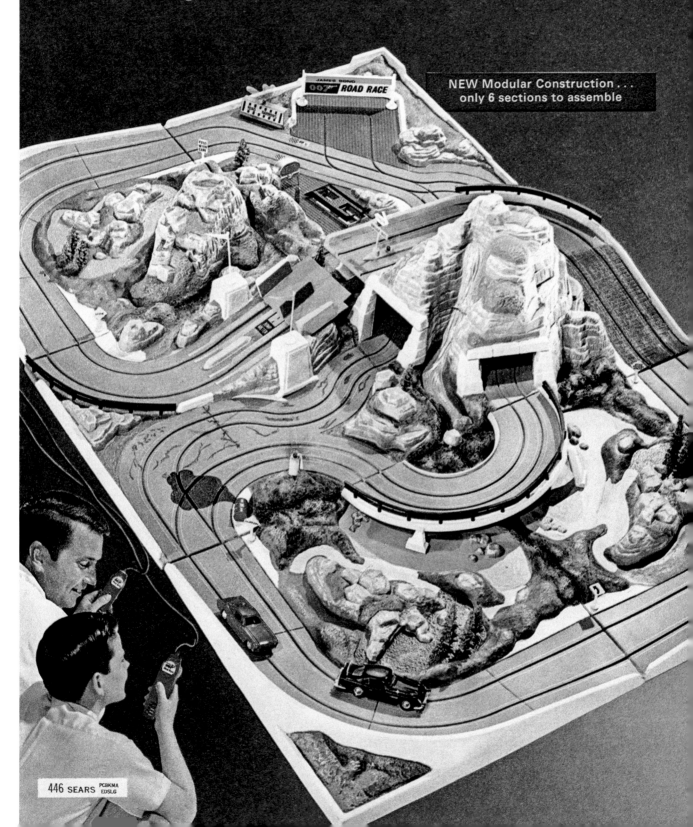

NEW Modular Construction . . .
only 6 sections to assemble

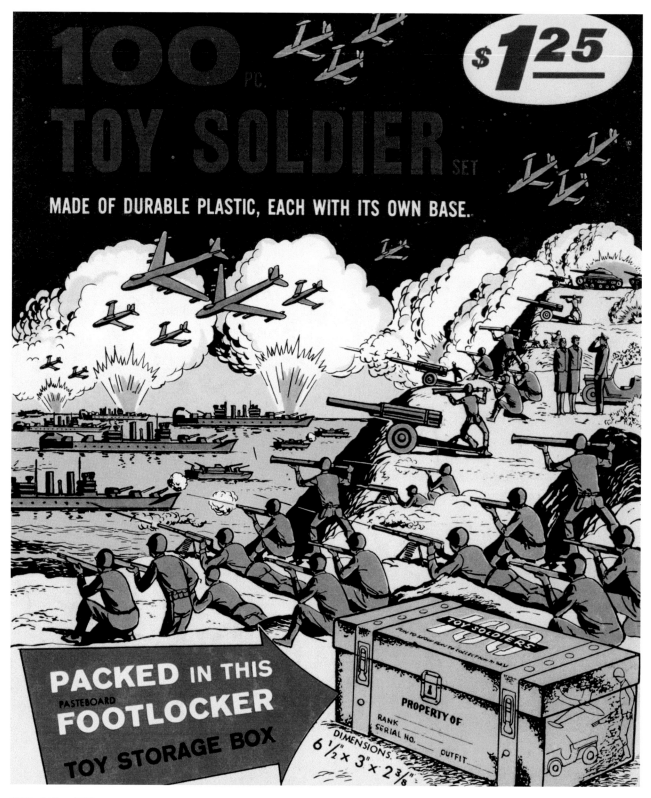

100 Toy Soldiers, 1965

Nabisco, c. 1963

SPACE CAPSULE FOR SALE!

The G-E PowerMite II — for all junior astronauts! 4′ 4″ high, big enough to sit inside. Complete with adjustable space helmet, battery-powered instrument panel, electric motor. Ten operating switches buzz, signal light flashes to send and receive Morse code, earth-path indicator scope shows world revolving. Of sturdy corrugated board, safe, educational, fun for any boy or girl. Easy to assemble. Just $5.00 and the front panel from any 12-pack of G-E Flashbulbs.

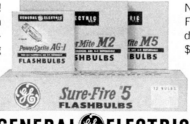

Now's the time to stock up on dependable G-E Flashbulbs. You'll need plenty for family pictures during the holidays. Pick up a supply, and send $5.00 (cash, check or money order made out to "General Electric Co." — no stamps, please) plus one front panel for every capsule ordered to: Capsule, Box 5500A, Cleveland 1, Ohio. Offer expires February 1, 1962. Limited to continental U.S.A. and Hawaii. Void where restricted or prohibited. Allow 3 weeks for delivery.

GENERAL ⊛ ELECTRIC

Photo Lamp Dept., Nela Park, Cleveland 12, Ohio

◄ General Electric, 1961

Montgomery Ward, 1969

In 1969, the space race reached its apex when astronaut Neil Armstrong walked on the moon. The Montgomery Ward Christmas catalog from that year shows how the competition between the U.S. and Soviet Union had infiltrated every aspect of American life, including toys.

Mit Neil Armstrongs Mondspaziergang hatte der Wettlauf der Supermächte ins All 1969 seinen Höhepunkt erreicht. Der Weihnachtskatalog des Versandhandelsunternehmens Montgomery Ward aus demselben Jahr zeigt, dass der Wettkampf zwischen den USA und der Sowjetunion alle Bereiche des amerikanischen Lebens infiltrierte, inklusive der Spielzeugbranche.

En 1969, la conquête spatiale atteint son apogée quand l'astronaute Neil Armstrong marche sur la Lune. Cette année-là, le catalogue de Noël de Montgomery Ward démontre combien l'affrontement entre les États-Unis et l'URSS s'insinue dans tous les aspects de la vie, industrie du jouet comprise.

► Rawlings, 1964

Fantastic
Acrobot
Exclusive at Wards

3⁵⁴

Walks on its hands, on its feet or crawls! Red lights blink when it moves and it makes strange robot-like mechanical sounds.

Amazing acrobatic robot is made of tough plastic with a blue body and red limbs. Arms and legs click into almost any position—straight up, forward, backward. You can make it sit, kneel, stand on one leg, do the splits, almost anything. Stands about 9½ inches tall and operates on 2 "C" batteries (not included—see pg. 368). Ship. wt. 1 lb. 4 oz.
48 T 23786 . . . . .3.54

SAVE THIS CATALOG
Use it to buy toys 'til
Aug. 31, 1970

He walks upright . . . or on his head . . . or on all fours He can sit down

"Great glove, Son!"

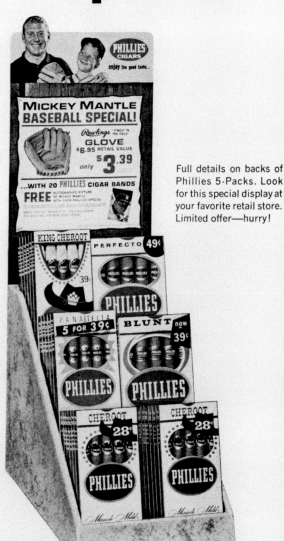

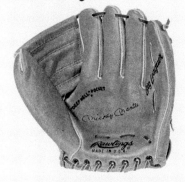

One-Man Field Patrol Helicopter

$8⁹⁹

without batteries

Snap the Helicopter on your back and be ready to takeoff on quick pretend trips . . A Sears Exclusive item

Explore the wilds, discover the mysteries of the jungle, penetrate behind enemy lines. Enjoy these and other imaginary adventures with this helicopter made of high-impact plastic. Press lever to "on" and the red and blue lights flash alternately. Press lever from the starting point to "low" and then further down to accelerate the rotor and spring the imagination into action. Replaceable bulbs. 25½ inches high. Helmet not included. Uses 2 "D" batteries (not included) . . order 1 package below. Use the phone if you want to order it the easiest way of all.

49 N 4208—Shipping weight 4 pounds............................$8.99

"D" Battery. Package of 2.
49 N 4660—Shipping weight 8 ounces..........................Pkg. 36c

Sears, Roebuck, and Company, 1967

▶ AMT, 1965

George Barris was the torchbearer of custom car culture, which was fueled by individuality, freedom, and status. Such was his influence on American culture at large that *Boys' Life* was advertising a miniature of his custom autos to kids who weren't yet old enough to drive.

George Barris war der Vorreiter des Custom-Car-Kults, bei dem es um Individualität, Freiheit und Status ging. Sein Einfluss auf die amerikanische Alltagskultur war so groß, dass in *Boy's Life* Minimodelle seiner Autos für Kinder beworben.

George Barris incarne la culture de la *custom car*, qui carbure à l'individualisme, à la liberté et au standing. Son influence est telle sur la culture américaine en général que *Boys' Life* fait la promotion de versions miniatures de ses voitures auprès d'enfants qui n'ont pas encore l'âge de conduire.

▶▶ Mattel, 1965

invent the wheel.
what we've done with it!

We've invented the fantastic
V-RROOM!®
X-15
™

It banks, it swoops, it steers with a joystick—and turns on a dime *on its rear wheels!* It's the most exciting ride ever—yet it's *safer* than a tricycle, because it's lots more tip-proof. Comes with a seat-belt, too, so kids stay safely snuggled in. And hear this: the X-15 has a brand-new V-RROOM! sound unit that needs *no* batteries! (It's even got a switch to turn it on—and off!) So why settle for pokey trikes and pedal cars? Give the kids a jet on wheels: Mattel's X-15!

This is a bike? It sure is—with shock absorbers and exclusive pivot-action for a safer, more comfortable ride...tough double frame... knobby tread tires...wide-track wheels and extra spokes. But it looks for all the world like a *motorcycle!* And even *sounds* like one—thanks to Mattel's famous V-RROOM! sound unit. (Quieting thought for Mom and Dad: you can also get the 20" BRONCO *without* V-RROOM!) In short: here's *one* BRONCO your rough riders won't bust!

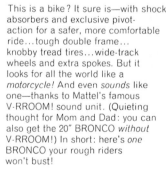

We've come up with the rugged
V-RROOM!®
BRONCO

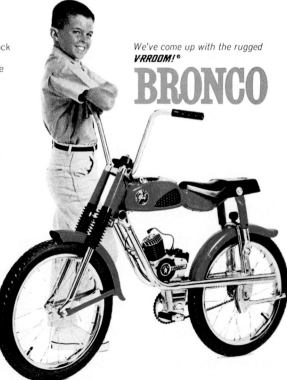

MATTEL, INC.
M
®

IF PRODUCT OR PERFORMANCE DEFECTIVE
★
Good Housekeeping
GUARANTEES
REPLACEMENT OR REFUND TO CONSUMER

Also available in Canada

©1965 Mattel, Inc. Hawthorne, Calif.

"V-RROOM! and X-15" are Mattel's trademarks for its VEHICLES.

Give your child enough Lego® and his imagination may get carried away.

It would take about three thousand boxes of Lego to build a giant elephant like this. But there are many simpler things a child can create with even the smallest Lego set. Those colored plastic bricks snap together to build houses and skyscrapers. They can be taken apart to build other things, even things that move with Lego wheels and gears.

There are 17 different sets for children from 3 to 12 years old. Sets start at $1.50. The 205-piece set shown at right fits any gift budget. Also available: Lego sets for making cars, trucks and trains that are motorized.

If you want to give a child something he won't get tired of in a day or a year, give Lego.

Have the kids enter Lego "Make a Model" contest
1st prize: week's free vacation. All expenses for two adults and two children at Colorado's famous Beaver's Guest Ranch, including Hertz rental car and first-class, round-trip air fare via CONTINENTAL AIRLINES 🦅 150 other prizes! Get entry blank at any participating Lego dealer.

Lego®...the thoughtful toy

Samsonite Corporation, Toy Division, Denver, Colorado 80217

Kenner Products Company, 1969

▶ Park Plastics Company, 1962

No. 105 **Park's**
SUB-MACHINE GUN
and DISPLAY RACK

Authentically styled Thompson repeater. Hundreds of shots without refilling. Long range. Jet black. Size 19". 1 doz., 7 lbs.

retail **98c**
Each

No. 116 **Park's**
WATERMATIC **(4 way action)**
WATER MACHINE GUN
and DISPLAY RACK

Shoots 4 ways... turn crank for 1200 water bursts per minute, with rat-a-tat. Sound may be set on or off. Also use crank without water... use trigger for single shots. 25" long, jet black plastic. 1/2 dozen/6 lbs.

retail **$1.69**
Each

No. 125 **Park's**
WATER GUN ASSORTMENT

- 2 dozen No. 124 PAR-KEE 19¢ ea. $4.56
- 1 dozen No. 100 WEE-GEE 25¢ ea.   3.00
- 1 dozen No. 106 LU-GEE 29¢ ea.   3.48
- 1 dozen No. 102 AUTOMATIC 29¢ ea.   3.48
- 1 dozen No. 107 LUGER 49¢ ea.   5.88

Shipping weight 5½ lbs. 4 to shipper / 22 lbs.

Total retail value of assortment **$20.40**

No. 126 **Park's**
COMBINATION WATER GUN PACK
with 3-D EASEL DISPLAY

- 3 dozen No. 124 PAR-KEE 19¢ ea. $6.84
- 2 dozen No. 100 WEE-GEE 25¢ ea.   6.00
- 1 dozen No. 106 LU-GEE 29¢ ea.   3.48
- 1 dozen No. 102 AUTOMATIC 29¢ ea.   3.48
- 1 dozen No. 114 ATOMEE 29¢ ea.   3.48
- 1 dozen No. 107 LUGER 49¢ ea.   5.88
- 3 only No. 105 SUB-MACHINE 98¢ ea.   2.94

Shipping weight 9 lbs. 4 to shipper / 36 lbs.

Total retail value of assortment

$32.10

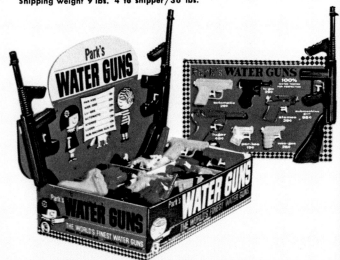

america's favorite

modeling compound
YOUR BASIC STAPLE TOY!

Parents . . . teachers . . . and children ask for Play-Doh Modeling Compound . . . **"the NAME they KNOW!"**

Consistent quality . . . new innovations in creative modeling ideas keeps **PLAY-DOH** way out front as your best bet for the popular-price toy or gift that means year 'round profit volume for you!

school canister

PD-99 . . .

Sugg. Ret., $1.50 (or less)
Re-Usable Metal Container For home . . . school . . . Sunday school. 3 full pounds of PLAY-DOH in permanent beautifully decorated playroom canister. Easy-lift lid. Modeling instructions on can. (Six to shipper; wt. 20 lbs.)

Popular FOUR-PAK
OVER 75 MILLION CANS SOLD . . . and the trend continues.

PD-259 Sugg. Ret., $1.00 (or less)
Easy modeling is real fun with PLAY-DOH Modeling Compound. Four 7-oz. cans; red, blue, yellow and white; colors blend. Pliable; non-toxic. Will not stain. Protected by ALCOA foil. Easy-off plastic lids. (12 to shipper; wt. 27 lbs.)

"Point-of-Sale" DISPLAY package PRE-SELLS Fun Factory and Forge Press Toys.

◄ Rainbow Crafts Company, 1963

Mattel, 1963

NEW ACTION GAME

High GearT.M. **Game** *#462 Retail Value: $6.00*
35,568 different gear patterns give this fast-action
maneuver game endless appeal for everyone age 7 to
adult! Two to four players spin and dial each move on the
Dial Gear, trying to guess which way all 10 gears will
spin to advance their pegs and send back "enemy" pegs!
Object of the game is to race all four of your pegs from
Gear No. 1 up to High Gear — speeding play by taking
chances to "Turn High Gear" or "Hold The Clutch." Easy
to learn, easy to play instructions. Game board and multi-
colored gears are high-impact plastic. Self-sell "demon-
stration" package lets customer examine game on counter.

TALKING HAND PUPPETS!

Pull the Chatty-RingT.M. and they say many different
things at random! All but Bugs have mouths you can move.
Cecil (The Seasick Sea Serpent)© – *#373 Retail
Value: $6.00*
In cuddly plush with black nostrils and wiggly eyes.
D. J. (Dishonest John)© – *#375 Retail Value: $7.00*
Has vinyl face and soft, pliable hands with cloth body.
Bugs Bunny© – *#376 Retail Value: $7.00*
In cuddly plush with famous Bugs' voice.
TV's Talking Horse Mr. Ed®–*#377 Retail Value: $7.00*
Colorful, cuddly plush with soft vinyl head.

"CECIL" & "DISHONEST JOHN" © 1950 ROBERT E. (BOB) CLAMPETT   "BUGS BUNNY" © WARNER BROS. PICTURES, INC.   "MR. ED" © 1962 BY MR. ED COMPANY   ©1962 BY MATTEL, INC.

◄ Five Star Toys, 1963

Mattel, c. 1966

Park Plastics Company, 1963

► Harmonic Reed, 1962

starmaster MONORAIL
mail train

Attention all future Space Engineers
...and Mailmen!

This Monorail train of the future really picks up mail bags —and discharges them at the flip of a youngster's finger. But most amazing it does all this without even stopping. Operator flips lever to control load or unload of bags. Battery operated, train runs over two hours on one D cell flashlight battery. Set includes Monorail mail train, 9 feet of flexible mono-track, six track supports, loading platform and mail bags.

- Safe for youngsters
  - Easy to set up track and operate
    - Extra track available
      - Complete instructions

Long and varied layouts can be made with additional track. Loading platform can be located wherever desired.

No. 10MR—Monorail Mail Train $5.00

No. 12MR—Extra track—9' with six supports $2.00

Monorail Mail Train approaches loading platform and is about to pick up mail bags. Notice control lever on side of platform is in "down" position, therefore allowing train to pick up mail bags.

Attractively packaged in strong corrugated display box 3" x 14" x 23".

EXPORT DEPARTMENT
1010 Schaff Building
Philadelphia, Penna.

PERMANENT DISPLAY
Room 809
200 Fifth Avenue, N. Y. C.

HARMONIC REED CORP., ROSEMONT, PENNA.

Barbie® TOYS

with Make-believe Cosmetics

Barbie®
manicures for a date with Ken

A dream comes true—Barbie's Manicure Set specially designed for Barbie fans. Everything's here, five different shades of play nail polish, polish remover, gloss, and even a jar of play nail cream. Includes three stylized plastic-handled applicator brushes, boxes of manicure sticks, emery boards, and Barbie's own facial tissue. Lifelike and Barbie-like, it's safe and fun—it's geeeorgeous! Size: 14½ x 10½ x 2¼".
No. 1125   Retail $1.98

Barbie®
makes up for a date with Ken

Wow! The works! Terrific and beautiful, little Barbies can primp all day. And take a look at that package! Every girl will want this set when her eyes fall upon it—strikingly highlighted by a new large-size real mirror. Three shades of play lipstick in new modern slim clear plastic holders, and two eye-shadow shades to go with them. Boxes of pressed play face powder and rouge, a box of Barbie puffs, and a boxed eyeshadow brush are included. Colorfully boxed. Size: 14½ x 10½ x 2¼".
No. 1126   Retail $1.98

Barbie® and "Merry"—two great names on a brand-new line of make-believe cosmetics. Sensational new grown-up looking, sophisticated toys, accompanied by the latest in packaging concepts. Set-up boxes in brilliant color for instant consumer appeal and impulse buying—and shrink film—it sparkles, it's pilfer proof, it sells!

"BARBIE" AND "KEN" Ⓡ AND © 1963. MATTEL. INC.

Mattel, 1963   ▶ Irwin, 1963

Fully-jointed Cartwright Family . . each with horse, 25 accessories $6⁶⁹ set

(5 thru 7) The Cartwrights are ready to ride the range. They're fully-jointed at head, shoulders, elbows, wrists, hips, knees and ankles . . take any pose for lifelike action. 9 inches tall. With hats, guns, holsters, clothes, canteens and more. Horses are equipped with ball-bearing hooves, saddle, bridle, reins, bedroll, saddle-bags. Durable plastic, realistic details.

Shipping weight set 1 pound 4 ounces.

(5) 49 N 59902—Little Joe and Horse . . . . Set $6.69
(6) 49 N 59903—Hoss and Horse . . . . Set 6.69
(7) 49 N 6087—Ben and Horse . . . . Set 6.69

for Little RODEO RIDERS

(1 and 2) Cowboy and Cowgirl 2-pc. Rodeo Suits. Festive embroidery accents authentic styling. Tapered broadcloth shirts have enameled metal snap front, cuffs; yoke and collar. Sateen slacks, skirts have elastic backwaist, belt loops, 2 front pockets. Sanforized® cotton . . max. fab. shrink. 1%. Machine wash, medium. Belts, hats not included. *State size 2, 3, 4, 5, 6, 6x.*

1 **Cowgirl Suit.** Plastic fringe skirt.
29 N 7878F—White
29 N 7880F—Red and white
Shipping wt. 10 oz.....Each $5.99

2 **Cowboy Suit.** Zip fly slacks.
29 N 7838F—Red and black
29 N 7840F—Blue and navy
Shipping wt. 11 oz.....Each $5.99

(3 and 4) Boys' and Girls' 2-pc. Western Suits. Pearlized plastic snaps on poplin shirts. Twill slacks have elastic backwaists, belt loops, front pockets, zip fly. Poplin skirts have all-around elastic waist. Sanforized cotton. Machine wash, med. Hats, belts not included. *State size 2, 3, 4, 5, 6, 6x.*

3 **Cowboy Suit.** With snap-on tie.
29 N 7829F—Red and black
29 N 7833F—Gold and brown
Shipping wt. 13 oz.....Each $3.99

4 **Cowgirl Suit.** Fringed skirt.
29 N 7839F—Red
29 N 7837F—Blue
Shipping wt. 9 oz.....Each $3.99

MEASURING CHART . . Order only sizes listed with each item					
Size (not age)	2	3	4	5	6	6x
Height (inches)	32½-35	35½-38	38½-41	41½-44	44½-47	47½-49

See facing page for Holster sets, Hats. Hats also sold on page 172. Boots sold on page 91C.

Sears, Roebuck, and Company, 1967

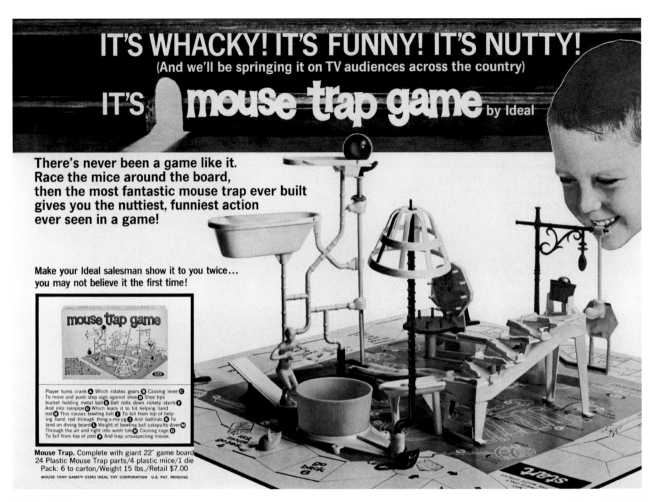

IT'S WHACKY! IT'S FUNNY! IT'S NUTTY!
(And we'll be springing it on TV audiences across the country)
IT'S mouse trap game by Ideal

There's never been a game like it.
Race the mice around the board,
then the most fantastic mouse trap ever built
gives you the nuttiest, funniest action
ever seen in a game!

Make your Ideal salesman show it to you twice...
you may not believe it the first time!

mouse trap game

Player turns crank Ⓐ Which rotates gears Ⓑ Causing lever Ⓒ
To move and push stop sign against shoe Ⓓ Shoe tips
bucket holding metal ball Ⓔ Ball rolls down rickety stairs Ⓕ
And into rainpipe Ⓖ Which leads it to hit helping hand
rod Ⓗ This causes bowling ball Ⓘ To fall from top of helping hand rod through thing-a-ma-jig Ⓙ And bathtub, Ⓚ To
land on diving board Ⓛ Weight of bowling ball catapults diver Ⓜ
Through the air and right into wash tub Ⓝ Causing cage Ⓞ
To fall from top of post Ⓟ And trap unsuspecting mouse.

Mouse Trap. Complete with giant 22″ game board
24 Plastic Mouse Trap parts/4 plastic mice/1 die
Pack: 6 to carton/Weight 15 lbs./Retail $7.00
MOUSE TRAP GAME™ ©1963 IDEAL TOY CORPORATION U.S. PAT. PENDING

Ideal Toy, 1963

▶ Topper Toys, 1966

▶▶ Bissell, 1965

*I baked
this cake in
my new oven.*

*I baked
this cake in
my new Suzy
Homemaker oven.*

Who is Suzy Homemaker???

She's every little girl who wants to be just like her mother. That's why all the Suzy Homemaker appliances look and work just like yours. They're big and beautiful—and work like real. The Suzy Homemaker Oven bakes cakes big enough to serve six! Top burners really heat. And it's completely safe! Oven door automatically locks when in use and won't open until oven cools. **The exclusive new Topper Safety Plug protects against electrical shock.**

The same kind of quality and care that goes into the Suzy Homemaker Oven **(A)** is in all Suzy Homemaker appliances. The Washer-Dryer **(B)**

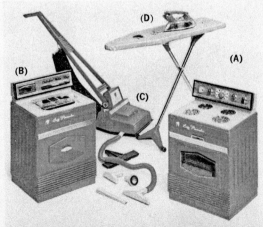

really washes clothes with agitator action, jet spray—and even spins dry! The Vacuum Cleaner **(C)** actually vacuums up dirt, comes complete with attachments. The Iron **(D**—with ironing board**)** has a jet spray sprinkler and it really heats! Completely safe with a red warning light and safety plug.

Never before could your little girl learn homemaking skills with appliances so big, so safe, so real! **Every Little Girl Wants Suzy Homemaker™ Appliances!**

TOPPER TOYS T.M.

De Luxe Topper Corp., Elizabeth, N.J. © DLT, 1966

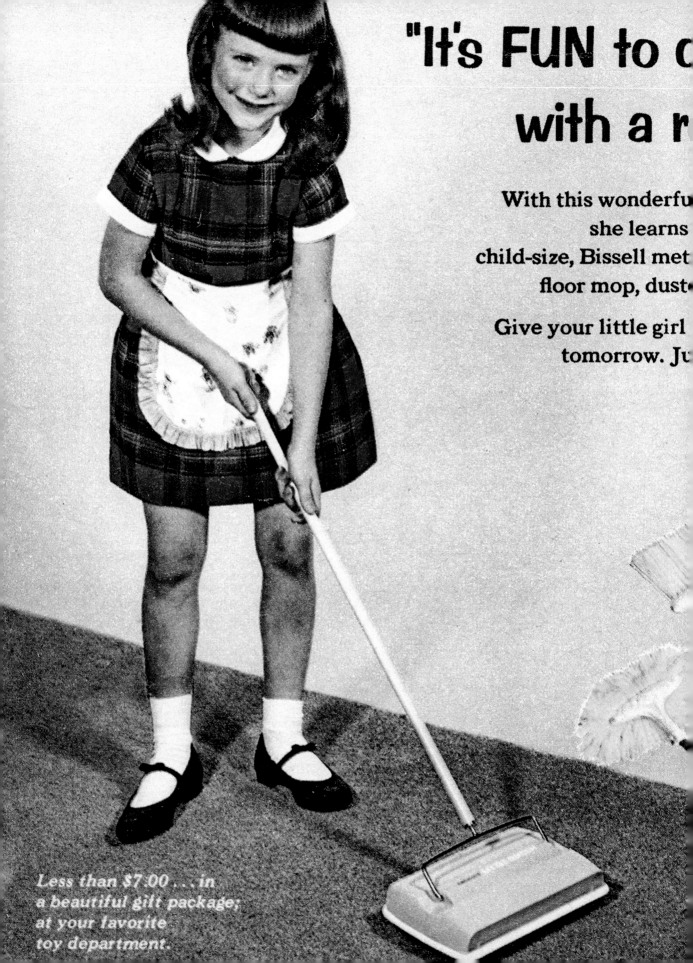

"It's FUN to c
with a r

With this wonderfu
she learns
child-size, Bissell met
floor mop, dust

Give your little girl
tomorrow. Ju

housework, mommy ---
I BISSELL® sweeper."

ece Deluxe *Susy Goose*® Housekeeping Set,
an house "for real!" She'll be thrilled with the genuine,
eper that really sweeps, a genuine Susy Goose
oom and dust pan, an apron and a real Dupont sponge.

s and hours of fun and activity. Guide her to useful tasks for
tch her eyes light up with joy this Christmas with
most wanted, most wonderful gift of all.

Susy Goose

"TOYS THAT MOLD CHARACTER"
JONESVILLE, MICHIGAN

Now–just in time for Christmas–
only at your Ford Dealer's!

MIDGET
MUSTANG

Specially priced at only

$12⁹⁵

While they last!

Here's a child's gift that'll look just as inviting under a Christmas tree as a 1965 Mustang will look in your driveway. The solid, all-metal Midget Mustang, that you might expect to see offered for $25.00, has easy-to-use pedals, make-believe shift lever and real rubber tires. Give

your child a Midget Mustang this Christmas—for a taste of the fun all Mustangers enjoy! Stop in at your participating Ford Dealer's and pick one up for only $12.95, suggested list price . . . at no obligation. For $2.00 more, dealer can order for delivery to your doorstep.

Gift idea for the whole family! 1965 Mustang—
the most successful new car ever introduced in America!

Best year yet to go Ford

MUSTANG!
MUSTANG!
MUSTANG!

A PRODUCT OF *Ford* MOTOR COMPANY

Ford Motor Company, 1965

▶ Garton, 1963

GARTON

Presents the SPIN-A-ROO

Introducing the newest, most exciting wheeled toy of the decade ... the SPIN-A-ROO by Garton. Here's a real "kid-pleaser" that has already become the talk of the trade. The SPIN-A-ROO not only drives forward and backward — it rares up and spins in a circle. It's safe. It's sturdy. It's sensational! The SPIN-A-ROO is profit-priced for fast turnover and year 'round sales. Makes your trip to the Toy Fair a complete success ... see the SPIN-A-ROO.

PREMIERE SHOWING
TOY FAIR
SPACE 407
1107
BROADWAY

She arrives Feb. 22nd! Get ready for

PEBBLES 3-D Display Available in Deal #1780-6

The most adorable doll to come along in a million years! PEBBLES . . . the brand new 15″ baby daughter of Fred and Wilma Flintstone. Pebbles' pixie face, and pony tail hair-do with the little pre-historic bone through it, will endear her to everyone. She wears a precious outfit of a sleeveless-smock top and bikini-style panties that let her little tummy peek through. Her jointed arms and legs allow her to be placed in many poses. Pebbles is an enchanting "stone-age" sweetheart sure to be loved by all children.

#1780-6 PEBBLES DOLL DEAL
Pack: 1 free display with mounted doll and a carton of 4 dolls individually boxed.
Weight: 16 lbs. Retail: $60.00

#0700-5 PEBBLES DOLL
Pack: 4 per ctn. Weight: 12 lbs. Retail: $12.00

FREE—Colorful window streamers and newspaper mats!

IDEAL TOY CORPORATION • 200 Fifth Avenue, New York 10, N. Y.

EVEN DOCTORS BUILD THESE "VISIBLE" MODELS...

because they're so incredibly accurate ...and such fun to build

Thanks to Renwal's famous "Visible" construction, you can actually see all superbly accurate details of bone structure, muscles, organs, nerve and respiratory systems.

Assembling a challenging Renwal Hobby Kit leaves you with a real feeling of accomplishment. You can take your impressive display apart and reassemble it again to show your friends the complexities of anatomy. After all, by that time, you'll be an expert.

The Visible Woman $4.98

The Visible Man $4.98

GOOD HABITS COME FROM GOOD HOBBIES RENWAL

The Visible Head $9.95

SEND FOR RENWAL'S FREE ILLUSTRATED BOOKLET

Renwal, Mineola, New York—Dept. BL-10
Please send me "Getting a Jump on the Future with a Renwal Hobby."

Name_____

Address_____

City_____ State_____

Renwal, 1963

▶ Dollac, 1963

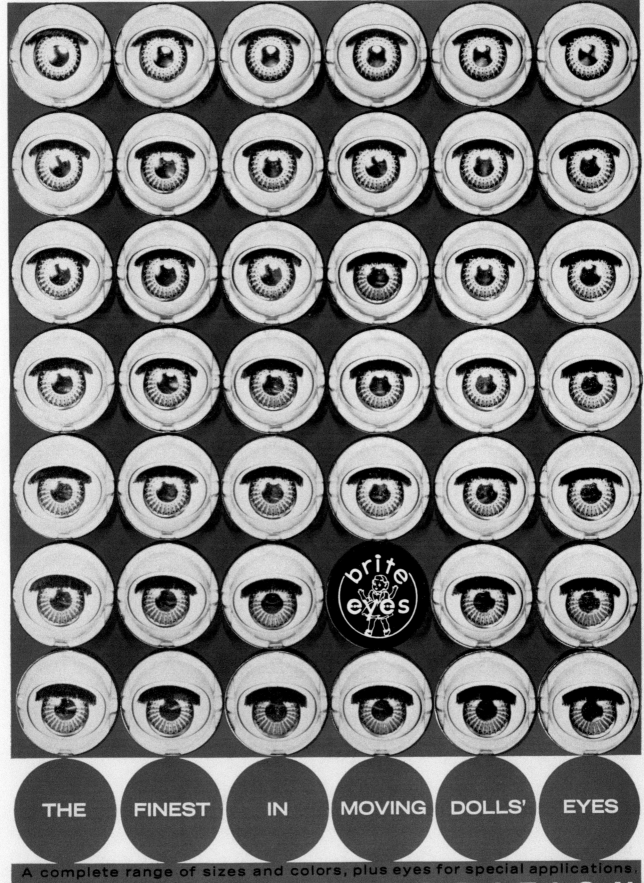

*2510-6 MR. MACHINE™ GAME

A fun-filled game centered around the beloved Mr. Machine character. A giant all plastic unit, designed to look like Mr. Machine, is used as the move and direction indicator. Players using miniature Mr. Machine movers, travel through a maze of exciting obstacle-filled roads. The objective is to get the Mr. Machine mover to his factory, trying to avoid hazards along the route. Each game offers new challenges and the unique Mr. Machine unit will add extra enjoyment to the game.   Retail **5.00**

SIZE	PACK	WEIGHT
19½" x 15" x 2"	½ doz.	13 lbs.

*2211-1 THE REBEL A board

game as exciting as the hit TV series it's based upon. Three raiders boldly pursue the Rebel through open and secret trails. The Rebel tries to outsmart and out-maneuver them in his attempt to get to the next town safely. Pursuit and capture are keynotes of the game. It's loaded with thrilling western adventures from beginning to end.   Retail **2.00**

SIZE	PACK	WEIGHT
19½" x 9¾" x 1¾"	1 doz.	21 lbs.

© 1961 The Rebel Co.

◄ Ideal Toy, 1961

Silly Putty, 1960

Daisy Manufacturing Company, 1960

▶ Park Plastics Company, 1960

No. 293 **Park's**

FAST DRAW TIMER
Target Set

One of the most interesting and challenging games
ever created. Man size target 32½" high.
Simple and fun to use . . . set timer, pull release
cord. Contestant draws and fires,
if target is hit anywhere, timer stops. Times draw
to split seconds. Specially designed timer
operates on a unique mechanical principle.
No batteries, no extras to buy. Complete with
giant cowboy target, Holster set, 6 darts,
Western style Fanning dart gun that can either
be triggered or fanned to fire darts.
PACKING: 6 only to master shipper, 20 lbs.

retail $4.98

TICK
TICK
TICK
TICK
TICK

Park PLASTICS CO   LINDEN, N. J.

ACTUAL UNRETOUCHED PHOTOS OF

OVER 11 INCHES TALL

FOUR BASIC PACKAGES: ACTION

AMERICA'S MOVABLE FIGHTING

AND ACTION BATTLE SCENES...

IN THE BOYS' MARKET. . . .

G.I. JOE™ HAS 21 MOVABLE PARTS!

STANDS, SITS, KNEELS! TAKES
ALL MILITARY ACTION POSITIONS! FIRING,
RUNNING, THROWING GRENADES!

HASBRO'S ASTONISHING G. I. JOE™!

SOLDIER,™ ACTION SAILOR,™ ACTION MARINE,™ ACTION PILOT™...

MAN™ WITH AUTHENTIC REALISTIC EQUIPMENT TO BUILD COMBAT TEAMS

G. I. JOE™ IS THE GREATEST OPEN END MERCHANDISING LINE EVER

DRAMATIC PACKAGING FOR MULTIPLE SALES!

G. I. JOE,™ AMERICA's MOVABLE FIGHTING MAN,™ is so realistic in construction, so authentic in equipment and battle gear, that he brings a new concept to the wonderful fun of "Playing Soldier." G. I. JOE™ comes in four basic packages...ACTION SOLDIER,™ ACTION SAILOR,™ ACTION MARINE,™ ACTION PILOT,™ equipped with fatigue uniform, cap, and boots. With the full line of authentic equipment available, any boy (AND HIS DAD) can build a whole new world of make-believe in their playroom, basement, or corner of the attic. Package after package of amazing equipment...all scaled from AUTHENTIC Government Issue in the Army, Navy, Marine Corps, and Air Force...G. I. JOE™ by Hassenfeld Bros., Inc. is the BIG ONE for 1964!

HASBRO'S
G.I. JOE™

G. I. JOE™ DIVISION, HASSENFELD BROTHERS, INC.   PAWTUCKET, R. I.

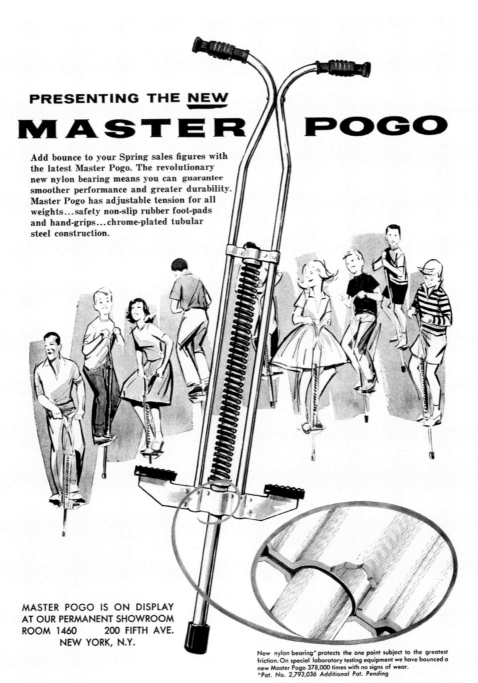

PRESENTING THE <u>NEW</u>
MASTER POGO

Add bounce to your Spring sales figures with the latest Master Pogo. The revolutionary new nylon bearing means you can guarantee smoother performance and greater durability. Master Pogo has adjustable tension for all weights...safety non-slip rubber foot-pads and hand-grips...chrome-plated tubular steel construction.

MASTER POGO IS ON DISPLAY
AT OUR PERMANENT SHOWROOM
ROOM 1460   200 FIFTH AVE.
NEW YORK, N.Y.

New nylon bearing* protects the one point subject to the greatest friction. On special laboratory testing equipment we have bounced a new Master Pogo 378,000 times with no signs of wear.
*Pat. No. 2,793,036 Additional Pat. Pending

MASTER JUVENILE PRODUCTS, INC.   HANSBURG ACRES   WALKER VALLEY, N.Y.

◀◀ Hasbro, 1964

◀ Aurora Plastics, 1967

Master Juvenile Products, 1963

TWISTER
The game that ties you up in knots
$2⁹⁹

"Right foot red" . . "left hand yellow"—each spin of the pointer tells you where to put your hand or foot. Quick, beat your opponent to the easy spots. Fall and you lose.

Even if you're 6, 16 or 60, you'll love this crazy fun game. Makes any party hilarious. Forces couple (even better, 3 or 4) to go through more contortions than they thought possible. Play it indoors in stocking feet, or outdoors in bare feet. 24-spot 6x4½-foot vinyl mat wipes clean and folds or rolls up for easy storage.

Shipping weight 2 lbs. 3 oz.
49 N 207................................$2.99

Push down lever to set pins

PLAY II
DIFFERENT GAMES

Including Dart Toss, Shuffle Board, Bowling with Automatic Pin Setter $13⁷⁹

A sports minded family will love this set. The bowling set has two 5-inch balls, and time-saving automatic pin setter. Play Shuffleboard with 4 pushers, 8 discs. Dart toss has 4 darts and target. They'll enjoy "Bounce the Checker," Tic-Tac-Toe, Bowling, Checker-Pitch, and golf. Also 3 racing games with 4 racing cars, horses, planes. 12x2-ft. printed linoleum. Plastic parts.
79 N 2548L—Shipping weight 18 pounds...Set $13.79

Sears, Roebuck, and Company, 1967

► Mattel, 1963

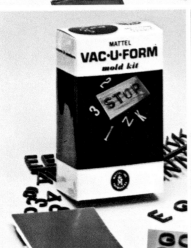
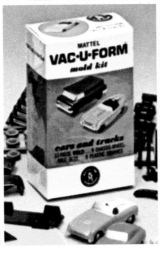
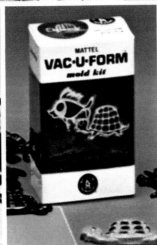

MOLDS PLASTIC...MAKES MOST ANYTHING!

Vac-U-Form Mold Kit Assort. #429 *Total Retail:*
$24.00
Contains 2 doz. assorted mold kits in self-service counter
container.

Vac-U-Form Material Pak Assort. #424 *Total Retail:*
$17.00
24 assorted paks of 4 different plastic Material Paks
affixed to a self-service counter card.

Vac-U-Form Mold Kits – #430-#436 *Retail Value:*
$1.00 each

Vac-U-Form Material Paks #425-#428
Colored Plastic – #425: 50¢
Clear Plastic – #426: 50¢
Metalized Plastic – #427: $1.00
Assorted Plastic – #428: $1.00

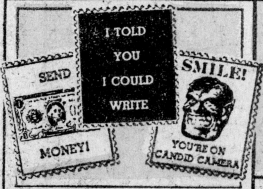

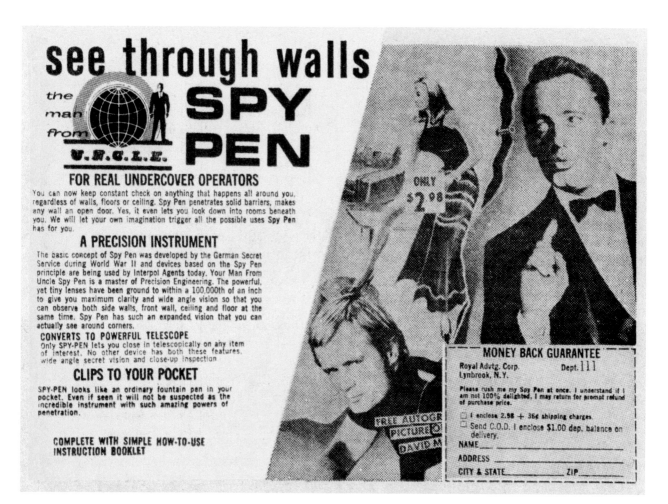

see through walls

the man from **U.N.C.L.E.** **SPY PEN**

ONLY $2.98

FOR REAL UNDERCOVER OPERATORS

You can now keep constant check on anything that happens all around you, regardless of walls, floors or ceiling. Spy Pen penetrates solid barriers, makes any wall an open door. Yes, it even lets you look down into rooms beneath you. We will let your own imagination trigger all the possible uses Spy Pen has for you.

A PRECISION INSTRUMENT

The basic concept of Spy Pen was developed by the German Secret Service during World War II and devices based on the Spy Pen principle are being used by Interpol Agents today. Your Man From Uncle Spy Pen is a master of Precision Engineering. The powerful, yet tiny lenses have been ground to within a 100,000th of an inch to give you maximum clarity and wide angle vision so that you can observe both side walls, front wall, ceiling and floor at the same time. Spy Pen has such an expanded vision that you can actually see around corners.

CONVERTS TO POWERFUL TELESCOPE

Only SPY-PEN lets you close in telescopically on any item of interest. No other device has both these features, wide angle secret vision and close-up inspection

CLIPS TO YOUR POCKET

SPY-PEN looks like an ordinary fountain pen in your pocket. Even if seen it will not be suspected as the incredible instrument with such amazing powers of penetration.

COMPLETE WITH SIMPLE HOW-TO-USE INSTRUCTION BOOKLET

FREE AUTOGR
PICTURE
DAVID M

MONEY BACK GUARANTEE

Royal Advtg. Corp.   Dept. 111
Lynbrook, N.Y.

Please rush me my Spy Pen at once. I understand if I am not 100% delighted, I may return for prompt refund of purchase price.

☐ I enclose 2.98 + 36¢ shipping charges.
☐ Send C.O.D. I enclose $1.00 dep. balance on delivery.

NAME
ADDRESS
CITY & STATE _____ ZIP _____

◀ Dollar Bargains, 1968

Royal Advantage, 1968

▶ Montgomery Ward, 1969

▶▶ Mattel, 1970

Walkie-Talkie — Talk with others with Base Station or walkie-talkie

AM Radio

CB Short Wave Receiver — Listen in on Citizen Band HAM" radio conversations

Wireless Code Sender — Send secret messages in code to friends who have a Base Station

ACTION PACKED **4-WAY BASE STATION** 26⁹⁹

[A] You need no license to operate this exciting communications toy! Use it as a walkie-talkie—you transmit and receive up to one mile over channel 14, talk with anyone who has a Base Station or walkie-talkie. Use it as an AM radio—hear your favorite music and sports. Use it as a CB shortwave receiver—listen in on all 23 channels. Use it as a wireless code sender—again it's channel 14, only this time use Morse code or your own secret code! Tap it out in dots and dashes—your friend will hear it on his Base Station. Headphone and mike incl. Operates on batteries (incl.), or house current (order adapter below). Abt. 13x6x6 in.
48 T 20188—Ship. wt. 9 lbs. 10 oz..**26.99**

AC adapter

[B] To operate Base Station on house current—saves batteries.
48 T 20028 X—Ship. wt. 8 oz.......**3.29**

THE "BIG EAR"

Birds in a nest 200 feet away—WOW! You can hear them. Tiny animals, cars—just zero in—you hear it loud and clear!

17⁹⁹

[C] Big 18-in. parabolic sound collector picks up sounds way off in the distance—amplifies them through stethoscope-type earphone. Point it into the brush—hear tiny animals you can't even see. Zero in on a parade—your buddy's secret message from his window across the street. Great for outings and "Jungle" adventures—you can hear wildlife without getting close enough to scare critters away. Hear most faint sounds 100 feet away; bird calls as far as 200 feet. Stands 40 in. high on sturdy wood legs (adjustable). Operates on 9-volt battery (not included—order from page 368). Ship. wt. 7 lbs. 3 oz.
48 T 20101 M.....................**17.99**

"Big Ear" broadcast accessory

Whatever "Big Ear" hears comes out radio

10⁹⁹

[D] Plugs into "Big Ear." Then sound comes out any FM radio speaker up to 30 feet away. Batteries incl. Ship. wt. 5 oz.
48 T 20102......**10.99**

Wrist radio broadcaster

You talk   He hears

Talk into it—your voice comes out FM radio 50 feet away! 10⁹⁹

[E] Hey—you're on the air! Your friends will flip when your voice comes over the radio. No wires. Wear it on your wrist—turn on and talk—your voice comes out any FM radio up to 50 feet away. Radio not included. Great for party fun or keeping in touch with the other room. Perfect as a sick-room monitor. Batteries included.
48 T 20106—Ship. wt. 6 oz.............**10.99**

Broadcaster kit 8⁹⁹

[F] Same as above, only you put it together yourself. Easy instructions.
48 T 20105—Ship. wt. 9 oz...........kit **8.99**

AM wrist radio— you wear it like a watch

12⁹⁹

[G] Everywhere you go you'll take along your favorite music and sports. Just the ticket for fishing trips, bike riding—anyplace you can't take a big radio, you can take this one as easily as a wrist watch! Get all the local AM radio shows loud and clear. Has its own tuner and mini-antenna. And you can listen 2 ways—from speaker or private earphone. Batteries included.
48 T 20104—Ship. wt. 6 oz................**12.99**

Wrist radio kit 10⁹⁹

10⁹⁹

[H] Same AM radio as above, only you put it together yourself. Easy instructions.
48 T 20103—Ship. wt. 9 oz...........kit **10.99**

Shop Early, PAY IN FEBRUARY   **Buy toys from this catalog till Aug. 31, 1970.**   BACKS WARDS 385

1970s

STAR WARS CREATES A LICENSING
JUGGERNAUT SERVING AS
A MODEL FOR TOY COMPANIES
AROUND THE WORLD.

THE "I WANT…" ERA

LEAVING THE 1960S, THE ADOLESCENT PERIOD OF TOY ADVERTIS-ING – AND A GROWTH PERIOD FOR TOYS IN GENERAL – THE '70S MARKED MORE MATURE TIMES. Toy companies were more confi-dent in their marketing prowess to reach their primary consumer (parents) through their principal drivers (children) with just the right balance of psychology and showmanship. The '70s was the "I Want…" era. Longing and desire were easily stimulated by Madison Avenue; the advertised toys were cost-efficiently manu-factured and produced in enough quantities to earn healthy profits.

Toys had long been electrically and battery operated (although usually batteries were not included), but a new technology — the computer — was just beginning to push its way into the pub-lic's consciousness. It was not, however, a perfect decade. The '70s brought massive global inflation, much of it caused by the

1970

Rubber-duck sales explode after Ernie starts singing about them on *Sesame Street*

Der Verkauf von Quietscheentchen geht durch die Decke, nachdem Ernie in der *Sesamstraße* sie besingt

Les canards en plastique s'arrachent quand Ernest leur consacre une chanson dans *Sesame Street*

1971

Later adapted by kids, glow sticks appear at a Grateful Dead concert

Leuchtstäbe tauchen bei einem Konzert der Grateful Dead auf und werden später zu Spielzeug

Les premiers bâtons lumineux apparaissent à un concert de Grateful Dead

1972

Native American pastime is appropriated by two friends in Oregon, christen it hacky sack

Ein Spiel der amerikanischen Ureinwohner wird von zwei Freunden aus Oregon Hacky Sack genannt

Deux amis de l'Oregon s'approprient un jeu de balle amérindien et le rebaptisent Hacky Sack oil crisis, which had a negative impact on sales and manufacturing costs. But on the optimistic side, with the Vietnam War over and the digital revolution rapidly progressing, the toy industry was poised to expand. *Pong*, the first video game to have commercial success, was released in 1975 with incredible long-term effects. In 1976, Steve Jobs and Steve Wozniak created the Apple Computer Company, which was, in its way, an outlier of things to come. In 1978, the bit-mapped video game *Space Invaders* was released, and the toy world began to swirl with new possibilities.

Nonetheless, the most influential new wave was not digital at all. *Sesame Street*, launched on PBS in 1970, was not only a unique children's educational concept — it was the birth of a toy franchise that continues today. Fisher-Price licensed the characters to produce toys, and because of its high production standards, the company was expected to make smart-looking ads to complement Grover, Cookie Monster, and the show's other creations. This was also a fertile period for making things. Lego was also a beneficiary of appealing art direction and copywriting. One of its effective ads for the New Lego Expert Builder Series read, "Move It! Steer It!

1973

1974

1975

Science-tinged activity toy Shrinky Dinks invented by two women in Wisconsin

Zwei Frauen in Wisconsin erfinden das naturwissen- schaftliche Actionspiel Shrinky Dinks

Deux femmes du Wisconsin inventent la feuille de plastique à cuire Shrinky Dinks

Fantasy role-playing game Dungeons & Dragons is released; imaginations run wild

Das Fantasyrollenspiel Dungeons & Dragons erscheint und lässt der Fantasie freien Lauf

Le jeu de rôles Donjons & Dragons sort et les imaginations s'embrasent

Atari releases a home version of *Pong* through Sears department store

Atari verkauft über das Kaufhaus Sears eine Home- Version von *Pong*

Atari édite une version domestique de *Pong* vendue dans les hypermarchés Sears

Shift It! Build It!" Headlines like that appealed to kids and sold the concept of empowerment. That, of course, did not mean that every advertisement was smart or clean — there were still plenty of ham-fisted comic book ads for novelties like Sea Monkeys. Yet many toy advertisements shed the old copy-heavy pulp look for the modern aesthetic — elegant typography and clean or conceptual photography that characterized mass-market magazine ads of the era. In terms of "creative" intelligence, Ideal's Mighty Mo truck and tractor line couldn't have had a better slogan than "Mo power to the little people!" Most toy ads still featured white children, but kids of different races were beginning to appear more frequently, leading the way to the more inclusive 1980s.

1976

Slime by Mattel oozes its way into pop culture

Slime von Mattel schleimt sich in die Popkultur ein

Le Slime de Mattel s'insinue dans la culture populaire

1978

Milton Bradley debuts Simon at New York City nightclub Studio 54

Milton Bradley lanciert Simon im New Yorker Nachtklub Studio 54

Milton Bradley fête le lancement du jeu Simon au Studio 54 de New York

1979

A former Chrysler designer creates the Cozy Coupe for Little Tikes

Ein ehemaliger Chrysler-Designer kreiert das Cozy Coupe für Little Tikes

Un ex-concepteur de Chrysler crée le Cozy Coupé pour Little Tikes

DIE QUENGELÄRA

Star Wars erzeugt ein Lizenzimperium, das zum Vorbild für die Spielzeugindustrie weltweit wird.

Durchlief die Spielzeugwerbung in den 1960er-Jahren ihre Pubertät, so brach mit den 1970ern die Zeit der Reife an. Die Spielwarenhersteller beherrschten das Marketing nun aus dem Effeff und erreichten die Primärkonsumenten (Eltern) über die Endverbraucher (Kinder) mit genau dem richtigen Maß an Psychologie und Effekthascherei. Die 1970er waren die Quengelära. Die Werbebranche schaffte es spielend, Bedürfnisse zu wecken. Und die beworbenen Produkte wurden kosteneffizient und in einer so hohen Auflage hergestellt, dass man gesunde Profite einfuhr.

Elektrische und batteriebetriebene Spielsachen kannte man schon seit einiger Zeit, nun bahnte sich eine neue Technologie – der Computer – langsam den Weg ins öffentliche Bewusstsein. Doch das Jahrzehnt brachte nicht nur Erfreuliches: Die Ölkrise und eine zum Teil daraus resultierende globale Inflation wirkten sich negativ auf Umsätze und Herstellungskosten aus. Andererseits war der Vietnamkrieg zu Ende, die digitale Revolution schritt rapide voran und die amerikanische Spielzeugindustrie befand sich auf Expansionskurs. *Pong*, das erste kommerziell erfolgreiche Videospiel, kam 1975 auf den Markt und sollte weitreichende Auswirkungen haben. 1976 gründeten Steve Jobs und Steve Wozniak die Apple Computer Company, Vorbote zukünftiger großer Dinge. 1978 erschien das grobgerasterte Videospiel *Space Invaders,* und die Spielzeugwelt taumelte neuen Dimensionen entgegen.

Die einflussreichste neue Welle war allerdings alles andere als digital. Die *Sesamstraße,* 1970 zum ersten Mal auf dem Sender PBS ausgestrahlt, setzte nicht nur ein einmaliges pädagogisches Konzept um, sondern begründete auch ein ganzes Spielwarenlizenzimperium. Fisher-Price erwarb die Lizenz, um aus den beliebten Charakteren der Sendung Spielfiguren herzustellen, und zu den hohen Produktionsstandards des Unternehmens passte natürlich eine entsprechend smarte Werbung, die Ernie & Bert, Grobi und das Krümelmonster ins rechte Licht rückte. Kreatives Spielzeug zum Selbermachen war in den 1970ern ebenfalls angesagt, und auch Lego setzte auf ansprechendes Design und clevere Texte. So heißt es in einer Werbeanzeige für die New Lego Expert Builder Series: „Beweg es! Lenk es! Verschieb es! Bau es!" Solche Schlagzeilen sprachen Kinder an und vermittelten ein Gefühl von zupackender Stärke. Natürlich war in dieser Zeit nicht jede Werbung smart oder stylisch – es gab immer noch jede Menge uninspiriert hemdsärmelige Anzeigen in Comicheften für Neuheiten wie die Sea-Monkeys (Urzeitkrebse). Doch viele Spielwarenanzeigen tauschten den billigen, textlastigen alten Look gegen eine moderne Ästhetik aus – mit einer eleganten Typografie und attraktiven konzeptionellen Fotos, die auch die populären Zeitschriften der Ära prägten. Ein gelungenes Beispiel für kreative Slogans war „Mo power to the little people!" (Mehr Macht den kleinen Leuten!) für die Laster- und Traktorenkollektion Mighty Mo der Firma Ideal. In den meisten Anzeigen dieser Zeit waren immer noch vorrangig weiße Kinder zu sehen, doch es tauchten nun auch vermehrt unterschiedliche Ethnien auf – ein Wegweiser zu den inklusiveren 1980er-Jahren.

► Questor, 1974

Child Guidance brings your child a little Sesame Street of his own.

With new Push Button Sesame Street, your child can play with the characters who live on Sesame Street.

Push a button and a matching geometric shape opens to reveal Ernie, Bert, Oscar, Cookie Monster or Big Bird. Or turn each button upside down and it becomes a stand for the matching character. Add a few hand puppets and Push Button Sesame Street almost becomes real.

So now when Sesame Street isn't playing on television, a little bit of it can still be playing right in your own home.

CHILD GUIDANCE

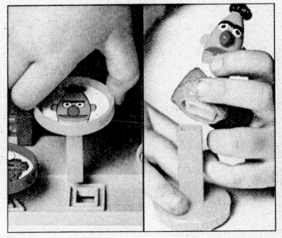

L'ÈRE DU « JE VEUX... »

Star Wars crée une révolution de la licence commerciale dont s'inspirent les fabricants de jouets du monde entier.

Après les années 1960 où la publicité pour les jouets a vécu son adolescence, alors que l'industrie du jouet en général était en forte croissance, elle acquiert dans les années 1970 une certaine maturité. Les fabricants de jouets mènent de façon plus assurée et assumée leur stratégie marketing, qui consiste à atteindre leur cible (les parents) par l'intermédiaire de leurs moteurs principaux (les enfants) en maniant savamment psychologie et grand guignol. Les années 1970 sont la décennie du « Je veux ». Les agences de Madison Avenue n'ont aucun mal à attiser l'envie et le désir compulsif des petits et des grands ; les jouets sont fabriqués à coût maîtrisé et produits en quantités suffisantes pour engranger des profits confortables.

Voilà longtemps déjà que les jouets sont électriques ou à piles (non fournies), mais une nouvelle technologie, l'informatique, commence tranquillement à s'installer dans les consciences. La décennie est loin d'être parfaite, elle connaît une inflation mondiale massive, en grande partie provoquée par la crise pétrolière, qui a un impact négatif sur les ventes et les coûts de fabrication. Dans une perspective plus optimiste, avec la fin de la guerre du Vietnam et la révolution numérique qui progresse en marche rapide, l'industrie américaine du jouet ne peut que prendre de l'ampleur. *Pong*, le premier jeu vidéo à remporter un gros succès commercial, sort en 1975. En 1976, Steve Jobs et Steve Wozniak créent la Apple Computer Company, une sorte d'anomalie au regard du chemin que prendra le secteur. En 1978 sort le jeu vidéo en mode pixel *Space Invaders* et le monde du jouet est pris de vertige face aux nouveaux horizons qui s'offrent à lui.

La tendance la plus marquante n'a cependant rien à voir avec les ordinateurs. *Sesame Street*, diffusée sur PBS à partir de 1970, n'est pas seulement une émission éducative pour enfants unique, elle marque aussi la naissance du jouet franchisé. Fisher-Price achète les droits sur les personnages pour en faire des jouets et l'exigence de qualité qui fait la marque du concept oblige l'entreprise à produire des publicités futées, cohérentes avec le ton de Kermit, Macaron, Elmo et leurs amis.

L'époque est propice à l'action. Lego collabore avec des directeurs artistiques et des auteurs de talent, notamment pour la campagne sur sa nouvelle collection Expert Builder : « Déplace ! Dirige ! Bouge ! Construis ! » Ce type de slogan véhicule une notion d'émancipation qui séduit les enfants. Pour autant, toutes les publicités ne sont pas malines ou saines – on trouve encore nombre d'encarts laids pour des gadgets comme les *Sea-Monkeys* (« singes de mer », des petites crevettes). La plupart des annonceurs abandonnent toutefois l'esthétique chargée des années *pulp* au profit d'un style moderne – typo élégante, photos claires ou conceptuelles – qui prend ses aises dans les magazines grand public. À propos d'intelligence « créative », le fabricant de jouets Ideal n'aurait pu trouver meilleur slogan pour le camion et le tracteur de Mighty Mo que : « Mo power to the little people ! » (« Plus de pouvoir pour les petits ! », en clin d'œil à la chanson de Lennon « Power to the people »). Les publicités montrent encore une majorité d'enfants blancs, mais d'autres couleurs de peau commencent à apparaître plus fréquemment ; une évolution qui se poursuivra dans les plus inclusives années 1980.

◄ Factors Etc, 1977

Welcome to the Fisher

Price Play Family Village.

Action Garage. Farm. House. Bath/Utility Room Set. Kitchen Set. Patio Set. School. Fun Jet.
Mini-Snowmobile. Musical Ferris Wheel. Merry-Go-Round. Fire Engine. Airport with Jet.
Play Family People. School Bus. Mini-Bus. Houseboat. All sold separately in individual sets.

STAR WARS

◄◄ Fisher-Price, 1972

◄ Star Wars Fan Club, 1978

Superhero Merchandise, 1978

It didn't take long after *Star Wars* debuted on the big screen in 1977 for a cornucopia of merch to follow. Comic books were prime targets, though the movie was so popular that the merchandising company could have advertised in the phone book and still sold out of its $4.69 Darth Vader costume.

Schon kurz nachdem *Star Wars* 1977 in die Kinos kam, überschwemmte das dazugehörige Merchandising den Markt. Die meisten Werbeanzeigen wurden in Comicheften platziert, obwohl der Film so erfolgreich war, dass das Darth-Vader-Kostüm für 4,69 Dollar auch ausverkauft gewesen wäre, wenn man im örtlichen Telefonbuch dafür geworben hätte.

Star Wars est à peine sorti sur les écrans en 1977 que les produits dérivés déferlent sur le marché. Leurs fabricants privilégient les comics pour en faire la promotion, mais le film remporte un tel succès que, même s'ils avaient opté pour le bottin, les costumes de Dark Vador à 4,69 dollars se seraient vendus jusqu'au dernier.

THE PERFECT TOY FOR PARENTS.
IT RECHARGES ITS OWN BATTERY.

The Poweride electric car is a parent's dream. Once you pay for it, you won't have to keep paying for it over and over again. Because this toy has its own rechargeable battery.

When it weakens, just plug it into any wall outlet just overnight to give your child seven more hours of fun.

Moving around and exploring his world is a thrill your child won't outgrow. And it's nice to know that from the time he's two till the time he's eight he'll be able to hop on his own car and go.

Because its most important parts are made from Allied Chemical's PLASKON® Nylon, Poweride will last that long.

But don't worry, he won't go too far.

Poweride only goes up to two miles an hour. Poweride. It's a small price to pay for the perfect toy.

Other models available: Poweride Super Cycle and Poweride Hot Foot Dragster.

POWERIDE™
Eldon Industries, Inc.

For you, with love and LEGO PreSchool.

It's an original, all right. But then so is she.

Miraculously, no two children are alike. That's why LEGO® Brand Pre-School Building Sets are perfect playthings.

They allow your child to explore, create, play and pretend to his or her curiosity's content.

The big, sturdy blocks snap together. Wheels roll, and doors open for the friendly LEGO figures.

When you watch your little one build and play with LEGO PreSchool Sets, there's no telling what

you'll see. And that's the whole, beautiful point.

LEGO PreSchool Sets 18 months and up.

Regular Bricks 3 yrs. & up

PreSchool Bricks 1½ yrs. & up

1978 ©LEGO Systems, Inc., Enfield, Ct. 06082.

LEGO® is a registered trademark of Interlego A.G.

Be a pilot

MACHING BIRD™   SKI GULL™   SKY SCRAPER™   STAR GRAZER™   CLOUD HOPPER™   REGAL EAGLE™

Fly the new HOT BIRDS™

Ready on the Flight Deck™. Check your HOT BIRDS equipment...Flaps...Dive brakes...Retractable landing gear. Connect the nearly invisible Sky Line™. Now — take-off! Fly! Soar! And bring her in for a perfect landing. You're the pilot!

Hot Birds™

NEW HOT BIRDS: Great-looking metal airplanes you fly.

MATTEL®

©1971 Mattel, Inc. "HOT BIRDS" is a U.S. Trademark of Mattel, Inc. for its TOYS.

MEET THE NEW KING OF THE SKY

INTRODUCING
the F-16 Fighter plane
from Monogram

World powers have selected the F-16 Fighter Plane to patrol their countries' skies in an air superiority role in the next few years.

But, you can build this king of the sky now with Monogram's realistic 1/48th scale plastic model kit. Monogram's F-16 has the same design innovation and advanced technologies as the real thing. That's because the data supplied from General Dynamics (makers of the F-16) was used.

Authentic? You bet! With a detailed cockpit, canopy that opens, external fuel tanks, Air Force decals, detailed wheel wells, 2 Side-winder missiles and a life-like pilot figure. The finished model is over a foot long with a wingspan of almost 8 inches. And you can finish your F-16 in authentic Air Force grey or the exciting air show presentation colors shown above.

The F-16 is the shape of things to come in fighter planes. Come and get yours wherever model kits are sold.

MONOGRAM MODELS, INC.
MORTON GROVE, ILL. 60053

New from our Air Force Collection

Introducing a whole

The Sunshine Family dolls™

Say hello to
The Sunshine Family.
A unique new
family of dolls
whose world
your children
can share-
and create.

new world of sunshine!

1 Mother, Dad and Baby have their own special house and furniture. But that's only the beginning.

2 The Sunshine Family dolls come with this book of "do-it-yourself" play suggestions. It shows your children how to make The Sunshine Family playthings & furniture with paste, string, scraps of fabric, crayons — and imagination.

3 They can, for instance, turn a milk carton into a table.

4 A berry-basket becomes a crib, and a spool can become a planter.

5 Bit by bit, your children can create The Sunshine Family world. And as they do, they share the fun and excitement of their own family adventures.

The Sunshine Family
The fun shines on and on.

The Ohio Art Company, 1971

Play-Doh.
So many ways to make
a little kid feel big.

Play-Doh® modeling compound lets kids make things all by themselves. Things they can really be proud of.

Like green cows and blue horses at Animal Farm. And ring-toss rings, and tiddly-winks discs to pop into a Funny Frogs™ mouth.

A kid can pump a real-looking fireman's hose right out of Pumper No. 9.™ And mold a rainbow of bricks and logs and building stuff with Fun Factory®.

And create hundreds more wacky, wonderful things.

Whatever it takes to give a pre-schooler a grown-up hunk of satisfaction, kids can make it with Play-Doh.

Kenner. General Mills

NET WT. 6 OZ. Play-Doh by Kenner

Play-Doh molds kids.

Don't watch TV tonight. Play it!

We're the games you play on your own TV set.

We're the Atari Video Computer System.™ (Remember "Pong™"? Well, that was just the beginning.)

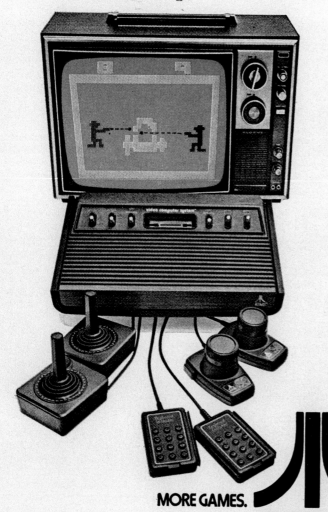

Atari is now a sophisticated, computerized programmable unit that hooks up to your television in a matter of seconds.

Atari features a greater selection (20 different Game Program™ cartridges, over 1300 game variations and options —and with many more to come!).

We're sport games. We're mind games. We educate. We entertain.

We can be played by one player (against the computer), two players, 3 or 4.

We're the system that's especially designed to change colors to protect and safeguard your TV tube from any damage.

We offer crisper colors (when played, of course, on a color TV).

We pride ourselves in truer-to-life sound effects, which play through your own TV's sound system.

We're Atari.

And if someone in your family hasn't asked for us yet, get ready.

They're going to.

MORE GAMES.   MORE FUN.

ATARI ®

YOU DON'T JUST PLAY GAMES WITH
THE BALLY ARCADE

Bally Sure. The Bally Professional Arcade™ Video Center comes to you with two of the most sophisticated, popular commercial arcade games in history built right in...Four-player Checkmate—the game of strategy; and Gunfight—the game of lightning reaction. But there's more.

The programmable microprocessor unit contains a 5-function, 10-memory printing keyboard calculator that scrolls on your TV screen. You can balance your checkbook, figure out your taxes or help your kids with their homework. This calculator is an exclusive feature offered only in Arcade.

And your Bally Professional Arcade is built for the future. Optional Videocade™ cassettes are available in a variety of programs that include an Educational Series, a Sports Series, an Action/Skill Series and a Strategy Series. And more are on the way!

The Bally Professional Arcade operates on ordinary house current and connects easily to your TV. The automatic shut-off switch prevents image burn on the screen.

Features like these allow you to experience new dimensions in a home TV entertainment center. Arcade. The computer video system that grows as you grow. By Bally. The people who make the games people play.

◄ Atari, 1978

Bally, 1977

RESCUE RIG™
Ready for any rescue mission! Talking Communications Center relays 6 calls! Rescue Boom for lifting and lowering. Basket opens to stretcher! 1 "D" battery and figures, not included.

0007-2290

Mattel, 1973

► Mattel, 1972

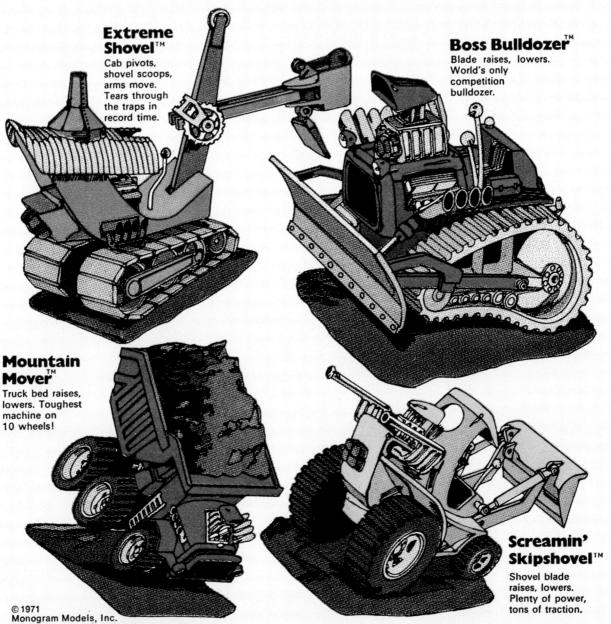

Martin B-26B Marauder

7002 (SEPTEMBER RELEASE)

Super-detailed 1/48 scale replica of famous American World War II bomber. Positive Alignment Locators for easy, precise assembly. Over 150 parts. Features include up or down landing gear, detailed bomb bay with open or closed doors, rotating turret, flight crew, removable engine cowling, authentic decal markings of 397th Bombardment Group.

Farrah's FOXY VETTE

3101 (JUNE RELEASE)

Supercar for a Superstar! Designed and built by George Barris, Farrah's Vette features radically flared fenders, louvered backlight, custom headlights and taillights, header sidepipes, "Vector" wheels, wide Goodyears and 454 V8 power. 1/25 scale.

◄ AMT, 1978

Louis Marx and Company, 1975

When Aces of the Sky appeared in
the Sears catalog in 1975, pinball was
still being banned in New York City
(from an ordinance going back to 1942)
for its supposed ties to gambling. The
ban would be lifted the following year,
just in time for the advent of modern
"solid state" machines.

Als Aces of the Sky im Sears-Katalog
von 1975 auftauchte, waren dank einer
Verordnung aus dem Jahr 1942 Flipperautomaten in New York noch verboten,
weil sie als Form des Glücksspiels gal-
ten. Im darauffolgenden Jahr wurde das
Verbot jedoch aufgehoben – gerade
rechtzeitig für die Ankunft von moder-
nen elektronischen Flipperautomaten.

Quand Aces of the Sky apparaît dans le
catalogue de Sears en 1975, le flipper
est encore interdit à New York (en
vertu d'un arrêté municipal de 1942)
pour ses liens supposés avec le jeu,
illégal. L'interdiction est levée l'année
suivante, à temps pour l'avènement
des massives machines modernes.

Aces of the Sky
Electric Pinball
by MARX

Operates on
standard household
current . . needs
no batteries
$29⁹⁷

Moonglow, 1970

▶ PSM Company, 1970

"I can make anything with Play-Doh®."

Jeff Strasser
Westchester, Ohio

"This looks like an elephant, but it's really a dog who grew a long nose because he told so many lies. He will change into a funny clown when I make a Play-Doh® princess and she kisses him on the nose. And I can make him into anything because he's Play-Doh.® Play-Doh® lets me make anything I think."

While your child is still a genius, keep him supplied with Play-Doh®.

As he squeezes and molds any fantasy his mind dreams up you'll see why Play-Doh® is the most important plaything you can provide.

Play-Doh® Modeling Compound comes in reusable containers and in a variety of fascinating sets.

Kenner

Kenner Products Company, 1973

▶ Playskool, 1978

YOUR CHILD MAY FALL IN LOVE WITH A BUG.

A pretend bug like Lucy Ladybug, Charlie Cricket, or Katie Caterpillar. Three soft, squeezable creatures who live in Playskool's fantasy-filled Bug World.

Children will love the water faucet elevator and the root chute slide that takes their new friends from their vegetable garden roof into their cozy little home.

They'll also enjoy taking them for rides in the walnut-shell car, putting them in the pea pod hammock at nap time, or making sure they're clean little bugs by pretending to bathe them in the eggshell shower. Brightly colored vegetables are really secret places to hide in.

So, this year, introduce your children to an underground fantasy world. Just be prepared for one thing ... they may fall in love with our bugs.

Playskool, Inc., A Milton Bradley Company

Dawn™ is the most beautiful doll in the world... yet she costs less than half the price!!!

Dawn is so much easier to get because she costs less than half the price of many other fashion dolls. She has the most fabulous clothes in the world. And they cost much less, too!

Dawn has a convertible car that really goes . . . a furniture set with a telephone that works . . . a handbag to carry Dawn in . . . a Dawn Music Box . . . beauty parlor . . . and the fabulous Dawn Fashion Show.

The Dawn Fashion Show. Dawn is the only doll in the world with a real revolving stage fashion show! Dawn and her friends walk and model, all by themselves!

Make a beautiful display like this of Dawn and her friends, Angie™, Glori™ and Dale™, wearing different outfits, right in your own room.

©1970-Topper Corp. Elizabeth N.J.

Every good cook has to start somewhere.

For her, there's no thrill quite like when she bakes that first Betty Crocker chocolate cake in her Easy-Bake Oven.

More than all the fun she'll have, Easy-Bake is a great way for her to create love in warm little bites.

Easy-Bake has built-in safety features, is U. L. approved and bakes with two ordinary light bulbs. And comes with real Betty Crocker mixes.

Easy-Bake. Because she'll love it.

Easy-Bake® Oven from Kenner

◀ Topper Toys, 1970

Kenner Products Company, 1973

One of the principles of Kenner was to make toys that would enable kids to do things they saw their parents doing. Using an incandescent light bulb as its heat source, Easy-Bake Oven gave the illusion of safety, which helped make it such a success. A Betty Crocker tie-in didn't hurt, either.

Eines der Prinzipien von Kenner war es, Spielzeug zu produzieren, mit dem Kinder ihre Eltern nachahmen konnten. Mit einer Glühbirne als Hitzequelle strahlten die Kinderherde der Marke Easy-Bake Oven Sicherheit aus, was zu ihrem Erfolg beitrug. Eine Kooperation mit der Marke Betty Crocker tat sicherlich das Ihre dazu.

Un des principes de Kenner est de fabriquer des jouets grâce auxquels les enfants peuvent faire la même chose que leurs parents. Le four Easy-Bake est chauffé par une ampoule à incandescence, ce qui rassure les grands et ravit les petits. L'association avec Betty Crocker participe bien sûr à son succès.

STAR WARS™

ACTION FIGURES

Twelve exciting action figures all in authentic STAR WARS costumes. All have movable arms and legs designed for great action poses; and they fit in other STAR WARS action toys and spaceships. Figures 2¼" to 4¼" tall.

CHEWBACCA™

LUKE SKYWALKER™

ARTOO-DETOO™ (R2-D2)

PRINCESS LEIA ORGANA™

HAN SOLO™

SEE-THREEPIO™ (C-3PO)

STAR WARS™

TIE FIGHTER™

Authentically detailed. Special buttons release two "solar panels" to simulate "battle damage". Lever raises seat and escape hatch — seat Darth Vader™ or other STAR WARS figures. Red laser cannon lights up and makes a whining laser sound.

Batteries not included.
Action figure not included.

LAND SPEEDER™

Special shift lever lowers the spring-loaded wheels for a "Floating Ride"! Open hood to find Turbo Reactor™ and Space Hatch storage compartment. Cockpit and rear deck seats up to four STAR WARS figures.
Figures not included.

STORMTROOPER™

DARTH VADER™

BEN (OBI-WAN)
KENOBI™

JAWA™

SAND PEOPLE™

DEATH SQUAD
COMMANDER

X-WING FIGHTER™

Spacecraft is complete with flashing light, laser sound, landing skid . . . the X-Wings even open and close! Cockpit canopy opens to put Luke Skywalker™ or other STAR WARS action figures in the pilot seat!

Batteries not included.
Figures not included.

DEATH STAR™ SPACE STATION

Help Luke™, Ben™, Chewbacca™ and Han Solo™ rescue Princess Leia™ from Darth Vader™. Manual elevator takes figures to any of the four floors. Top floor has an exploding laser cannon, third floor contains a manually operated light bridge, second floor houses the control area and the first floor features the famous Trash Compactor — complete with removable garbage and Trash Monster! Over 22″ tall.

Figures not included.   **Assembly Required**

Safety study shows Marx Big Wheel most stable tricycle design tested in U.S.A.

DELUXE BIG WHEEL
The original Big Wheel with two new features. A handy saddlebag, and a firm-grip handbrake that lets him slow down and stop without dragging his feet. For kids 4 to 7 years old, weighing up to 65 pounds and 40 to 55 inches tall.

MINI WHEEL
The smallest of the Big Wheel line. For tots 1½ to 3, weighing up to 45 pounds and 30 to 38 inches tall.

SPORT WHEEL
Like the Big Wheel, only smaller. And just as safe. For the 3-year-old up to the 6-year-old who is short for his age. 60 pounds maximum. 40 to 55 inches.

LITTLE WHEEL
A scaled-down Big Wheel for 2½-to 4-year-olds. Features low-slung stability. Scoop contour seat. Oversized front wheel. For kids 38 to 45 inches tall, weighing up to 50 pounds.

A five-month study* on the safety performance of the best-known tricycle designs in the United States has just been completed for the Department of Health, Education and Welfare's Bureau of Product Safety. Of all the tricycles tested, the design of the Marx Big Wheel was found to be most stable for children six and under.

Marx designed the Big Wheel especially for safety. The low-slung seat and extra-wide-track rear wheels prevent turnovers. The oversized front wheel and ground-hugging suspension won't let your child tip over backwards. Notice that none of the wheels have spokes to catch jeans. It can't rust. It can't dent. And it's built to take punishment.

*Calspan Corporation—An Evaluation of the Safety Performance of Tricycles and Minibikes.
Contract No. Food & Drug Administration 72-91.

And now Marx has incorporated this same Big Wheel safety design into a whole line of tricycles for smaller children. Pick the model best suited to your youngsters' age, size and weight. They'll have the thrill of their young lives ...and you'll have the confidence of knowing you're giving them the most stable tricycles you can buy.

Marx
If we make it...it can take it!

Good Housekeeping GUARANTEES

PARENTS' MAGAZINE GUARANTEED

◄ Kenner Products Company, 1978

Louis Marx and Company, 1973

► Playskool, 1978

Though Alphie was not the first commercial robot, this version released by Playskool in 1978 was a harbinger of things to come. "Right out of the space age," it was released a year after *Star Wars*, so parents were primed for their children to have an electronic companion like C-3PO.

Alphie war zwar nicht der erste kommerzielle Roboter, diese von Playskool 1978 lancierte Version erwies sich aber als Vorläufer zukünftiger Entwicklungen im Spielzeugsektor. Er kam „direkt aus dem Weltraumzeitalter" ein Jahr nach *Star Wars* heraus. Eltern waren also schon mental auf einen freundlichen elektronischen Spielgefährten wie C-3PO für ihre Kinder eingestellt.

Alphie n'est pas le premier robot proposé sur le marché, mais ce modèle Playskool de 1978 préfigure l'avenir du secteur. « Venu tout droit de l'ère spatiale », il est lancé un an après la sortie de *Star Wars*, si bien que les parents ont très envie d'offrir à leurs rejetons un compagnon comme 6-PO.

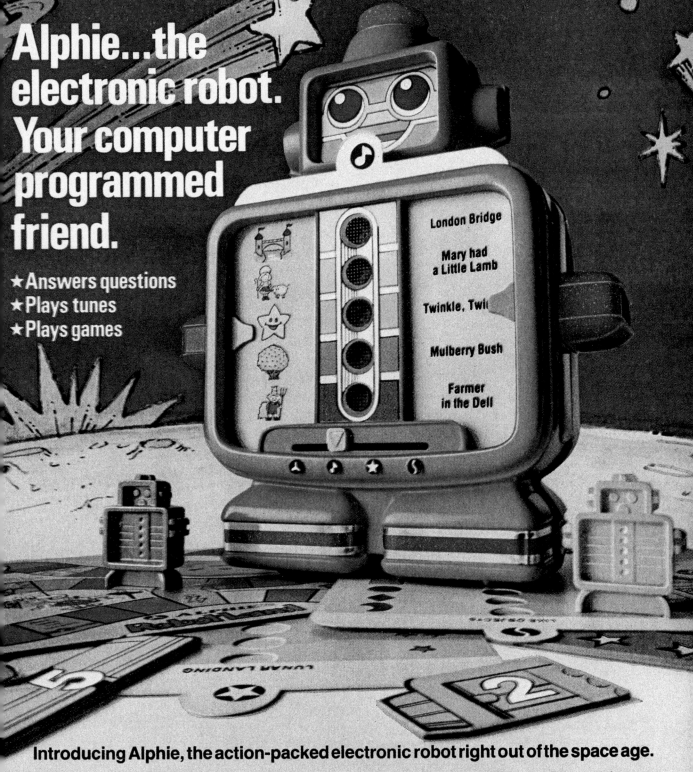

Alphie...the electronic robot. Your computer programmed friend.

★ Answers questions
★ Plays tunes
★ Plays games

London Bridge

Mary had a Little Lamb

Twinkle, Twi

Mulberry Bush

Farmer in the Dell

Introducing Alphie, the action-packed electronic robot right out of the space age.

Alphie's a 21st century teacher, super exciting, challenging, and lots of fun.

He talks with robot sounds and flashing lights. He plays "Stars And Stripes Forever" to tell a child an answer is right...and makes a mild "buzz" when the answer is wrong — and then Alphie shows what the answer should have been by flashing the right light.

Alphie teaches pre-schoolers color and picture matching, and five to eight year olds more advanced word matching and counting games. He even teaches music appreciation by conducting a sing-along to five popular children's songs. And to save the battery, Alphie shuts off his power automatically when not in use. So, if you want to make learning fun for your children, introduce them to Alphie. You'll be giving them a teacher they'll never forget.

J. C. Penney, 1970

▶ Parker Brothers, 1979

HE REALLY SMOKES

Mr. Brain can be programmed for six different patterns

1 9⁹⁹

Circular

Zig-Zag

Square

WATCH OUT!

All kinds of robots are on the move

3 TV Robot
3⁷⁷

Rudy the Robot
2 9⁹⁹

Space Robot
4 4⁷⁷

Mr. Amaze-A-Matic
Can be programmed to run six different patterns
5 9⁹⁹

Easy to program

There he blows!

EXPLO

Explo® Robotron
Put him together, then watch him blow apart
6 2⁹⁹

Gofer® Robotron
7 2⁹⁹

GOFER

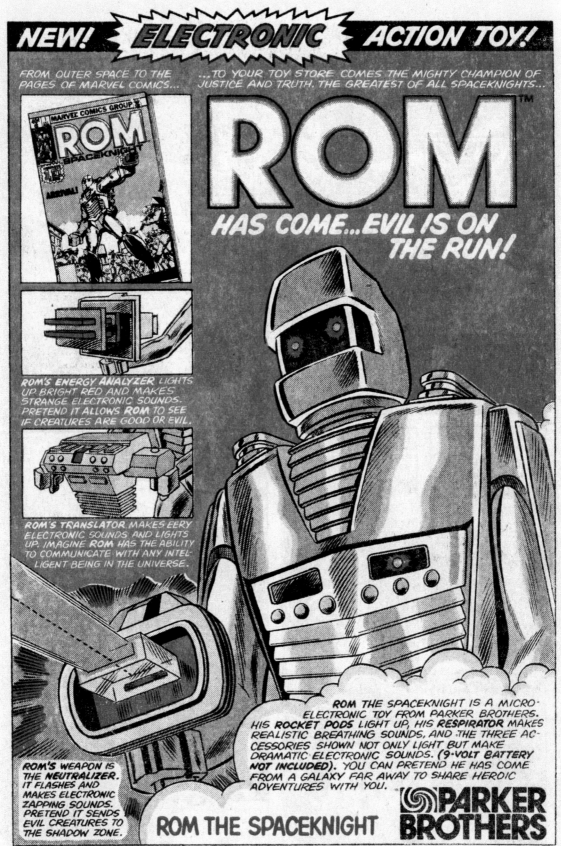

HOBIE SKATEBOARDS

STEP UP TO A HOBIE

Top to Bottom, a. Sundancer, b. Hustler, c. Competition

The new line of Hobie Skateboards offers top quality equipment for the fastest growing sport in the world. Check out our new 1976 models today!

- Fiberglass skateboard chassis in standard or kicktail styles.
- All wheels have double-sealed, precision bearings for fast, quiet, trouble-free riding.
- The Sundancer features the amazing new "Solo Suspension System," while the Competition and Hustler utilize the finest conventional trucks available.

On display at Hobie Surfboards (34195 Pacific Coast Highway, Dana Point), and available at finer surf, skate, bike, sporting goods, and department stores everywhere.

Dealer inquiries welcome: write or call

Hobie Skateboards P.O. Box 812, Dana Point, CA 92629 (714) 646-2404

In competition with automobiles, skateboards finish dead last. Be careful. Skate safe.

◄ Parker Brothers, 1975

Hobie Skateboards, 1976

Carlisle, 1971

▶ AMF, 1970

EASY RIDERS

BY ROADMASTER
AMF

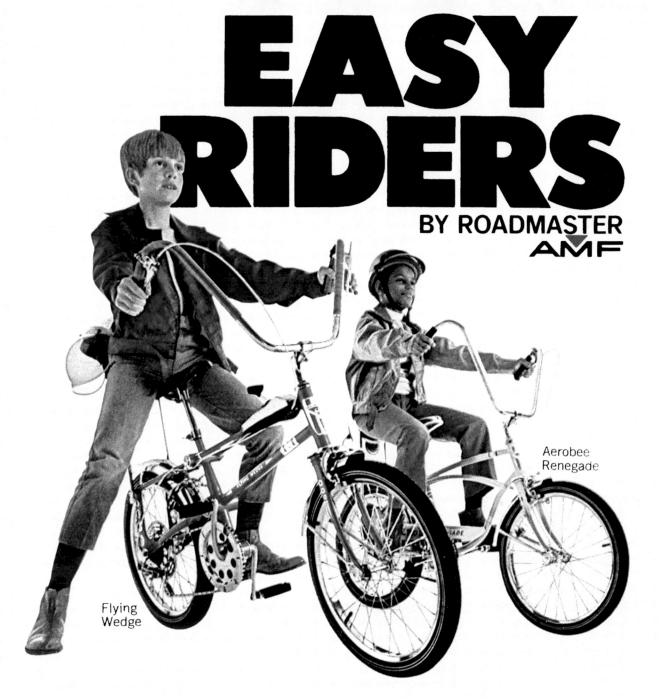

Aerobee
Renegade

Flying
Wedge

The Super Bikes. You don't just ride 'em, you cruise on 'em.

You can choose either the Flying Wedge with a 5-speed Stick Shift or the Aerobee Renegade with dependable coaster brake . . . or any one of 41 other AMF Roadmaster models. For the name of your nearest dealer, call free 800-243-6000. AMF Incorporated, Wheel Goods Division, Olney, Illinois 62450.

The Flying Wedge features a 5-speed stick shift control and Derailleur gear.

Even the chain guard on the Renegade says *action!*

sta·ple

(stā′pəl), *n., adj.*

A principal commodity in a mercantile field; goods in steady demand or of known or recognized quality.

This standard dictionary definition is a pretty good description of Magic "8-Ball." For more than a quarter-century, Magic "8-Ball" has been a **principal commodity** in the toy field creating a **steady demand** and **recognized** as a **quality** item of exceptional play value. Today it is better than ever with all-plastic safety construction plus bright new impulse-sales packaging. Its exciting sister item, ZODIAC BALL for astrology and horoscope buffs, is making cash register music. Stock the items with all the answers—Magic "8-Ball" and Zodiac Ball from Alabe.

Let the "8-Ball" get behind you! ⑧

alabe crafts inc. *1632 Gest Street · Cincinnati, Ohio 45204 · (513) 251-0886*

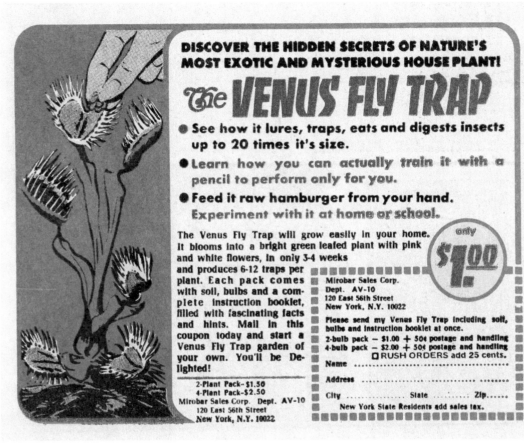

◄ Alabe Crafts, 1972

Mirobar Sales, 1971

YOUNG FUN

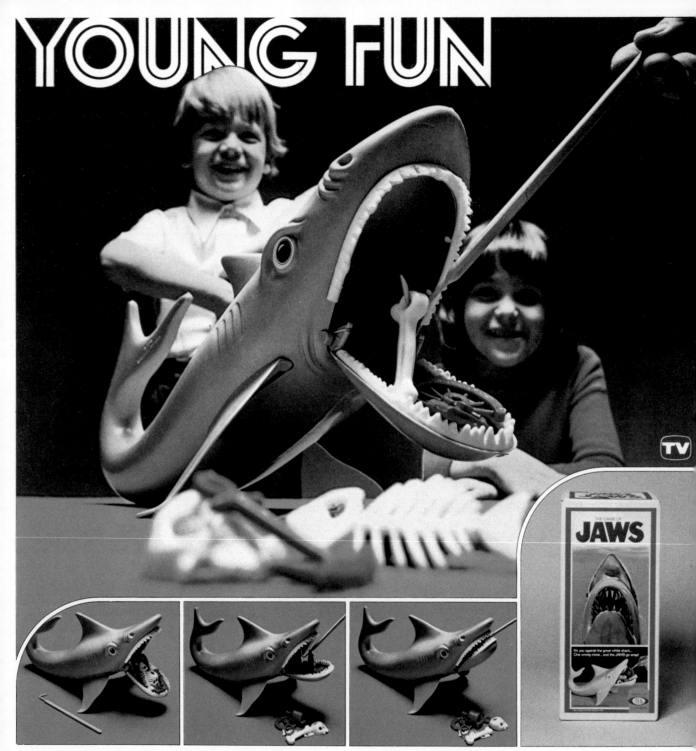

TV

JAWS™ GAME
2008-1

Lights! Action! Roll'em! It's you against the Great White Shark, in this game of skill that captures all the suspense and terrifying swiftness of the movie, "Jaws." The idea is to carefully remove pieces of junk—like a camera, an anchor, a fish, an old tire—from the shark's gaping jaws, using a gaff hook. The first player to remove four pieces of junk is the winner. But look out—as junk is removed, the shark's jaws start to quiver... then to move ever so slightly. If you make a wrong move now— CLACK! the terrible jaws snap shut! If it happens to you, you have to put back any junk you've removed, and start over. Everyone's talking about the movie, "Jaws"—the biggest box-office blockbuster of all time! Over 45 million people have already seen it, and it'll continue to be shown across the country right through 1976. A sequel, "Jaws II," is now being produced! With all this publicity behind it, you might say the possibilities for this game of Jaws are...wide open! Some assembly required.

Age group: 6 and up.
Pack: 6 pcs. Wgt: 11 lbs.

◀ Ideal Toy, c. 1976

Mattel, 1970

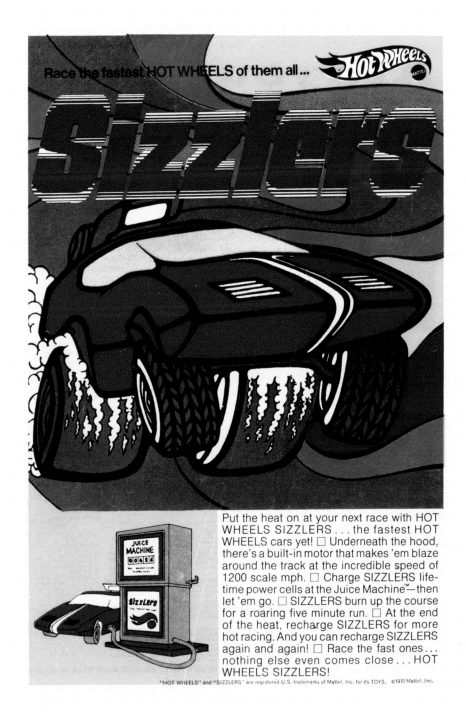

Race the fastest HOT WHEELS of them all ... Hot Wheels

Sizzlers

Put the heat on at your next race with HOT WHEELS SIZZLERS ... the fastest HOT WHEELS cars yet! ☐ Underneath the hood, there's a built-in motor that makes 'em blaze around the track at the incredible speed of 1200 scale mph. ☐ Charge SIZZLERS lifetime power cells at the Juice Machine™—then let 'em go. ☐ SIZZLERS burn up the course for a roaring five minute run. ☐ At the end of the heat, recharge SIZZLERS for more hot racing. And you can recharge SIZZLERS again and again! ☐ Race the fast ones ... nothing else even comes close ... HOT WHEELS SIZZLERS!

"HOT WHEELS" and "SIZZLERS" are registered U.S. trademarks of Mattel, Inc. for its TOYS. ©1970 Mattel, Inc.

Flash Gordon™ Playset . . . one side is Emperor Ming's castle . . . the other side is Flash Gordon's space room, complete with computer

Only $12⁸⁸ without figures

Help Flash and Dr. Zarkov™ rescue Dale from the evil hands of Emperor Ming!

8

(9 thru 12)
$4⁸⁵ each

11

12

9

10

Set folds to become carrying case

Sears, Roebuck, and Company, 1978

▶ Chiquita Brands, 1979

Nobody knows how to talk to kids like See'n Say® talking toys.

Tweety™

Daffy Duck™

Bugs Bunny™

Sylvester™

Road Runner™

Porky Pig™

Mattel Preschool See'n Say talking toys make your child's make-believe more real.

With a pull of the string, your child's imagination comes to life with the voices of his favorite cartoon characters and beloved storybook friends. Even animals have their say! And your child has so much fun, he doesn't even realize he's learning.

Maybe that's why there are more See 'n Say toys talking to more kids out there than any other talking toy.

Talking TV

The Zoo Keeper Says
The Farmer Says

Mother Goose Says

Bugs Bunny™
Talking Phone

Holly Hobbie®
by Knickerbocker®

A doll she'll remember with love

Holly Hobbie® will remind you of the rag doll you once loved.

You'll understand why little girls fall in love with Holly Hobbie® at first hug.

That's why Holly Hobbie® is fast becoming an American tradition.

Holly Hobbie® and her friends, Heather and Amy are soft, huggable rag dolls. And there are tiny versions with complete playsets—dresses to change, carriages to wheel, flowers to water, kitchens to cook in and a doll-size Gazebo.

Knickerbocker makes toys with loving attention to detail and to quality. So one day the little girl you love can give her Holly Hobbie® dolls to the little girl she loves.

Made to love
Made to last
by
Knickerbocker Toy Co., Inc.
1107 Broadway, N.Y, N.Y. 10010

Each doll is 6" tall

Holly Hobbie® is copyrighted by American Greetings Corporation.

Ideal Toy, 1973

► Revell, 1974

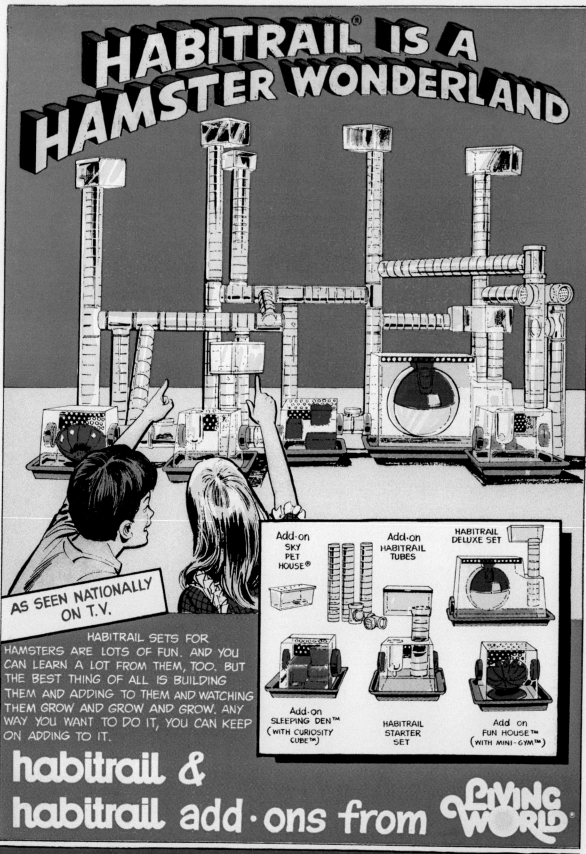

For those who required a bit more excitement than a stationary, non-biological toy could offer, the Habitrail afforded children the opportunity to give their pet hamster a lavish domestic environment including a "Fun House (with Mini-Gym)." The ability to keep adding features is emphasized, though keeping your hamster alive was the real trick.

Kindern, die sich mit leblosem Spielzeug langweilten, bot Habitrail die Möglichkeit, ihrem Hamster ein üppiges Domizil zu bauen, inklusive „Spaßhaus (mit Minifitnessstudio)". Betont wurde, dass man immer neue Teile anbauen konnte, die wahre Herausforderung lag jedoch darin, den Hamster am Leben zu erhalten.

Aux enfants qu'un jouet inerte n'exalte pas follement, Habitrail propose de composer un environnement grand luxe pour hamsters, notamment « une baraque de foire (avec minisalle de gym) ». Les accessoires peuvent être rajoutés à l'envi, à condition de garder la bestiole en vie assez longtemps pour qu'elle en profite.

Nature House, 1971

► Sears, Roebuck, and Company, 1989

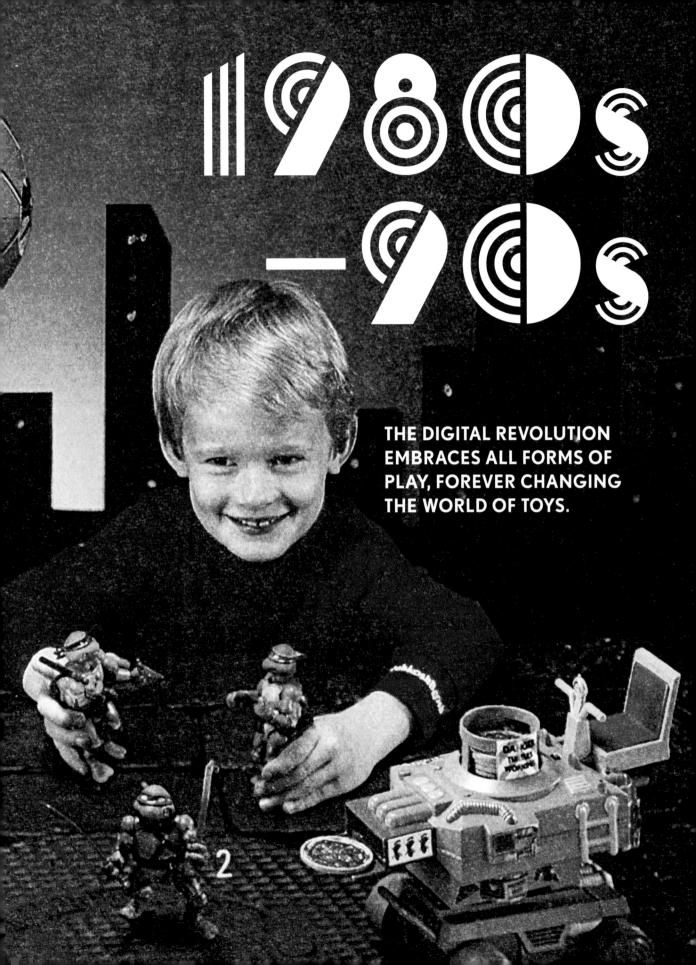

1980s–90s

THE DIGITAL REVOLUTION EMBRACES ALL FORMS OF PLAY, FOREVER CHANGING THE WORLD OF TOYS.

FOR CHILDREN OF ALL AGES

BY THE 1980S AND '90S, TOYS HAD BECOME MORE THAN MERE PLAYTHINGS DESIGNED TO EXCITE YOUNG ONES. They were advertised as fashionable, trendy status symbols—and some even as luxury items. These two decades prompted nostalgia for toys as they were in the decades of innocence, before the big chain stores dominated the market—not for the toys themselves, but for the spirit that they evoked.

Two films captured the contrast between toy culture of the past and present. *A Christmas Story* was Jean Shepherd's semifictional retelling of his childhood from the perspective of Ralphie Parker, whose sole desire in life was to be presented with a Red Rider air rifle—"the best present he had ever received or would ever receive"—on Christmas morning. The film expressed how during the Depression and World War II eras, before the tsunami

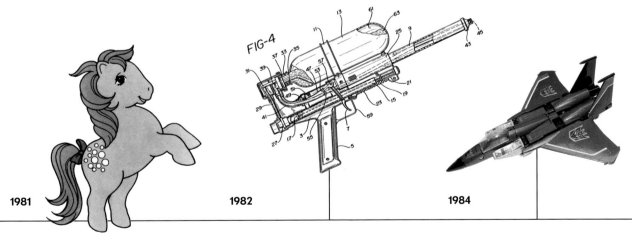

1981

My Pretty Pony, the precursor to My Little Pony, gallops into stores

My Pretty Pony, Vorreiter von Mein kleines Pony, galoppiert in die Läden

My Pretty Pony, précurseur de Mon Petit Poney, entre sur le marché au galop

1982

NASA engineer Lonnie Johnson creates prototype for Super Soaker

NASA-Ingenieur Lonnie Johnson kreiert den Prototyp der Wasserpistole Super Soaker

L'ingénieur de la NASA Lonnie Johnson crée le prototype du Super Soaker

1984

Transformers take the American market by storm

Die Transformers erobern den amerikanischen Markt im Sturm

Les Transformers prennent le marché américain d'assaut

of postwar consumption, one simple toy could thoroughly capture a child's imagination. In *Big*, Tom Hanks, as 12-year-old Josh Baskin, is granted a wish to become big (he literally became adult-size while keeping a child's brain). Inconceivably, he is hired by a major toy company and becomes an executive in charge of testing. The company looks more at the bottom line than pleasing children, so the plot includes the idea that childhood is a gift and should not be manipulated by branding experts in global corporations — toys should bring joy, right? Obviously, the lesson was not entirely learned.

By the '80s, many toys came with forced obsolescence built in. Atari was huge until it was overtaken by more advanced handheld units. Does anyone even remember Tengen games? Increasingly, more movie, cartoon, and comic books tie-ins flooded the market. Print advertising was squeezed as mass-market national magazines closed, so it was impossible to see a film or TV show (like *Teletubbies* and *Teenage Mutant Ninja Turtles*) without being targeted right between the eyes as a toy customer. There were still model airplanes to be built from kits and cakes to be baked

1985

1989

1992

Garbage Pail Kids trading cards make big bucks on bad taste

Die Sammelkarten der Garbage Pail Kids verwandeln schlechten Geschmack in riesige Umsätze

Les cartes à échanger des Patoufs, où comment faire fortune avec du mauvais goût

Nintendo releases Game Boy for gamers on the go

Nintendo bringt für Gamer unterwegs den Game Boy heraus

Nintendo édite la Game Boy, pour les joueurs qui ont la bougeotte

The popularity of *Barney & Friends* leads to a purple plush dinosaur frenzy

Die Beliebtheit von *Barney & Friends* führt zu einer enormen Begeisterung für lila Plüschdinos

La popularité de *Barney* déclenche un raz-de-marée de dinosaures violets en peluche in little homemaker stoves, but toys during these decades were coming out of the oven fully cooked in the research sense and ready to play. Some toys, such as the ones made by Playskool and Fisher-Price, were more educational than others. Some were more interactive. Toys were personalized, too. Cabbage Patch Kids and Beanie Babies came with their own backstory narratives. The worlds of make-believe had a new cast; Barbie had more friends — some were even minorities — and Playmobil offered new fantasy experiences. Toys had preset story lines that children were obliged to follow. The most significant shift in advertising, however, was the dual focus on child and parent. The baby boomers had grown up, but they still wanted toys to play with, too. *Toy Story*, another film that bears witness to that, evoked a time when everyone who loved toys wanted to believe they had secret lives.

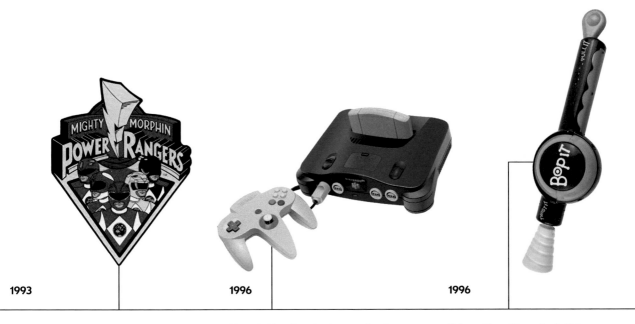

1993

Mighty Morphin Power Rangers debuts on TV, spawning a merchandising gold mine

Die Serie *Power Rangers* feiert ihren TV-Start und entpuppt sich als Merchandising-Goldmine

Les *Power Rangers* font leur apparition à la télé et inaugurent une nouvelle mine d'or

1996

Nintendo 64 is released with a groundbreaking new controller

Nintendo 64 kommt mit einem bahnbrechenden neuen Controller heraus

La nouvelle Nintendo 64 est équipée d'une manette de jeu révolutionnaire

1996

Kids must "bop it," "twist it," or "pull it" in a new game by Hasbro

„Drücken", „drehen" oder „ziehen" heißt es in einem neuen Spiel von Hasbro

Avec le Bop it! de Hasbro, les enfants « tordent », « tirent » et « tapent » à la demande

FÜR KINDER ALLER ALTERSGRUPPEN

Die digitale Revolution erfasst alle Spielsparten und verändert die Welt des Spielzeugs nachhaltig.

In den 1980er- und 1990er-Jahren waren Spielsachen mehr als einfach nur Gegenstände, die Kinder bei Laune halten. Sie wurden als stylische, trendige Statussymbole beworben – manche sogar als Luxusgüter. In diesen zwei Dekaden kam Nostalgie für das Spielzeug der „guten alten Zeit" auf, in der die großen Warenhausketten noch nicht den Markt beherrschten – eine Nostalgie, die sich nicht auf das Spielzeug selbst bezog, sondern auf die generelle Geisteshaltung, die man damit verband.

Zwei Filme fingen den Kontrast zwischen der Spielwarenkultur der Gegenwart und der Vergangenheit ein. In *Fröhliche Weihnachten* erzählt Romanvorlagen- und Drehbuchautor Jean Shepherd halbfiktional seine eigene Kindheit aus der Perspektive von Ralphie Parker, der sich nichts sehnlicher wünscht, als zu Weihnachten ein Luftgewehr der Marke Red Rider zu bekommen. Der Film drückt aus, wie in Zeiten von Wirtschaftskrise und Zweitem Weltkrieg – vor dem Konsumtsunami der Nachkriegszeit – ein einfaches Spielzeug die Fantasie eines Kindes vollständig gefangen nehmen konnte. In *Big* wird dem zwölfjährigen Josh Baskin (gespielt von Tom Hanks) der Wunsch erfüllt, groß zu sein; er wächst auf die Körpergröße eines Erwachsenen heran, behält aber sein kindliches Gehirn. Josh wird erstaunlicherweise von einem großen Spielzeugunternehmen als Produkttester eingestellt, die Firma ist aber mehr am Profit interessiert als daran, Kindern zu gefallen. Und die Moral von der Geschicht: Kindheit ist ein Geschenk und sollte nicht von den Branding-Experten globaler Konzerne manipuliert werden. Doch diese Lehre wurde offensichtlich nicht von allen beherzigt.

In den 1980ern war vielen Spielwaren von vornherein nur eine kurze Lebensdauer bestimmt. Atari-Videospiele beherrschten den Markt, bis technisch fortschrittlichere kleinere Spielkonsolen auftauchten. Wer erinnert sich heute noch an Tengen-Spiele? Auf Filmen und Comics basierendes Spielzeug überflutete den Markt förmlich. Die Printwerbung nahm kontinuierlich ab, weil einstmals weitverbreitete Zeitschriften eingestellt wurden, und gleichzeitig wurde es im Privatfernsehen nahezu unmöglich, einen Film oder eine TV-Sendung (wie *Teletubbies* und *Teenage Mutant Ninja Turtles*) zu sehen, ohne von Spielzeugwerbung bombardiert zu werden. Natürlich konnten Kinder immer noch aus Bausätzen Flugzeugmodelle basteln oder in kleinen Spielzeugherden Kuchen backen, aber die Spielwaren dieser Dekaden erreichten den Verbraucher tendenziell schon fix und fertig. Einige Produkte, wie die von Playskool und Fisher-Price, waren pädagogischer, andere interaktiver. Spielsachen wurden außerdem häufig personalisiert. Die Cabbage Patch Kids und die Beanie Babies bekamen individuelle Hintergrundgeschichten. Und die Welt des Rollenspiels mit Figuren bekam neue Darsteller: Barbie hatte mehr Freunde (einige davon sogar Angehörige ethnischer Minderheiten) und Playmobil lockte mit neuen Spielewelten. Spielfiguren hatten vorgegebene Geschichten, denen die Kinder folgen sollten. Die auffälligste Verschiebung in der Werbung war jedoch der duale Fokus auf Kind und Eltern: Die Babyboomer waren zwar inzwischen erwachsen, wollten aber auch etwas zum Spielen haben. *Toy Story*, ein weiterer Kinofilm mit nostalgischem Blick auf die Spielzeugvergangenheit, beschwor eine Zeit herauf, in der alle, die ihre Spielsachen liebten, glauben wollten, dass diese ein geheimes Leben haben.

▶ Acclaim Entertainment, 1991

Hello, fellow humans!
Bartholomew J. Simpson
here, with a big secret:
Space mutants are invading Springfield!
Yours truly is the only one who can see 'em—so it's
up to me to stop 'em. I've gotta spraypaint things, get radical on my skateboard, and in general
behave like a nuisance, man. It's a good thing I've got the rest of the Simpsons to help me out.
So if you're a decent person, a patriot, save the Earth! *Buy this game!*

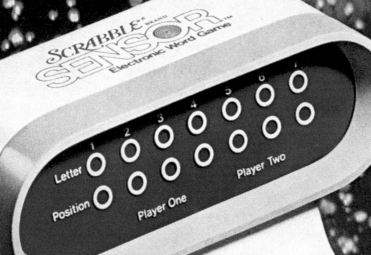

POUR LES ENFANTS DE 7 À 77 ANS

La révolution numérique s'empare de toutes les formes de jeux, changeant à jamais la face du jouet.

Dans les années 1980 et 1990, les jouets sont devenus plus que des produits ludiques destinés à exciter les plus jeunes. Ils sont vendus comme des objets de mode, de statut, de caste, et parfois même de luxe. Ces deux décennies sont teintées de nostalgie pour le temps de l'innocence où les grandes chaînes commerciales ne dominaient pas encore le marché, pas tant pour les jouets eux-mêmes que pour l'esprit qu'ils convoquent.

Deux films incarnent ce contraste entre le passé et le présent de la culture ludique : dans *A Christmas Story*, Jean Shepherd relate un épisode semi-autobiographique de son enfance du point de vue du jeune Ralphie Parker, dont le seul vœu est de se voir offrir une carabine à air comprimé Red Ryder – « le plus beau cadeau qu'il aurait jamais » – le matin de Noël. Le film montre combien pendant la Dépression et la Seconde Guerre mondiale, avant le tsunami consumériste de l'après armistice, un jouet unique pouvait fasciner un enfant jusqu'à l'obsession. Dans *Big*, Tom Hanks incarne Josh Baskin, 12 ans, dont le vœu de devenir grand s'est soudain réalisé (il a grandi, mais a conservé son cerveau d'enfant). Il se retrouve engagé par un gros fabricant de jouets qui le charge de superviser les phases de test. L'entreprise s'intéresse plus aux gros sous qu'au plaisir des enfants, si bien que l'intrigue incorpore l'idée que l'enfance est un don qui ne saurait être manipulé par les experts en identité de marque des multinationales – les jouets sont supposés apporter la joie, non ? À l'évidence, la leçon n'a pas été bien apprise. Dans les années 1980, nombre de jouets sont frappés d'obsolescence programmée. Atari est un géant du secteur, jusqu'à ce que les consoles portables prennent le dessus. Qui se souvient encore des jeux Tengen ? Peu à peu, le marché a été envahi par les produits dérivés de films, de dessins animés et de bandes dessinées. La publicité imprimée s'amenuise avec les magazines nationaux grand public où elle paraissait jusqu'alors, si bien qu'il est impossible de voir un film ou une émission de télévision (comme les *Teletubbies* ou les *Tortues Ninja*) sans être pris pour cible par les vendeurs de jouets. Les enfants peuvent encore construire des maquettes d'avions ou cuire des minigâteaux dans des minifours, mais les jouets de ces dernières années du siècle sortent tout chauds du four, prêts pour des heures de jeu. Certains, comme les produits Playskool et Fisher-Price, sont plus éducatifs que d'autres. Certains sont plus interactifs. Les jouets se personnalisent. Les Patoufs et les peluches Beanie Babies ont chacun leur histoire. Le monde du « faire semblant » s'anime de nouveaux personnages : Barbie a davantage d'amis, parfois issus de minorités, et Playmobil propose de nouvelles aventures imaginaires. À chaque jouet correspond une intrigue, une grille à laquelle les enfants doivent se conformer. Le virage le plus marquant qu'opère alors la publicité est cependant l'importance qu'elle accorde à la fois à l'enfant et au parent. Les baby-boomers ont grandi, mais ils ont encore envie de jouer. *Toy Story*, autre film qui témoigne de cet attachement au jouet, évoque une époque où tous ceux qui aimaient les jouets souhaitaient de toutes leurs forces qu'ils aient des vies secrètes.

◄ Selchow and Righter, 1980

Strawberry Shortcake.™
The lovable doll that smells like the berry in her name.

You've never seen a doll quite like Strawberry Shortcake. She's the berries! From her berry big hat, to her berry pretty face, to her berry nice strawberry smell.

She has three little Friends–Huckleberry Pie, Apple Dumplin' on Tea Time Turtle, and Blueberry Muffin. They're all less than six inches tall, and all smell like their names. And they all have combs for combing their berry soft hair.

They can ride in Strawberry Shortcake's Snail Cart and sell pies and jams in her Berry Bake Shoppe. These pretend playsets and the dolls are all sold separately.

Ask your little girl to smell Strawberry Shortcake. She'll fall in love at first sniff.

She's the berries!

Kenner

◄ Kenner Products Company, 1980

In 1980, girls "fell in love at first sniff" with Strawberry Shortcake, the doll that smelled of strawberries. The character was originally produced as greeting card art by the American Greeting Corporation, but Kenner licensed it in 1979 and it was an instant success thanks to her novel scent.

1980 war die Begegnung mit Emily Erdbeer, einer Puppe, die nach Erdbeeren duftete, für viele Mädchen „Liebe auf den ersten Riecher". Die Figur wurde ursprünglich als Grußkartenillustration von der American Greeting Corporation produziert, aber Kenner erwarb 1979 die Lizenz und machte die Puppe zum olfaktorischen Renner.

En 1980, les filles « tombent amoureuses » de Charlotte aux fraises, « au premier reniflement ». Le personnage figure au départ sur des cartes de vœux éditées par l'American Greeting Corporation, mais Kenner en achète les droits en 1979 et son succès est instantané, grâce à son arôme inédit.

Mattel, 1983

There were times when a little girl couldn't say how she felt.
But now, there's Poochie to help your little girl put it into words. On Poochie notepaper, with Poochie pencils and Poochie stamps that say all sorts of things.
There are Poochie stickers, Poochie combs, and mirrors, even Poochie purses.
With Poochie this and Poochie that, your Poochie girl will make quite an impression.

A Poochie girl says what's on her mind.

At one time, a little girl couldn't say what was on her mind. Now, she can say it with Poochie. **Give your little girl a style of her own.**

Poochie

Memos

YOU DRIVE ME CRAZY

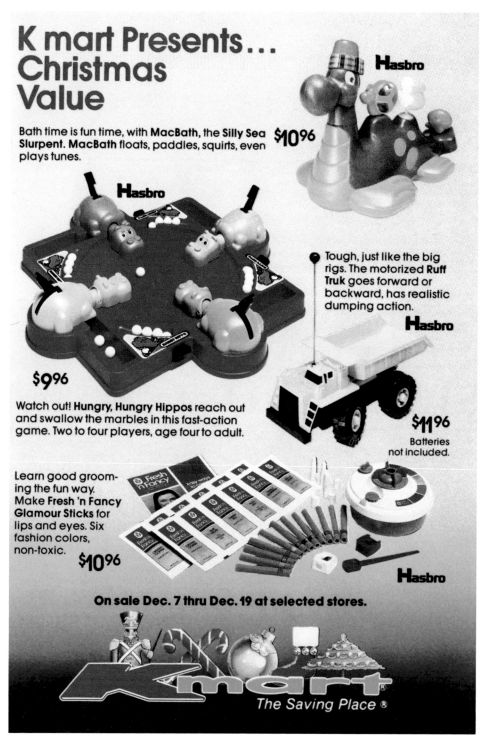

K mart Presents... Christmas Value

Kmart, 1981

▶ The ERTL Company, 1984

Bath time is fun time, with **MacBath**, the **Silly Sea Slurpent**. MacBath floats, paddles, squirts, even plays tunes.

Hasbro

$10⁹⁶

Hasbro

$9⁹⁶

Watch out! **Hungry, Hungry Hippos** reach out and swallow the marbles in this fast-action game. Two to four players, age four to adult.

Tough, just like the big rigs. The motorized **Ruff Truk** goes forward or backward, has realistic dumping action.

Hasbro

$11⁹⁶
Batteries not included.

Learn good grooming the fun way. Make **Fresh 'n Fancy Glamour Sticks** for lips and eyes. Six fashion colors, non-toxic.

$10⁹⁶

Hasbro

On sale Dec. 7 thru Dec. 19 at selected stores.

Kmart The Saving Place ®

Michael Jackson™ and Rainbow Brite.™
Gifts to keep children singing.

As long as there are songs to sing and nursery rhymes and ABCs to recite, children five and older will be enjoying their Vanity Fair phonographs. And you can give them their favorite this Christmas—with superstar Michael Jackson* or Rainbow Brite** and her magical flying horse, Starlite™.

Be assured you're giving

the best quality children's phonograph. Vanity Fair builds them to handle a child's enthusiasm and to play any 45 or 33⅓ RPM record. Either phonograph has a kid-tough case, solid-state circuitry, child-tested safety plug, the nearly unbreakable SuperArm™ and a five-year warranty.

Your little star can even

sing along with the Michael Jackson phonograph on its remote microphone and hear his or her voice through the big four-inch speaker.

Give a Vanity Fair phonograph and you give years of fun. What a good idea!

VANITY FAIR
by ERTL

THE ERTL COMPANY
Dyersville, Iowa 52040
Subsidiary of Kidde, Inc.

Toys "R" Us, 1989

▶ Gym-Dandy, 1984

NOW PLAYING IN YOUR BACKYARD

STAR WARS
RETURN OF THE JEDI

SCOUT WALKER COMMAND TOWER™ WITH SPEEDER BIKE RIDE™

FEATURING A 4-SOUND ELECTRONIC CONSOLE

Gym-Dandy® brings Jedi™ excitement to America's backyards. Little Jedi Knights can swing on the sturdy Speeder Bike™ and activate 4 great sound effects: Laser Cannons™, Turnstile Guns™, Scout Walker™ and Proton Torpedoes™!

To find the Gym-Dandy dealer near you, dial toll free: 800-447-4700.

GYM-DANDY.
The trusted one.

9 Volt Battery required (not included). © 1984 CBS Inc.

© 1985 THE ERTL COMPANY © 1985 BIGFOOT 4X4 TM

BIG AND CRUNCHY.

BIGFOOT It's mean. It's nasty. It'll eat anything that gets in its way.

And now you can build a 1/25th scale plastic model kit of your own.

With 460 cubic inches of Ford Power Plant. Monster off-road tires and super heavy duty rims.

It even has four wheel drive, a winch and a roll bar.

Pick up Bigfoot at your favorite store. It comes complete with AMT's exclusive facts manual. Full color decals. A destructive personality. And one, very bad reputation.

amt

Laugh,
Gund,
laugh.

Gotta
Getta
GUND®

© 1984 Gund, Inc.

◄ Gund, 1984

R. Dakin and Company, 1983

WELCOME ABOARD
HASBRO

WE'RE TAKING OFF IN NEW DIRECTIONS!

Make plans now to join the Cabbage Patch Kids® licensing
program as we launch new projects and explore new frontiers.
Contact Original Appalachian Artworks today for exciting
licensing opportunities and be prepared for take off!
P.O. Box 714 • Cleveland, GA 30528 • 404-865-2171

©1989 Original Appalachian Artworks, All Rights Reserved.

(Circle No. 38 on Reader Inquiry Card)

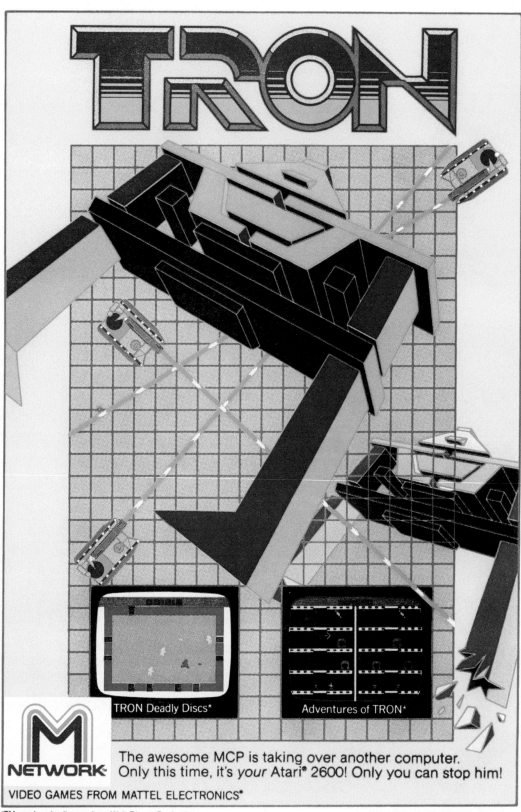

TRON Deadly Discs*

Adventures of TRON*

◄ Mattel Electronics, 1983

Atari, 1983

One of the most recognizable video games of all time was conceived when the Nintendo Co.'s landlord – Mario – dropped by looking for rent, inspiring his incorporation into a new game. Although made for the arcade, it was soon licensed for the home market by Atari but had a slow start due to the video game crash of 1983.

Die Idee für eines der bekanntesten Videospiele aller Zeiten wurde geboren, als der Vermieter der Firma Nintendo Co. – ein gewisser Mario – eines Tages vorbeischaute, um die Miete einzutreiben. Ursprünglich als Spielhallenspiel konzipiert, wurde Super Mario schon bald von Atari für die Heimkonsole lizensiert, kam aber wegen des Zusammenbruchs der Videospielindustrie ab 1983 nur langsam in die Gänge.

Ce jeu vidéo parmi les plus reconnaissables de tous les temps est né après que le propriétaire des locaux de Nintendo – Mario – a débarqué en quête du loyer, ce qui inspira l'idée à l'équipe de l'intégrer dans un nouveau jeu. Conçu pour l'arcade, il est bientôt breveté pour le marché domestique par Atari mais les ventes tardent à décoller, car en 1983 le secteur du jeu vidéo est en crise.

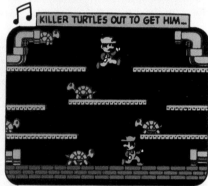

*Mario Brothers by Nintendo Trade Marks and © Nintendo 1983.   †Trademark of Sears, Roebuck and Co.

The fun never ends with **simon**

The classic computer memory game of lights and sounds

Three skill levels. 2 to 4 players. Five ways to play. Different every time. Ages six to sixty. Great family fun. Bright lights and computer sounds.

Milton Bradley, 1983

▶ Remco, 1986

The Karate Kid was released in 1984, grossed $91 million at the domestic box office, and spawned a line of toys and merchandise to capitalize on karate fever. For kids who weren't ready to join a dojo, Remco offered an action set that allowed them to "chop, twist, and kick" like the Karate Kid, Daniel LaRusso.

Karate Kid kam 1984 in die Kinos, spielte 91 Millionen Dollar ein und brachte eine ganze Palette von Spielwaren und Merchandising-Produkten hervor, die auf der Karatewelle schwammen. Für Kinder, die keinem Dojo beitreten wollten, bot Remco ein Actionset an, mit dem sie wie Karate Kid Daniel LaRusso „schlagen, sich drehen und treten" konnten.

Karaté Kid sort en 1984 et rapporte 91 millions de dollars de recettes nationales. Évidemment, la ligne de jouets et accessoires dérivés suit. Les enfants qui ne se sentent pas prêts pour le dojo peuvent se rabattre sur la figurine de Remco, qui « frappe, tord et fouette » comme le jeune Daniel LaRusso.

PUT THE POWER OF KARATE AT YOUR FINGERTIPS.

Miyagi

Sato

Karate Kid

Chozen

Attack Alley and Training Center

Johnny

KARATE KID TRI-ACTION™ FIGURES AND PLAYSETS

You've never seen action like this before. All Karate Kid Tri-Action figures chop, twist and kick. There's Daniel, the Karate Kid ...Miyagi...Johnny...Sato... and Chozen. Each comes with its own breakaway accessory.

The Karate Kid™

REMCO

Available at your favorite toy store.

Competition Center

The Adventure Is Yours

With DUNGEONS & DRAGONS®
Fantasy Adventure Games

D&D® Basic Set opens your world to adventure . . .
D&D® Expert Set gets you involved!
Our D&D® game is the world's most
talked about role-playing adventure. And
for good reason. It's a complete game SYSTEM.
In fact, our Basic game sets the pace for
the additional excitement and character
development you'll find in our Expert Set.

So if you think our Basic Set is great,
GET INVOLVED . . . capture even more
adventure in our Expert version.

◄ TSR, 1983

In its nascent years, Dungeons & Dragons was accused of steering kids in nefarious directions that could result in withdrawal from society or even death. Therefore, it was important that the ads cast the game in a more wholesome light — it was not witchcraft, but "adventure."

Anfangs wurde am Spiel Dungeons & Dragons kritisiert, dass es Kinder negativ beeinflussen und zu einem Rückzug aus der Gesellschaft oder sogar zum Tod führen könne. Umso wichtiger, dass die Werbung das Spiel in einem positiveren Licht darstellte – es ging also nicht um Zauberei und Hexenwerk, sondern um „Abenteuer".

À ses débuts, Donjons & Dragons est accusé de pervertir les enfants, de les marginaliser, voire de les pousser à la mort. Il est donc capital que la publicité redore son blason – il ne s'agit pas de sorcellerie mais d'« aventure ».

Mattel Electronics, 1983

► TSR, 1984

►► MPC, 1981

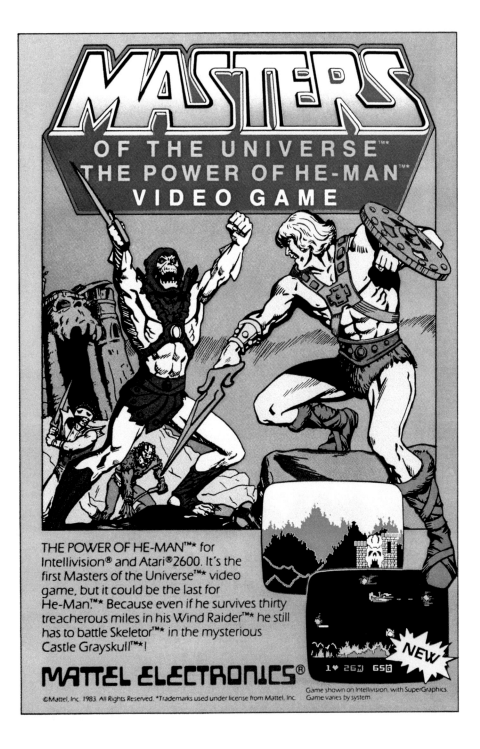

THE POWER OF HE-MAN™* for Intellivision® and Atari®2600. It's the first Masters of the Universe™* video game, but it could be the last for He-Man™* Because even if he survives thirty treacherous miles in his Wind Raider™* he still has to battle Skeletor™* in the mysterious Castle Grayskull™*!

MATTEL ELECTRONICS®

©Mattel, Inc. 1983 All Rights Reserved. *Trademarks used under license from Mattel, Inc.

Game shown on Intellivision, with SuperGraphics. Game varies by system.

BUILD THE WORLD'S MOST ADVANCED DEFENSE SYSTEM.

You've built the deadliest aircraft. The most awesome tanks. And the mightiest warships. Now, maybe, you're ready for Robotech Force.™ Super-powered robots equipped with radar-directed, rapid fire lasers. And powerful computerized brains, programmed to seek and destroy all enemies. So protect the world from attack. Put yourself in command of the most awesome defense system that the world has ever known. Robotech Force.™

Revell® ceji

◄ Revell, 1984

Huffy, 1985

BMX started in the backyards of
Southern California in the early 1970s.
The sport was invented by kids who
were inspired to emulate their favorite
motocrossers on modified Schwinn
Stingrays. By the '80s, companies such
as Huffy were capitalizing on the trend
by manufacturing race-ready bicycles
and advertising them in comic books.

BMX kam in den frühen 1970ern in
den Hinterhöfen Südkaliforniens auf,
erfunden von Kids, die ihre Motocross-
idole auf aufgepeppten Schwinn-
Stingray-Fahrrädern nachahmten.
In den 1980ern schlugen Firmen wie
Huffy aus dem Trend Kapital, indem
sie coole Räder produzierten und sie
in Comicbüchern bewerben.

Le BMX est né dans les arrière-
cours de Californie au début des
années 1970, inventé par des gosses
qui modifiaient les Stingrays de
Schwinn pour imiter les champions
de motocross. Des sociétés comme
Huffy s'en emparent dans les
années 1980 et promeuvent leurs
vélos de course dans les comics.

Lego Systems, 1986

▶ Marvel Comics Group, 1981

SPIDER-MAN: SPINNING A WEB OF SUPER SALES

*S*pider-Man's spinning his way into 26 all-new half-hour cartoons to be sold directly into first-run syndication, beginning September 1981 and heading for an audience impact peak at the Christmas selling season.

THE MARVEL MEDIA MASTER PLAN: STEP ONE

The Spider-Man cartoons are the first project created by Marvel's animation studio in California, and the first step in Marvel's ongoing commitment to the development of broadcast media.

POPULARITY PROOF

Over 100 million Marvel comic books are consumed by kids every year. With a 45% share in the U.S. market, an unparalleled 100% awareness level, and a presently syndicated Spider-Man package that's number one in 75% of its markets, Marvel's got popularity proof!

Don't miss the excitement that all Marvel SUPER HEROES generate.

MARVEL AND KIDS
The Best of friends.

Contact:
Licensing Department
MARVEL COMICS GROUP
575 Madison Avenue
New York, New York 10022
212/838-7900

MATTEL ELECTRONICS®
FOOTBALL 2

Passing! Running! Kicking! You call the plays. Computer's on Defense. Watch out for interceptions, blitzes or a two-point safety! Football 2 by Mattel Electronics® is like taking the field! You drop back to pass, scramble, hit the receiver downfield! Touchdown! Three-point field goals and punts. Kickoffs, too-- even runbacks! This is the all-pro edition of the #1 electronic football game! Simulated game sounds include "Ref's whistle", "Charge", "Victory" tune for TD's & field goals. Status key gives down, field position & yards to go. Score key gives score & time remaining! New wider screen, 4 playing speeds, 4 directional keys! Field & scoreboard light up separately.

#1050 Std. Pak 6

Operates on 9-volt transistor battery, not included.
Pocket electronic game for 1 or two players.

#1050 Football 2

◄ Mattel Electronics, 1980

Parker Brothers, 1983

Mattel Electronics, 1983

▶ American Greetings, 1986

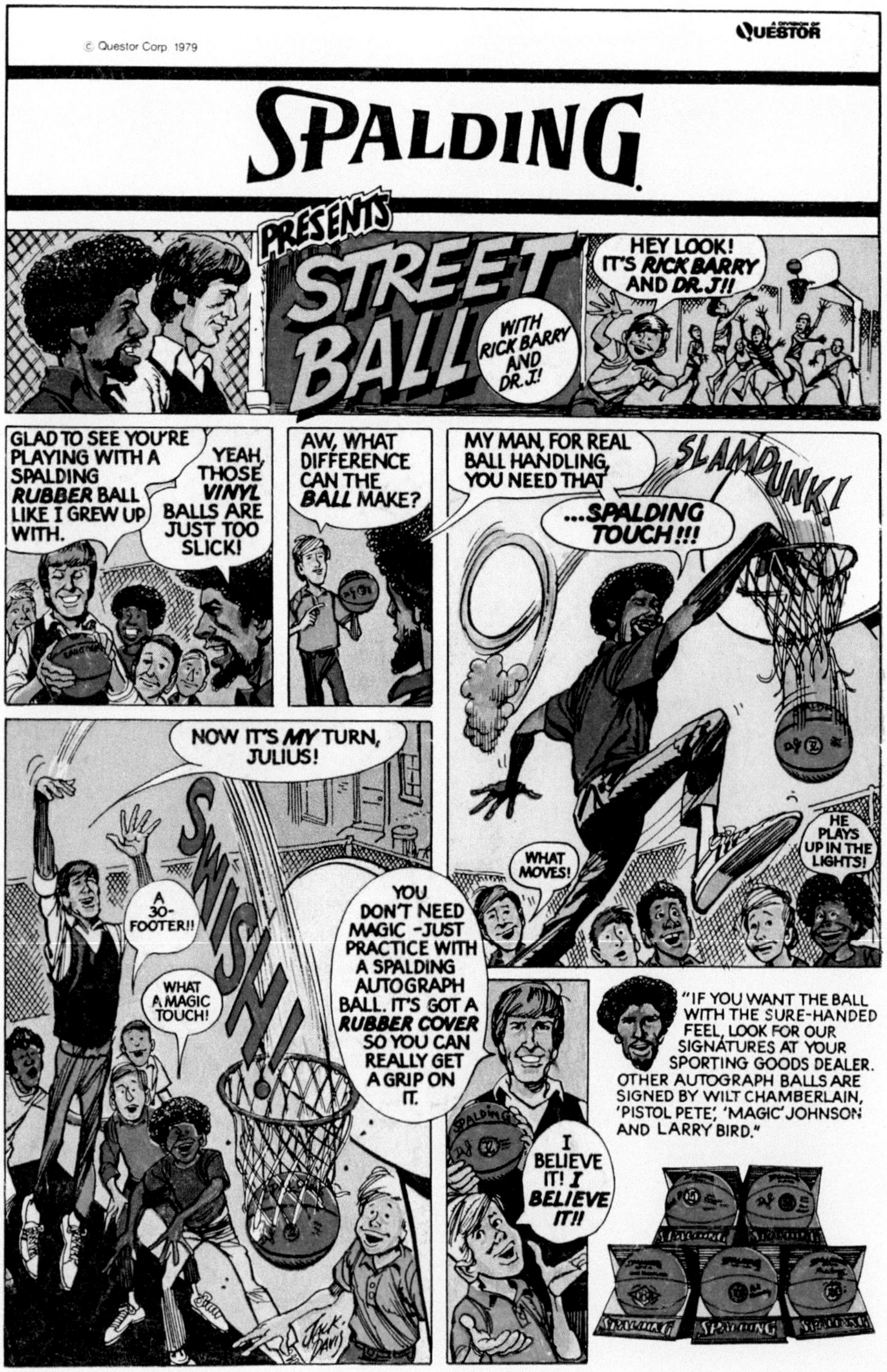

Questor, 1980

▶ Matchbox, 1989

Still at #1!

PEE-WEE HERMAN™ TALKING DOLL

3500

As the Emmy Award Winning network TV show enters the 1988/1989 TV season "Pee-wee's Playhouse" continues to be the #1 rated Saturday morning network TV show among children aged two to eleven years old.

In addition to the Saturday morning shows. 1989 will also offer several prime time specials *and* a new movie scheduled for release in the Summer!

As hot as ever our 17" Pee-wee Herman Talking Doll features:

■ Poseable arms and legs the famous grey plaid suit, red bow tie
■ and white bucks
■ surface washable

Just pull the string to hear six famous Pee-wee lines recorded with his own voice . . .

"Hello, I'm Pee-wee Herman"
"I love you"
"Aargh"
"Hey, what's that! Made you look"

(no batteries required)
Non-talking version 3510 also available.

Individual Package Size:
10" × 9¹³⁄₁₆" × 20⁷⁄₁₆"

Master Carton Size:
28" × 20" × 20⁹⁄₁₆"

Pack: 6

Weight: 22.5 lbs.

Cube: 6.7 cu. ft.

AS SEEN ON TV!

LOCK'N'CHASE™*
LOCK OUT THE POLICE AND GRAB THE GOLD. BEFORE THE POLICE GRAB YOU!
17360 17360
MATTEL ELECTRONICS®
INTELLIVISION®
*Used under license from Data East Inc. © 1981, 1982 Data East Inc.
©Mattel, Inc. 1982 All Rights Reserved.

ATTACK THE ALIENS

Strange creatures from outer space are threatening our planet. Who are these aliens and what do they want? No time for questions now. Your mission is to destroy the aliens with your laser cannon before they reach Earth. Hit a space invader and score points. But just when you think you've destroyed them all, new invaders appear.

Remember, the aliens have weapons, too. If you're hit with their laser bombs three times, you're lost in space forever. **112 Games**

Look at the friends you can make with Play-Doh®!

clean   non-toxic
Ages 3 and up

Play-Doh
MODELING COMPOUND
by Kenner®

Play-Doh® brings its friends into the homes of kids everywhere
There's the world of Strawberry Shortcake*…all the Sesame Street†
neighbors…the adventurous characters of Star Wars**…and
those comical Stone Age people, the Flintstones††. They all add to
the fun children can make with Play-Doh Modeling Compound!

Fisher-Price

◀ Kenner Products Company, 1981

Fisher-Price, 1990

Kirsten® Larson

♥

A pioneer girl of strength and spirit growing up on the prairie in 1854.

THE AMERICAN GIRLS COLLECTION™

Pleasant company for American girls.

*The American Girls Collection®
is just the kind of pleasant company
girls want, need, and love.*

*Books about five lively girls
who grew up long ago are the heart
of the collection. Lovable
dolls that have beautiful
clothes and accessories make
these stories of the past come alive
for American girls today.*

♥

*Available exclusively from
Pleasant Company.*

*For a FREE catalogue of books,
dolls, dresses, and other delights
for girls 7 and up,
call 1-800-845-0005.*

*Or write: Pleasant Company
Dept. 83170, Middleton, WI 53562-0497*

NAME	
ADDRESS	
CITY	
STATE	ZIP
	83170

PLEASANT COMPANY®

Pleasant Company, 1995

Started in 1986, each American Girl doll came with a detailed backstory, such as Kirsten Larson, "a pioneer girl of strength and spirit growing up on the prairie in 1854." Parents loved them because they taught lessons about U.S. history; kids loved them because they felt like real people whom they actually *knew*.

Jede Puppe der 1986 lancierten Reihe American Girl hatte ihre eigene detaillierte Hintergrundgeschichte. So war Kirsten Larson zum Beispiel „ein starkes und mutiges Pionier-mädchen, das 1854 in der Prärie aufwuchs". Eltern liebten die Girls, weil sie US-Geschichte vermittelten; Kinder liebten sie, weil sie ihnen wie echte Menschen vorkamen, die sie persönlich kannten.

Depuis 1986, toutes les poupées American Girl sont accompagnées d'un petit livret biographique, comme Kirsten Larson, « une fille de pionniers forte de corps et d'esprit dans la grande prairie en 1854 ». Les parents les adorent parce qu'elles enseignent l'histoire américaine et elles plaisent aux enfants qui ont la sensation de les *connaître* comme de vraies personnes.

▶ Ideal Toy, 1983

SOME OF YOUR BEST CHILDHOOD FRIENDS HAVE NEVER GROWN UP.

Thumbelina.® You loved her then, your daughter will love her now. It's a feeling girls never outgrow.

Thumbelina.® Betsy Wetsy.® And Tiny Tears.® They're Ideal's Classic Dolls. As loved today as yesterday.

IDEAL CLASSIC DOLLS

IDEAL®

FREE!

LONE RANGER WESTERN TOWN!

THE LONE RANGER
and SILVER

GENERAL
GEORGE
CUSTER

BUFFALO
BILL CODY

BUTCH CAVENDISH
and SMOKE

TONTO and SCOUT

Figures and horses not included.
© 1982 Lone Ranger TV Inc.

HERE'S HOW TO GET YOUR FREE WESTERN TOWN.

Purchase any 4 Lone Ranger figures or horses shown above. Cut out the name of the figure or horse (the name in big white letters) from the front of each package as your proof-of-purchase. Then fill out the coupon below and send it to us with all 4 proofs-of-purchase. We'll send you the town that brings the Old West back to life.

The exciting Lone Ranger Western Town includes Arbuckle's Hotel, the Carson City Bank, Bok's General Store, the Gold Nugget Saloon and Casino, and lots more.

All with colorful, realistic detail, on the front and back. Plus, this great scene for wild west action is the perfect size for all Lone Ranger 3¾" action figures and horses. Some assembly required.

Gabriel®

© 1982 Gabriel Industries, a division of CBS Inc.

G.I. JOE EXTREME™

ONLY G.I. JOE EXTREME™ GIVES YOU LONG DISTANCE ULTRA SLAM FIREPOWER™!

Freight™

Metalhead™

Lt. Stone™

Ballistic™

Iron Klaw™

Wreckage™

Detonator™

Spitfire™

New!

81225 G.I. Joe Extreme™ Deluxe Figure Asst.

- Bulked-up, and ready for battle – these guys mean business!
- Each deluxe figure features long distance Ultra SLAM Firepower™!
- Ready them up for any mission with detachable battle armor!

Ages: 5 and up.
Pkg. Type: Blister Card **Pk:** 6

Tv

New!

81235 G.I. Joe Extreme™ Heavy Artillery™ Asst.

- Bring on the heavy artillery!
- G.I. JOE Detonator™ with exclusive Sgt. Savage™ figure hones in on the enemy and slams the firing button to launch long distance Ultra SLAM Firepower™!
- SKAR™ Spitfire™ with exclusive Inferno™ figure blasts long distance Ultra SLAM Firepower™! into unsuspecting troops. Incoming missiles that hit their target cause massive battle damage, toppling platform and figure!

Ages: 5 & Up
Pkg: Closed Box **Pk:** 6 **Tv**

OddzOn Products, 1989

▶ Hasbro, 1996

NERF
BRAND
SPORTS™

00281 Nerf® Ball 2 -Pack
- Two 4" balls in rackable polybag with header card!
- Bright colors!
  Ages: 3 & Up
  Pk: 6

New!

60483 Instant Baseball
- Complete portable baseball game... just add kids!
- Bat, ball, bases and home plate all store neatly together!
- Scoring and inning indicators included on home plate
  Ages: 6 & Up **Pk:** 4

Tv

New!

60438 Nerf® Turbo Jr.™ Football
- The right size and weight to build basic skills!
- Easy to grip, throw and catch!
- Multi-use — ideal for indoor or outdoor play!
  Ages: 4 & Up
  Pkg: Shrink Wrap Sleeve
  Pk: 6

00215 Turbo Grip™ Football
- Grooved and balanced for perfect passes!
- Explosive neon colors!
- New packaging establishes performance positioning.
  US Patent No. RE33449.
  Ages: 4 & Up
  Pkg: Open Carton **Pk:** 6

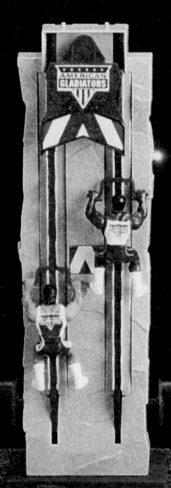

A

AMERICAN GLADIATORS

B

C

D

Super Soaker, 1997

Super Soaker, the brainchild of former NASA engineer Lonnie Johnson, took a ham-fisted approach to selling its water guns in 1997 with celebrity wrestler Sycho Sid. After the enormous success of his product in the '90s, Johnson went on to produce several other products, including a diaper that plays a song when wet and a solar energy converter.

Wasserpistolen der Marke Super Soaker, eine Erfindung von NASA-Ingenieur Lonnie Johnson, wurden 1997 ziemlich grobschlächtig mit Promi-Wrestler Sycho Sid beworben. Nach dem enormen Erfolg dieses Produkts in den 1990ern produzierte Johnson noch andere Dinge, zum Beispiel eine Windel, die Musik spielt, wenn sie nass ist, und einen Energie-umwandler für Solarstrom.

L'ancien ingénieur de la NASA Lonnie Johnson ne lésine pas sur les moyens pour vendre son pistolet à eau Super Soaker en 1997 puisqu'il embauche le célèbre catcheur Sycho Sid. Après le succès phénoménal de ses produits dans les années 1990, Johnson inventera notamment une couche qui joue une chanson quand elle est mouillée et un convertisseur d'énergie solaire.

Reunite with an old friend.

You Could Win an Exciting Flying Adventure!

It's time to re-enlist with G.I. Joe®.

Remember when you and G.I. Joe could save the world? When you and he could take on any challenge? You still can. All the fun and excitement of G.I. Joe live on in a larger than ever variety of 12-inch figures. The USMC Boot Camp, the USAF Crew Chief, the US Army Cold Weather G.I. Joe and Army and Navy Football players — all are exceptional quality, fully outfitted in hand-sewn attire and authentically styled equipment.

And now, in the G.I. Joe® Fighter Pilots USA® Sweepstakes, you can reunite with your old friend G.I. Joe and take a friend on an amazing real-life aerial simulated combat flying adventure. Win a chance for you and a friend to fly in a real "light attack fighter trainer" with a former military fighter pilot.

This adventure is brought to you by the one and only G.I. Joe — the first name in authentic military. Act now to purchase these remarkable figures that are a timeless addition to any home and a must for a collector of any age. Enter now for your chance to win the G.I. Joe® Fighter Pilots USA® Sweepstakes.

**GI.JOE®
CLASSIC COLLECTION**
The First Name In Authentic Military

Fighter Pilot USA Sweepstakes, 1998

► Mattel, 1993

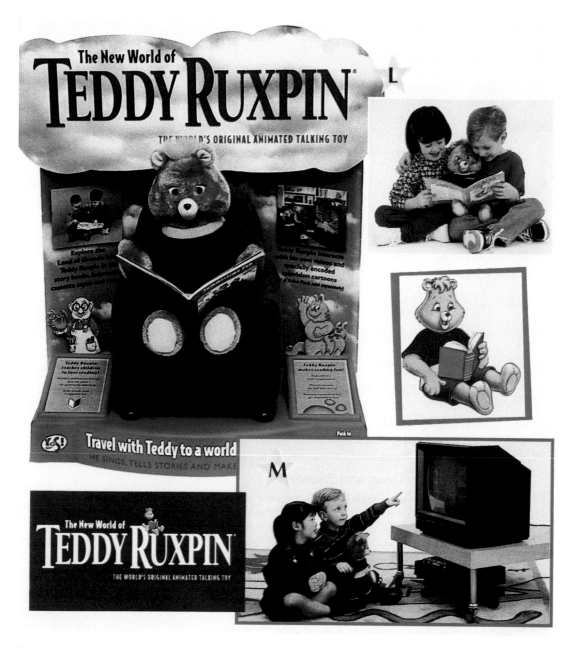

The New World of

TEDDY RUXPIN

THE WORLD'S ORIGINAL ANIMATED TALKING TOY

Sears, Roebuck, and Company, 1998

▶ Bandai Company, 1997

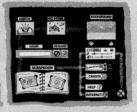

Where you get the best dolls under the rainbow!

And the best deals, too!

ROYAL WEDDING COUPLE
11 1/2". Ages 3-up
OLMEC **$19.99**

HOT SKATIN' BARBIE
11 1/2". Ages 3-up
MATTEL **$10.99**

ASHA ROYAL PRINCESS
11 1/2". Ages 3-up
MATTEL **$14.99**

BAYWATCH BARBIE
11 1/2". Ages 3-up
MATTEL **$14.99**

LOWER prices BIGGER selection GUARANTEED

If you find a lower price in any current toy ad...just show us the ad and we'll match it. GUARANTEED!
Competitor must have advertised item in stock and ad must show specific item and price. Prices are matched
after Toys "R" Us savings have been deducted from original price. Does not apply to percent-off sales.

Play for keeps.

*She'll keep playing & playing & playing with her **Power Wheels**® Barbie™ Corvette.®*

*Play cellular phone–
essential for Barbie™
business calls
and hours of chit chat.*

*Detailed dash,
shift console with
an ignition key,
and glove
compartment.*

*More play!
Power Wheels also
makes road signs,
and stoplights
that really light.*

STOP

*Play with confidence:
Power Wheels
patented safety
braking system that
stops the car
the minute her
sneaker leaves
the pedal.*

*Real doors that
open and close!*

*Runs on
Power Wheels
exclusive
Super 6-volt
system with
rechargeable battery.
Goes 3 mph
forward
and reverse.*

*Behind this
symbol is a
well-made toy:
Power Wheels
builds in quality
with Corvette-
perfect styling
and super tough
construction.*

**POWER
WHEELS**®
FT. WAYNE, INDIANA

The world's leading maker of battery-powered vehicles.

Good Housekeeping

Call toll-free 1-800-348-0751 if you'd like our catalog, more information or help with a problem.

©1988 Kransco   BARBIE and associated trademarks are owned by and used under license by Mattel, Inc. ©Mattel, Inc. 1988. All Rights Reserved.
CHEVROLET CORVETTE is a trademark of GENERAL MOTORS CORPORATION and is used under license.

◄ Toys "R" Us, 1995

Mattel, c. 1990

Sears, Roebuck, and Company, 1991

MC Hammer's third album, *Please Hammer, Don't Hurt 'Em*, was such a mainstream success (rare for a rap album at that time) that one year after its release, you could open the Sears *Wish Book* and find a toy version of singer/dancer in his trademark "parachute pants" alongside Barbie.

MC Hammers drittes Album *Please Hammer, Don't Hurt 'Em* war ein solcher Mainstream-Erfolg (damals für ein Rap-Album eine Seltenheit), dass man ein Jahr später im Wish Book von Sears gleich neben Barbie eine Spielzeugversion des Sängers und Tänzers inklusive der für ihn typischen ausladenden „Hammer Pants" finden konnte.

Le troisième album de MC Hammer, *Please Hammer, Don't Hurt 'Em*, remporte un tel succès (fait rare pour un album de rap à l'époque) qu'un an après sa sortie le catalogue de Sears propose à côté de Barbie une figurine de l'artiste vêtu de son célèbre « pantalon parachute ».

Sears, Roebuck, and Company, 1992

Sears, Roebuck, and Company, 1998

▶ Fisher-Price, 1990

▶▶ Hasbro, 1994

Fisher-Price presents the joy of cooking.

Look at what we've cooked up for your little one—The Fisher-Price® Toddler Kitchen—a child-sized kitchen that cooks up a huge portion of fun.

Here's the secret recipe: Take one colorful, spinning "burner." Add a toaster with 2 slices of toast that "boing" up and down. A bread board that sorts shapes. And a door that clickety-clacks. Then stir it all gently with a spoon that smiles.

In addition to the kitchen, we have some extra treats you can pick up for your little gourmet—like Wiggly Wobbly Eggs and a Moo Sound Milk Bottle.*

What a wonderful way to feed a young imagination.

RED DRAGON THUNDERZORD
THE RED RANGER'S POWERFUL NEW ZORD

Warrior Mode

Firebird Thunderzord*

+

Unicorn Thunderzord*

+

Lion Thunderzord*

+

Griffin Thunderzord*

THUNDERZORD ASSAULT TEAM
FOUR POWERFUL NEW ZORDS

THUNDER MEGAZORD

WHITE TIGERZORD

MEGA TIGERZORD
(Combination of Thunderzord Assault Team & White Tigerzord)

*Not Sold Separately.

TOR THE SHUTTLE ZORD
WITH ELECTRONIC SOUND

Warrior Mode

Combination of Red
Dragon Thunderzord
and the Thunderzord
Assault Team)

Attack Mode

THUNDER ULTRAZORD

The Ultimate Battle System!
(Combination of Red Dragon Thunderzord, Thunderzord
Assault Team, White Tigerzord, and Tor.)

Warrior Mode

Nintendo, 1990

▶ Acclaim Entertainment, 1991

INDEX

INDEX

▶ Tootsietoy, 1931

TOOTSIETOYS

DOLL HOUSES
AND
FURNISHED DOLL HOUSES

Tootsietoy Mansion

Authentic architectural design of "Modern Spanish" with easy access to all five rooms. Made expressly for the New Tootsietoy Furniture. Heavy bookboard construction, nine washable colors. Size 27 x 20 x 18 inches. Five dollar retailer. Comes knocked-down—packed in attractive carton.

N15077. . . . . $6.00 Each

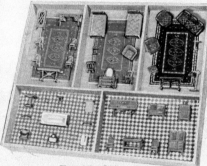

Furnished Mansion

Five complete rooms of furniture as pictured and mansion (as shown above) all packed in shipping carton 24 x 20 x 4 inches. Weight 17 lbs.

N15079. . . . . $13.00 Each

Baby Grand

Piano with lifting top, closing keyboard, moving music rest and bench with upholstered top. Four color choices—Chinese red, jade green, mahogany and gold. Attractive Lithographed Box, size 6¾ in. x 5 in.

N15075. . . . . $8.00 Per Doz.

Tootsietoy Doll House

Modern suburban design. Heavy board in eight waterproof colors. Rooms easily reached from front or rear. Shipped knocked down. Size 20 x 16 x 11½ inches.

N15076. . . . . $4.00 Each

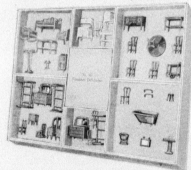

Furnished Doll House

Outstanding value. Complete furnishings for Livingroom, dining room, two bedrooms, bathroom and kitchen. 39 pieces altogether. Entire set and house strongly packed in shipping carton. Measuring 27 x 18 x 3 and weighing 13 lbs.

N15078. . . . . $9.00 Each

CREDITS & IMPRINT

Frontispiece: Wham-O, 1967
Pages 4–5: Mattel, 1984
Pages 522–523: Sears, Roebuck, and Company, 1998

All images are from the Jim Heimann Collection unless otherwise noted.
Any omissions for copy or credit are unintentional and appropriate
credit will be given in future editions if such copyright holders contact
the publisher.

Images courtesy of: Jon Gothold 116–117, 119, 122, 125, 129, 144–145,
148, 172–173, 178, 179, 182, 192, 208, 221, 230, 232, 255, 290;
Tommy Steele 56

Text © 2021 Steven Heller (essays)
Text © 2021 Ryan Mungia (captions and timelines)

The publisher would like to thank Teena Apeles, Jon Gothold,
Justin Sayles, Tommy Steele and Scott Bryan Wilson for their invaluable
assistance in getting this book produced.

To stay informed about TASCHEN and our upcoming titles, please
subscribe to our free magazine at www.taschen.com/magazine,
follow us on Instagram and Facebook, or e-mail your questions to
contact@taschen.com.

EACH AND EVERY TASCHEN BOOK PLANTS A SEED!
TASCHEN is a carbon neutral publisher. Each year, we offset our
annual carbon emissions with carbon credits at the Instituto Terra,
a reforestation program in Minas Gerais, Brazil, founded by Lélia and
Sebastião Salgado. To find out more about this ecological partnership,
please check: www.taschen.com/zerocarbon
Inspiration: unlimited. Carbon footprint: zero.

© 2021 TASCHEN GmbH
Hohenzollernring 53, D-50672 Köln
www.taschen.com

German translation: Ronit Jariv, Cologne
French translation: Alice Pétillot, Bordeaux

Printed in Slovakia
ISBN 978-3-8365-6655-1

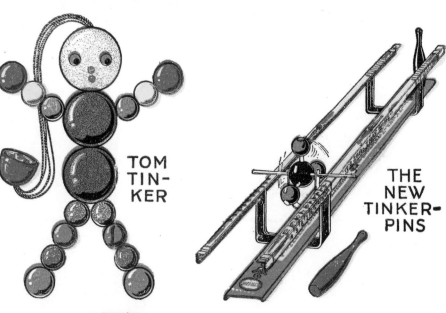

TOM TIN-KER

THE NEW TINKER-PINS

TINK

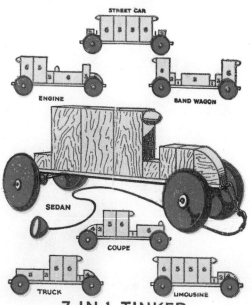

STREET CAR

ENGINE

SAND WAGON

SEDAN

COUPE

TRUCK

LIMOUSINE

7 IN 1 TINKER

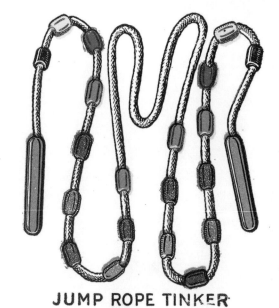

JUMP ROPE TINKER

SIREN TINKER

PONY TINKER